Backstage at **THE TONIGHT SHOW**

Backstage at THE TONIGHT SHOW

from **Johnny Carson** to **Jay Leno**

Don Sweeney

Foreword by **Ed McMahon**

TAYLOR TRADE PUBLISHING
Lanham • New York • Boulder • Toronto • Oxford

Copyright © 2006 by Don Sweeney
First Taylor Trade Publishing edition 2006

This Taylor Trade Publishing paperback edition of *Backstage at the Tonight Show* is an original publication. It is published by arrangement with the author.

Published by Taylor Trade Publishing
An imprint of The Rowman & Littlefield Publishing Group, Inc.
4501 Forbes Boulevard, Suite 200, Lanham, Maryland 20706

Distributed by NATIONAL BOOK NETWORK

Library of Congress Cataloging-in-Publication Data
Sweeney, Don, 1952–
  Backstage at The tonight show : from Johnny Carson to Jay Leno / Don Sweeney ; foreword by Ed McMahon.— 1st Taylor Trade Publishing ed.
    p. cm.
  Includes bibliographical references and index.
  ISBN-13: 978-1-58979-303-3 (pbk. : alk. paper)
  ISBN-10: 1-58979-303-X (pbk. : alk. paper)
  1. Tonight show (Television program) 2. Celebrities—Anecdotes. I. Title.
  PN1992.77.T63S94 2006
  791.45'72—dc22

2005035531

♾ The paper used in this publication meets the minimum requirements of American National Standard for Information Sciences—Permanence of Paper for Printed Library Materials, ANSI/NISO Z39.48-1992.
Manufactured in the United States of America.

Thanks to
David Blume
Kathryn Krenz
Gloria Pollack
Catherine Sweeney
Who made this book sound like the Queen's English.

Thanks to Cory Carson, Jeff Sotzing, Jay Shanker, Jerico, Phil Greenfield, Kevin Sweeney, Arlene Sweeney, Elizabeth Gardner, my parents, Eileen and John Sweeney, and especially to my wife, Catherine, and my son, John, who have had to listen to me tell these stories over and over again.

Contents

What goes on backstage, stays backstage. Many times performers try to hide the fact that they are nervous, unprepared, or God forbid, normal. Producers don't want the audience to see that the show is sometimes held together with duct tape and glue. This book takes what went on behind the scenes at *The Tonight Show* and brings it all front and center. It provides you with a glimpse of what it was like to work for one of the greatest variety shows in the history of television.

The first person I ever asked for an autograph was Joe Penner, a radio comedian who was famous for his saying, "Wanna buy a duck?" I wasn't collecting autographs; it was just a reason to go up to someone I admired and have some sort of conversation with him.

The opportunity to be backstage at *The Jack Benny Show* or to carry on a conversation with the great W. C. Fields would have been something I would have cherished for the rest of my life.

The Tonight Show was a daily parade of everyone and anyone in show business. Many of the artists were just starting out and eager to get a chance to establish themselves on national television. Getting their "big shot" on *The Tonight Show* could make or break their career. In that same procession of performers were the legends of show business, the icons of the industry, who more than confirmed their ability to entertain an audience.

The studio audience had the thrill of seeing the show from a much different perspective than what they would view at home. They were able to see what went on when the show would cut away to a commercial break. Besides being able to hear the thunderous Tonight Show Band play uninterrupted for a whole two or three minutes, they sometimes witnessed something the home viewers didn't get to see. Whether it was a word that couldn't be uttered over the airwaves or something as simple as watching an artist get primped by the hair and make-up people seconds before Johnny would say, "We're back," the studio audience had something to tell all their friends when they got back home.

Imagine being able to watch that show from behind the curtain line, to witness the program each day from the daily production meetings to when the very last studio light was dimmed.

For nearly twenty years, Don Sweeney worked in the music department of *The Tonight Show* and had the privilege to interact with the many talented performers who walked through the doors at Studio 1 at NBC in Burbank. Don was able to capture some of those moments from his point of view, backstage at *The Tonight Show*.

Ed McMahon

The King of Late Night and I

Follow the yellow brick road to the land of Carson. Unknowingly, I was on that magic road to become one of the privileged people to work with one of the greatest celebrities in the history of television. Along that road I met up with several characters, sometimes similar to the characters Dorothy and Toto encountered trying to get to the Wizard. My wizard was Johnny Carson.

When Johnny Carson took over *The Tonight Show* after Jack Paar stepped down, I was ten years old. I lived with my mom and dad, my older sister Arlene, my younger brother Kevin, and my little sister Elizabeth in Elmhurst, New York, in a neighborhood known as the Matthew Homes. They were about eight square blocks of attached apartments made of orange and yellow bricks built before World War II. I know this because my next door neighbors found some photographs taken of their apartment when it was a World War II recruiting office.

Anyone who has taken the Long Island Expressway into Manhattan on a regular basis would know where the Maspeth gas tanks were. Alongside the expressway were two immense gas tanks about 100 yards in diameter that would raise and lower from four stories high to about ten stories high. The local news reporters would use these tanks as a marker when giving the morning traffic reports. We lived just down the block from the tanks. My grandmother lived up the street from us just across from them.

My mom told me that my grandmother was one of the first people in the neighborhood to own a television set. Her house was one of those homes where sometimes the whole block would be sitting in the living room to watch such shows as *The Texaco Star Theater*, *Your Show of Shows*, and *I Remember Mama*. Somewhere around 1962 my grandmother also bought one of the first color televisions. I can remember bringing a few of my friends up to Nana's house to watch *Bonanza, The Perry Como Show, The Andy Williams Show* and *The Wonderful World of Disney.*

My grandmother was a widow who raised her five children alone. Her husband passed away when her oldest child was eleven and her youngest was barely seven months. Thirty years later, her children were all grown and Nana lived in a Grand Avenue apartment with her oldest son, a construction worker, my uncle Jimmy Gillen.

The woman who lived next door to them was Mrs. Dalton, a wardrobe mistress for all of the shows done at 30 Rockefeller Plaza at NBC Studios in Manhattan. She invited my mother to bring my sister Arlene and me to NBC Studios to be in the Peanut Gallery.

Those of you who are old enough know what the Peanut Gallery was. For anyone too young, the Peanut Gallery was the audience section of children on the *Howdy Doody Show.* My sister was eight years old and I was five. We both were very much into Doodyville, Phineas T. Bluster, Flub-a-dub, Buffalo Bob Smith and Howdy Doody. Except for Buffalo Bob, all were marionette characters on the show that lived in the fictitious town of Doodyville. Any television historian will tell you it was the hottest show of the '50s.

Although I was only five, the one memory that I still can recall was that my sister and I were placed in the front row of the Peanut Gallery and we were told that the boy sitting next to us was the son of Clarabell the clown. I kept looking at his son and looking at Clarabell thinking to myself, "How could he be Clarabell's son? The little boy doesn't have any clown make-up on his face." Toward the end of the show, Clarabell shows up wearing roller skates and carrying a dozen eggs. Buffalo Bob warns him to be careful not to drop those eggs. Eventually, Clarabell looses his balance, falls on the floor and winds up with broken eggs all over him. I looked at his son again and thought, "That's what your father does for a living?"

Mrs. Dalton encouraged my mother to try to get on some of the game shows. She gave us the name of a woman who worked for Goodson and Todman, headed by Mark Goodson and Bill Todman, two of the biggest game show producers in television at that time. My mom called and made an appointment for the whole family to go into the city for an interview.

Goodson and Todman had offices on one of the top floors of the thirty-story Seagrams Building in New York City. The woman we had the appointment with was Agnes Nixon. She became very famous later on in the seventies as an executive producer of the daytime series *All My Children*. The Seagrams Building was famous for its glass exterior and at the time was considered very modern. When we were escorted into Ms. Nixon's office, I immediately went over to the floor-to-ceiling glass windows that surrounded her office to have a look at the traffic below. My mother has a fear of high places and she really freaked out that my little brother Kevin and I were leaning against the window. My mom wasn't too thrilled about taking an elevator, much less seeing her two sons, a two-year-old and five-year-old, with their noses pressed against a glass window exclaiming that the people below looked like ants. The interview was a simple one. My parents filled out a lengthy questionnaire while I simply had to answer questions like, "Where'd you get all that red hair?" and "What's your favorite television show?" They took some pictures of us all and told us they would call us if anything came up.

Eventually, we got called to do a show. My dad and I were picked to be contestants on *Play Your Hunch* with its host, Merv Griffin. The show was simple. Two teams of married couples competed to solve problems and answer questions. When I came out I was supposed to try to fool the two teams with a stunt.

Days before I went to perform on the television show, they told my mom to have me practice balancing silver dollars on my forehead. One of our neighbors had a jar full of silver dollars, so I practiced. I was able to balance up to twenty-five of them on my own, which was pretty good for a seven-year-old.

When we got to the TV rehearsal we met a man named Ira Skutch, one of the producers of *Play Your Hunch*. Ira was the person in charge of dreaming up the scenarios for the participants to fool the contestants. Suddenly, I was given a tall top hat and told that Merv Griffin was to place the chips upon my hat and the contestants would have to guess how many I could balance. I had been told that I would be able to keep any of the silver dollars I would balance. For a seven-year-old, ten to twenty-five bucks was a lot of money in 1959. Ira turned to an assistant on stage and told him to go downstairs to the bank and get as many silver dollars as he could. While we waited for the silver dollars to arrive, Skutch took my dad and me to meet the show's host, Merv Griffin.

When we went into Merv's dressing room he was lying on a chaise lounge chair, wearing a white terrycloth robe and a towel wrapped around his neck. He looked like a movie star. He was very friendly to my dad and me and helped to put us at ease before our live television debut.

Our wardrobe mistress friend, Mrs. Dalton, dropped by to see how things were going. We had some time to kill, so she was nice enough to take us on a little tour of the NBC Studios. She took us to Studio 8H (where they now tape *Saturday Night Live*), which was set up to tape some segments for NBC's *Your Hit Parade*.

We eventually went to her office area. It was practically a closet. It was filled with hanging costumes, hats, gloves, an ironing board and boxes of all sorts of costume-related items. Mrs. Dalton took out one large box and said to me, "Here's one you might want to see." She opened the box and pulled out a giant head of a dog costume. It wasn't just any dog's head. It was the head of JumPup. JumPup was a costume somebody wore weekly on the *Shari Lewis Show*. Mrs. Dalton showed me that one of the ears on the costume was torn, and she needed to sew it up. I grew up watching the *Shari Lewis Show* and watched JumPup dance with Shari Lewis at the end of each show. Although I always knew it was a guy in a dog outfit, I was clearly frightened when she took it out of the box. She saw my reaction and decided to put it away. And the Wizard said, "Pay no attention to the person behind the curtain."

I guess if I had to pinpoint where my spark for wanting to work in television started, it had to be this day. Little did I know that the very studio we were in was NBC Studio 6B, the same studio used to tape *The Tonight Show* in the evenings when Jack Paar was the host. Four years later, Johnny Carson would begin his thirty-year reign as the "King of Late Night" in the same studio. I was on a game show hosted by someone who would later become a talk show host with a show of his own, competing against Johnny Carson. The yellow brick road can be a winding one sometimes.

Play Your Hunch aired weekday mornings live on the NBC television network. Depending on where you lived in the United States and if your affiliate local station opted to carry this show, you may have seen it in your area. It wasn't live to the entire nation, but it was aired live locally in New York. My mom was home at my grandmother's house watching us on color television along with my grandmother and the principal of my grammar school.

As the show wore on and it came time for my segment, I remember the television lights being bright and hot. I stood alongside Merv while he asked me who I was and where I lived but I was preoccupied with the microphone he was pointing my way. As I answered his questions, I could hear my voice coming out of speakers at the back of the studio. The lights were so bright; I couldn't see the cameramen or the staff. All I could see were the feet of the stage crew. I said something that triggered a laugh from the studio audience but I couldn't see them out there in the dark. I don't even think I was told there was going to be an audience.

When it came time for me to do my trick with the silver dollars, I assumed the position looking straight up to the ceiling of hot lights with my two arms extended outward like I was an airplane. Although we were unrehearsed, they told me Merv would put the coins on my forehead for me. As he placed the coins in a stack on my head I could feel his hand shake and he was not placing them as neatly as I would have. When we got to ten coins, they fell to the floor. When I started to go after some of the coins that rolled away, Merv laughed and called me back to his side. But I wasn't about to let those people in the dark walk off with my ten bucks.

In the next segment, my dad and two other men came out, each one supposed to be my father, each one with cards in front of him labeled X, Y and Z. They each had a story ready to tell about what I was going to do with the money I just won.

My dad and I do not look alike. I had flaming red hair, pink skin and freckles. My dad had dark brown hair with a long face and darker features. The other two men had rusty brown curly hair with ruddy complexions. The first man said I was into science and was going to buy a chemistry set with the winnings. The other man said I was very much into sports and was going to buy myself a new baseball mitt. My father told the real story: that the next day was my older sister's birthday and I was going to buy her a birthday present. We fooled the contestants. They never thought a five-year-old would spend his hard-earned coins on his sister.

When we finished the show and headed home on the subway, we had a ten-block walk to our apartment in Elmhust. It was Halloween, but it was a school day. As we passed by my grammar school, my dad asked me if I wanted to go to school. There still were a few hours left in the school day and he thought I would want to go tell my friends of my television appearance. I chose to take the rest of the day off and get ready for Halloween. The next day was really my sister's birthday and I bought her the home version of the television game *Concentration*. I received a free home version of *Play Your Hunch*, but my sister was a big fan of the show *Concentration*.

Many years later I met up with Merv Griffin when he was appearing on *The Tonight Show* and told him this story. He was so elated to hear it that every time I saw him afterward he would always be sure to say hello to me and talk about the old days.

My grandmother owned and operated a greeting card store in Woodside, New York, and after work she and Uncle Jimmy would have dinner at our apartment and walk up the block to their one-bedroom apartment on the second floor. Sometimes my uncle's job would take him out of town, so I would help my grandmother home with her packages. Whenever I had the next day off from school or it was a Friday night, I would always ask if I could stay overnight. The main attraction was Nana's color TV. My uncle slept in a hide-a-bed next to the television. I lay awake watching television until the wee hours of the morning. When I was ten I was especially interested in the new host of *The Tonight Show*, a very young and witty Johnny Carson.

Johnny was particularly alluring to a young boy like me because he was a wise guy. He'd poke fun at New York Mayor Lindsay, Fidel Castro, Nikita Khrushchev, the President of the United States, anybody who was in the news that week. Johnny would do sketches, take-offs on commercials, movies, and other television shows, always with an impish gleam in his eye, or a sarcastic smile. He and his big guy sidekick, Ed McMahon, would smirk at their own jokes as if they couldn't believe they were getting paid to have this much fun.

As time went on and I got a little older, my parents would let me stay up to watch Johnny's monologue. My parents were also avid fans of *The Tonight Show*. They were Jack Paar fans too. I remember hearing my mom talking on the phone with my Aunt Sheila about how Jack Paar said this and Jack Paar said that. At the time, I didn't know who Jack Paar was, so whenever I envisioned him, I always pictured Bert Parks, the guy who hosted *The Miss America Pageants*. It wasn't until Jack Paar left *The Tonight Show* and started *The Jack Paar Show* on prime time that I discovered yet another talk show wise guy. Jack Paar was witty and sarcastic but, to me, not as charismatic as Johnny Carson. Steve Allen was slightly before my time, although I am sure I would have enjoyed watching his show. After all, he invented *The Tonight Show*. Red Skelton was the funniest man I have ever heard and Johnny Carson had a lot of Red's silliness about him. And why wouldn't he? At one time, Johnny was one of Red Skelton's writers.

By the time I was in high school, I was watching Johnny's monologues every night and began to recite his jokes at the lunch table the next day. My friends didn't stay up late enough to realize that I was stealing Johnny's jokes. They thought I was just some witty guy who liked to tell jokes about articles in the daily newspapers. It wasn't until I was in my senior year that my friends caught on to me. Because of my lunch room stand-up experience, I wound up hosting the annual high school talent shows and stole every joke I could from the likes of Bob Hope, Jack Carter and, of course, Johnny Carson.

To add to my Carson addiction, I was able to go into Manhattan when I was thirteen and fourteen, sometimes alone (New York and life in general were totally different in 1965 than they are now) and learned how to sneak in to watch *The Tonight Show* rehearsals. As I got older and became a familiar face to the Tonight Show Band members and stage crew, I was able to stay at rehearsals when others were asked to leave.

One time, my friend Richie and I went in to Manhattan to spend the day in NBC. If you got there before 9:00 a.m. they would hand out free tickets to see mostly game shows, such as *Password*, *What's My Line?*, *Beat The Clock*, *Snap Judgement*, and a very early version of *The Match Game*. These shows were always fun to see as a young teenager. I got to see people like Soupy Sales, Orson Bean, Sam Levenson, Peggy Cass, Harry Morgan, Gene Rayburn, Larry Blyden and a whole list of very witty, likeable and entertaining people. For those insomniacs or those lucky few who know how to set their VCRs, these people can still be found on the Game Show Network in the wee hours of the morning.

After many visits to NBC Studios, I learned that security wasn't as secure as Johnny Carson would have liked. My friend Richie and I would take the NBC tour in the early afternoon. The tours would be closed to the fifth and sixth floor after 3:00 p.m. due to *The Tonight Show* rehearsal. But if you took the tour at 2:30 p.m., by the time the tour got to *The Tonight Show* studio, you would be the last ones in to see the empty stage before they would cut off the area to tours. When the tour guides, also known as pages, would herd their tours down the hall to the elevators, Richie and I would suddenly have to go to the bathroom. We would hide in there until the tour was entirely gone and then sneak back into the studio audience seats. We were smart enough to know that if we dressed up in our Sunday best clothes, we would look like a couple of kids who came into the city with our parents. There was a client booth along the sidewall of the studio that was basically a glassed in living room overlooking the studio. Richie and I sat there and watched the rehearsal. The NBC pages were ushers and tour guides who were also assigned to police the area during a broadcast. Suddenly one of the NBC pages came up behind us and said, "Excuse me, boys. Who are you with?" Without a beat, I turned to him and said, "Oh, my dad works upstairs and said we could sit here." NBC Studios is at 30 Rockefeller Plaza, a thirty-story office building where such businesses as Shell Oil and RCA headquarters were located. I knew this and so did the page. I guess he wasn't about to eject a couple of well-dressed teenagers for no apparent reason on the chance that they might be the sons of someone who signed his paycheck. He said we could stay there as long as I put away the Insta-matic camera I was holding. I had no intention of snapping a photo knowing that the flash would be like sending up a flare in the middle of a nighttime jailbreak. I was so wrapped up in watching what was going on down on the stage, I totally forgot the camera was in my hand. I quickly put the camera in my coat pocket and now had a new friend, the page.

After several studio sneak-ins, it got easier as other pages recognized me as a familiar face and a harmless son of whomever. Little did they know that my dad didn't work anywhere near NBC Studios. He worked in the U.S. Post Office in Flushing, New York.

The layout of *The Tonight Show* in Studio 6B had the studio orchestra with half the band facing away from the audience and the saxophones along the right wall looking across to Johnny and his guests. (It is actually a mirror of Conan O'Brien's band's set up. In fact, Conan's studio is Studio 6A, directly across from where Johnny used to do his show. Studio 6B was completely remodeled when Johnny moved to Burbank and is now used for the local news and Dateline NBC.) This Studio 6B layout allowed me to sit on the far right side of the audience at rehearsal and look directly over the drummer's shoulder. Grady Tate was the regular drummer. He was always friendly and said hello, but rarely turned to talk to me. But in later visits, drummer Ed Shaughnessy was there. He was always eager to point out drum tips for me. (I had been playing drums since I was eleven years old.) After I started to take drum lessons from Ed, I would get security clearance to sit and watch the rehearsals and sometimes I would get to stay and watch the taping of the show rather than having to sneak in. I was sixteen, but you were supposed to be eighteen to watch the taping, so I was very lucky.

The first time I got to see Johnny Carson in person was during one of my visits to NBC to see the game show *Snap Judgement* with Gene Rayburn as the host. Johnny's second wife, Joanna, had made a rare guest appearance on *The Tonight Show* the night before and said she was going to be a panelist on *Snap Judgement*. Somehow, I knew if I went to see that show I would have a chance of seeing Johnny. Sure enough, I got in to see the taping of the game show, and Joanna Carson was one of the panelists. During the course of the game, one of the answers to one of the questions was "Johnny Carson," and Joanna got the answer wrong. The correct answers were displayed on the wall behind the panelists. When Joanna didn't get the answer right and it was revealed that the answer should have been "Johnny Carson," a hand from backstage came through the slot in the wall and slapped the set. Rayburn quipped, "Oh look, that must be Johnny backstage. He's not too happy that you didn't get that answer right." The audience all laughed and figured it was the hand of a stagehand just playing around, when suddenly, out from behind the wall stepped Johnny Carson. I knew he was going to be there.

GREETING JOHNNY CARSON

Whenever Buddy Rich was on his way through New York or Canada, he would appear on *The Tonight Show*. Johnny Carson was clearly one of Buddy Rich's biggest fans.

Buddy was appearing for a week at the Manhattan nightclub Barney Googles and made an appearance on *The Tonight Show* to promote it. When Buddy's spot was nearly over, Buddy asked Johnny when he was going to come over and hear the band. Johnny teased Buddy about not having the time. "I'm sorting my socks this weekend," Johnny said as one of his lame excuses. Buddy kept at him and cornered Johnny into giving him some kind of an answer. Just before the show went off for the night, Johnny said he would come by and see the band the following night.

I made it my business to be there too. I had never met Johnny in person, and this would be a kick to see both him and Buddy outside of *The Tonight Show*.

It was my first date with a beautiful girl I had met. My band was playing in her father's restaurant, the Far East in Whitestone. She was the cashier. Her name was Dorkus Chin. I once asked her what Dorkus meant in Chinese. She told me it meant fawn or young deer. She then continued to say, "My last name is Chin." She then grabbed the end of her chin and said to me, "Chin, you know, this part." She was a professional model and was going to school at Bard Women's College in upstate New York.

We got to Barney Googles and watched Buddy's first set. There was a two-drink minimum and they delivered both of our drinks at one time. I nursed the drinks for the first show and continually looked around for Johnny Carson. He wasn't there.

They cleared the room for the second show. I asked if we could stay. The waitress explained we could stay where we were if we ordered two more drinks. We ordered. Dorkus didn't drink, so I ended up drinking her drinks as well. The room was definitely moving halfway through Buddy's second set. I had given up on Johnny making an appearance, but I enjoyed hearing Buddy play.

At the end of his second set, Buddy came out front to joke with the audience. While he was talking, somebody threw a rubber chicken past Buddy's head. It was Johnny Carson. Buddy joked with Johnny, who was sitting near the front of the stage. Buddy thanked us all for coming and gave a special thanks to Johnny, and then Buddy disappeared backstage. Everyone in the club got up and left and Johnny was still sitting at his table. I walked over to meet him. As I got up, the eight glasses of booze I had consumed during the two shows took me over and suddenly Barney Googles became a floating cloud. I managed to stay on my feet and approached Johnny. I probably scared the hell out of him. I slurred out my name and shook his hand. As I swayed back and forth in front of him, he had a look on his face as if to say, "Please don't hurt me." To me, his head looked as if it were three sizes too big for his body. His voice sounded as if it were coming through a transistor radio. As I told him over and over what an honor it was to meet him and how I have watched his show every night since he started, Johnny kept saying thank you and nodding and blinking at me in fear. I left before I did something really stupid, like throwing up all over him.

There I was with two of the men I admired most in show business, and I was too drunk to realize it until the next day when I was getting over a really bad hangover.

WORKING FOR JOHNNY CARSON

I started taking drum lessons from Ed Shaughnessy in 1970. Besides getting to know Ed from sneaking my way into *The Tonight Show* rehearsals, I was actually introduced to Ed by Buddy Rich.

My only regret was that I should have started taking drum lessons from Ed Shaughnessy when I was younger. I was eighteen when Ed started giving me lessons. Ed is a master at solving problems and usually solving those problems with one sentence. He liked to use analogies. For instance, when he taught me how to practice drum rolls and rudiments, Ed said, "Hold your hands as if you were putting them through a chain link fence. You can't move your arm up, down or sideways." Many years after taking lessons from him I would go to him with a drum problem to solve. One time I was doing a show that included a "West Side Story" medley. Every time we rehearsed it, the conductor would accuse me of speeding up the tempo during the song "America." I told Ed I did not have my face buried in my music; I was staring at the conductor who would wave his arms wider but never changed his tempo. Ed gave me one of his one sentence problem-solving ideas. He said, "Look at him at the beginning of the song and don't look back, and he will follow your tempo." The next time I rehearsed the medley I did exactly as Ed instructed and when the medley was over, the conductor was very happy with the tempo and shouted to me, "Now you've got it!"

Ever since I turned eighteen I tried to get hired at NBC. I must have filled out a job application every three months. I would have liked to start out as a page. I would have made a great page. I could learn to talk and walk backwards without tripping or bumping into anything. My friends and I became experts after taking the tour so many times, we almost could move our lips to match the memorized banter the pages would recite as they showed us around NBC.

The tour didn't change much over the years. Sometimes the tour was altered because of show taping schedules or they might take the tour to a different studio to show a set of an NBC special that was taping. There was one part of the tour where we would meet up with another tour and the two guides would take us into a room where they would demonstrate how sound effects were used in radio. The two pages would turn out all the lights and act out a short soap opera drama scene using a creaky door, thunder and rain, or a galloping horse. The scene would always end with a gun shot and a loud scream. When the lights would come back on they would show us how they created all of the sound effects. My friends and I would later verbalize our personal reviews, comparing their performance to the other times we took the tour.

When _The Tonight Show_ moved from New York to Burbank, I was lost without it. There no longer was any thrill in taking the NBC studio tour. Ed Shaughnessy moved to California with the show, so I lost the best drum teacher anyone could ever hope for. The times that Johnny took the show out to California for a week or two were always like a series of specials. A different cast of characters would do the show, such as Dean Martin, David Jansen, Burt Reynolds, Michael Landon, and the Las Vegas–type performers, such as Sammy Davis, Jr., Ann Margaret, Debbie Reynolds and Frank Sinatra. When the show was in New York, the guests were more Broadway-type performers, comedians, newspaper columnists or movie stars passing through New York to go shoot a movie in Europe, such as Richard Harris, Bert Convy, Soupy Sales, Joey Heatherton, Myron Cohen, Jackie Leonard, or Tiny Tim. Not that the New York shows were inferior in any way, but the Burbank shows were jam-packed with special guests to boost the ratings during sweeps weeks when the networks would survey audience sizes to determine the price of commercial time. These times always pay off well for the viewer. It was these trips to Los Angeles that first sparked my interest to live there. It always seemed to be bright, sunny and cheery. It always seemed like summertime and that movie stars could be seen everywhere. In the spring of 1972, six months after *The Tonight Show* permanently moved to Burbank, my friend Giz and I took a cross-country trip by car. The ultimate goal was to see what life in Los Angeles was like and if I would like to move there.

Our entire trip across the United States took us four weeks. On the way to California we drove through New Jersey, Delaware, Pennsylvania, Ohio, Indiana, Illinois, Missouri, Oklahoma, Texas, New Mexico, Nevada, and Arizona. On the return trip we went through Utah, Wyoming, Iowa, and Michigan, while backtracking through a few of the states we passed through going west. Eighteen states if you count New York and California. We saw a good portion of the United States and got a taste of what California was like. As soon as I got back to New York I announced to my parents that I was moving to Los Angeles. My parents told me I could do whatever I wanted to do after I turned twenty-one. Seven months later, when I turned twenty-one, I moved to Los Angeles.

I shared an apartment in Hollywood with one of my best friends, Phil Greenfield, who came out to Los Angeles with me from Flushing, New York. We had a beautiful apartment where Sunset Boulevard and La Cienega intersect. We had two bedrooms, a back porch, two car ports, a pool, all utilities included (except the telephone), for $190 a month.

Philip and I enjoyed going to NBC to watch the tapings of a show called *The Midnight Special*. The show did not have a permanent host. Each week another celebrity (usually a musical act) would host the show and would introduce the other acts. The show's only consistency was its off-camera announcer, Wolfman Jack.

"The Wolfman" was a gravelly-voiced radio personality widely known across the Mid-West in the early '50s. He later became even more famous as result of his appearance in the film "American Graffiti," where he played himself. On *The Midnight Special* the Wolfman would come out and talk to the audience members while the stage crew set up for the next band. In later years, home audiences also would get to know the Wolfman when the producers eventually put him in front of the cameras and occasionally let him introduce some of the acts.

The first show was hosted by singer Helen Reddy, the second by Mac Davis. Phil and I went to the Davis taping. The show aired Friday nights on NBC at 1 a.m. following *The Tonight Show*. (Shouldn't it have been called the 1 a.m. Special?) They taped the show on a Tuesday to be aired a week from the coming Friday. So, as Mac taped show No. 2, show No. 1 had not aired yet.

Because of the ten-day delay in airing the taped show, we caught Mac in somewhat of an error. He was introducing one of the acts they had taped the week before. The group was still high on the charts with one of their songs, so the show was going to make it look as though they were bringing them back a second time to perform their hit. They were actually on videotape. When Mac introduced the Spinners, he said, "And here they are, brought back by popular demand, the Spinners." We asked him on the break between camera takes, how could they be back by popular demand? The viewing audience had not seen show No. 1 yet. Embarrassingly he answered, "Well, that's just one of those show business expressions we try to get away with once in a while."

While I am on the topic of Mac Davis, I want to add a side note about him. At that same taping, we were able to talk with the artists between camera takes. That was one of the reasons we enjoyed going to the tapings. On one of the breaks, I asked Mac why he always wore the same blue denim pants and shirt. Did he have a closet full of blue denim, or was that the same outfit? His reply was one of surprise. "I wear other outfits, don't I?" he asked the audience. The audience all said in tandem, "No." Suddenly he realized that he had been wearing the same outfit again and again. Ever since that night, whenever I saw Mac on other shows, he never again wore blue denim. In fact, he became quite flashy in the clothes he wore from that time on. I like to think I had something to do with it.

In the beginning, *The Midnight Special* could not get the superstar-level performers they would have had on the show. They didn't quite realize that they were presenting the superstars of tomorrow. On the early episodes they had the Doobie Brothers, Steely Dan, the Spinners, the Hollies and anyone else who had a record climbing up the Billboard Top 40 charts. Phil and I would check out the new TV Guide when it went on sale at the supermarkets. The issue that appeared on Monday was for the following week. All we had to do was check the listings for *The Midnight Special* and we would know who was going to be taping on Tuesday, the following night. Sometimes we'd be surprised to find an added attraction of someone not listed in TV Guide.

This being 1973, the entertainment industry would mix music styles and entertainers without concern. One week George Burns was booked on *The Midnight Special* in order to plug the opening of his latest movie, "Oh God." John Denver, who also starred in the movie, was hosting the show that week, so it seemed like the right thing to do to have Burns appear with all of these pop and rock acts. Definitely a corporate decision!

Burns, after doing a few jokes with Denver, was warmly received by the young audience—mainly because he was George Burns. Denver then proclaimed that George was going to sing a song for us—a song that Burns had recorded that was actually climbing the pop charts, called "I Wish I Was Eighteen Again." He performed the song without a hitch and the audience cheered.

If that were not enough, he was scheduled to do a second song, his rendition of "Mister Bojangles," a tune that we were all familiar with from the Nitty Gritty Dirt Band's 1968 version. George Burns was familiar with the song from hearing Sammy Davis Jr. perform it. Sammy had made it his classic closing dance routine for his Vegas act.

Now in 1973, George was a ripe 76 years old. We thought he was old then. He just wasn't able to get through the song without flubbing the lyrics. Take after take, he would lose it somewhere in the middle of the song. Each time we would have to applaud as though he was just introduced. After about 10 takes we were getting tired, and so was George. It must have been the 20th or 30th take before he finally made it to the end of the song. The audience was so relieved that we gave him a standing ovation.

A week later, when we watched the show at home, our ovation was well edited into the program. One would think that we all loved George Burns dearly. Well, some of us really did, but in this particular case, the ovation was not for his performance.

When I first arrived in Los Angeles it took me nine months to find a job. When I lived in New York, I had worked for the United States Postal Service for three years. I had saved up enough money to barely get me through six months of unemployment. Having been a postal worker, department store clerk, bus boy and a movie theater usher wasn't enough experience to get a job as soon as I got into town.

I looked for job postings that listed "no prior experience" or "trainee accepted." The clerks at the unemployment office would say, "Oh, I know it says no experience, but they want someone with some experience." Or when it called for trainee, the clerk would again dismiss the job offer because it was "in the Valley." They would say it was too far for me to have to drive every day.

After being so discouraged from the clerks at the unemployment office, I took the Sunday newspaper and circled three jobs similar to employment I had when I was in New York. The first one was an ad for a ticket taker at a movie theater, the second job listing was for a delivery driver (I just drove nearly three thousand miles from New York), and the third was for a department store clerk.

As I drove up to the movie theater, it was a showing the movie "Deep Throat." When I worked at the RKO Keith movie theater in Flushing, New York, the projectionist told me when a theater would get shut down for showing pornography, the first person arrested is the projectionist because he physically is showing the movie. The second person arrested would be the ticket taker because he physically is letting the people into the theater. As I sat across the street, leering at the large marquee brandishing the words "Deep Throat," I envisioned being taken away in handcuffs and all my friends and relatives back East thinking, "He's gone porno." I did not apply.

The second job listing was for a store clerk in Glendale. I had to take the freeway for a few miles to get there. It was a very hot day and my air conditioner was not working, so I had the windows opened. The slip of paper with the address and telephone number on it was sitting on the console next to me one minute and began to fly all around my car interior the next. I frantically tried to retrieve the scrap of paper while driving fifty miles an hour and trying to stay in my lane. It eventually disappeared and I thought it must have flown out the window.

I took the third job for one hundred bucks a week driving a delivery truck for Melrose Stationers in Hollywood. The only reason they hired me was because I was from New York. The store owner's wife was originally from there and had a soft spot for any New Yorker. If nothing else, this job helped me learn how to get around town. Each day I delivered office supplies from the San Fernando Valley to Culver City. I stayed at this job for three years. Four months after starting my new job, while cleaning out my car, I found the slip of paper from the second job listing.

Phil Greenfield and I lived in an apartment building in the heart of Sunset Boulevard, just down the block from the Continental "Riot" House. If you've seen the motion picture, "Almost Famous," you'd have a pretty good idea what it was like in the seventies in Hollywood. The girls portrayed in that movie were just like the girls who lived in my building. The Comedy Store was within walking distance from my place. I would go there to try out my stand-up comedy act. I was probably in line with other aspiring young comics such as Arsenio Hall, Fran Drescher, Ben Stiller and . . . oh yeah, Jay Leno. They were all starting out back then but I didn't meet any of them. The deal at the Comedy Store was, you waited in line and got a number. That number was the order that comics would perform that night. I usually got a high number that put me on at about twelve-thirty in the morning. The few times I got a low number, I still went on at one or two in the morning because the comics with agents or TV deals would show up and get the primetime spots without needing a number. The place was packed at nine or ten o'clock at night. By twelve o'clock, the only people in the audience were other comics waiting to get on stage. I also had one problem with my comedy career. I could get up in front of an audience and say anything without being nervous, I just needed writers.

I was new to Los Angeles so I bought a ten-speed bicycle to get around town. I thought I could get by without a car. I was walking back to my apartment at 8400 Sunset Boulevard after dropping my bicycle off at the Hollywood Bicycle Center on Beverly Boulevard. It was a great bike ride from my place, all down hill. But a long walk back. I was at the corner of Santa Monica and Crescent Heights when I saw a poster for the Ace Trucking Company. It said they were appearing that weekend at a place called the Starwood. I literally took about ten steps when a car cut in front of me at a driveway to the Top Hat Dry Cleaner. The driver was Fred Willard, one of the Ace Trucking Company players. I went up to his car, excited and amazed and I told him I just saw the sign about his appearance and suddenly he whisked in front of me. It was truly a coincidence. "I've got to come see you guys!" I told him. "Yeah, we're at the Starwood tonight, tomorrow and Sunday," he smiled. He was about to head off to the cleaners when I asked him, "Hey Fred, where is the Starwood?" His smile changed slowly from a smile to a look of disbelief and said, "Uh, it's right across the street." Directly across from the cleaners there was a two-story marquee on the Starwood that read, THE ACE TRUCKING COMPANY TONIGHT THRU SUNDAY. I felt like such a nerd.

When I got back to my apartment I called a friend of mine, Nancy Patano, and asked if she would want to go with me and see the show. She knew nothing of the Ace Trucking Company but said she would love to join me. Suddenly Nancy and I had our first date.

After a hilarious evening we had some coffee and talked about the show. I commented on how the Ace Trucking Company reminded me of the Three Stooges, only there were five of them. The original Ace Trucking Company was Fred Willard, Patty Deutch, Bill Saluga, George Frakus and Michael Mislove. When I mentioned the Three Stooges, Nancy explained that she worked as a nurse's aide at the T.V. and Motion Picture Hospital in Calabasas. Knowing that I was a fan of the Three Stooges she asked, "Would you like to meet one of the Stooges?"

My job at Melrose Stationers took me two or three times a week to a Rolls Royce repair shop on Santa Monica Boulevard just outside of Beverly Hills. The woman had a photo of the Three Stooges at her desk and it was signed by Moe Howard. I asked the lady if she ever met Moe. "Oh yeah," she said, "He gets his Rolls fixed here from time to time." When I saw that photo, I thought what a thrill it would be to meet one of the Three Stooges. And so, when Nancy asked me if I wanted to meet one of the Three Stooges, I answered as Curly would say, "Woo, woo, woo, woo, woo woo!!"

Nancy set it up for me to come to the Motion Picture Hospital the next day to meet Larry Fine of the famous trio. Larry had had a stroke and was recuperating at the hospital. The Motion Picture

Hospital is a retirement home for anyone who worked in a union connected with the entertainment industry. Carpenters, lighting grips, producers, directors, writers and even musicians are eligible to go to this hospital for treatment and retirement. All of those unions contribute to it and many other hospitals like it across the country.

I was escorted through several large recreational areas and corridors leading to a large lodge-like sitting room. It had a huge stone fireplace and clusters of people were sitting at various tables playing cards or just talking to one another. Larry was seated at one of the tables with a few other men when Nancy brought me over for an introduction. Larry was almost midget size, but not quite. He was much smaller than I imagined him to be. When I looked back at some of the Stooges' short features after I met him, I surmised that the other actors were short in stature as well. If Larry was five feet tall, then Vernon Dent, who played the boss or angry husband chasing after them in most of the films, was maybe five foot eight. I had always assumed that he was taller. Larry was also seventy-two years old. He may have shrunk a little with age. He was not quite the size of a Munchkin, but he was still very small in stature. I clearly was following the yellow brick road.

Larry's hair was slicked down and combed back. Everyone remembers him as the one with the hair like a "porcupine." He was the one with the curly hair while Curly was the one with a shaved head. Larry was wearing a brown hounds-tooth sport jacket and seemed excited to meet me. Larry soon was told by one of the nurses that he would have to get a blood pressure reading done at his room. He motioned for me to follow him. He walked with the help of a walker, so it was a slow walk.

His room was similar to a hospital room. As you walked in there was a bathroom to the right with the large door to accommodate a wheelchair or walker. Further into the room there was a large hospital bed. Larry was sitting on the edge of the bed. His feet barely touched the floor.

After the nurse took her readings, Larry and I sat and talked about the Stooges. I had a million questions. I asked him if there were any out takes from any of their films. He said that there were no out takes because they used everything. The films were made for such a small budget that they couldn't afford more than one take.

Later on, I would learn through Moe Howard's book that the pie fights were dangerous after the first take. They would run out of pies and scoop up whatever was salvageable from the floor and make new pies out of them. When they scooped up the cream from the floor, they would also scoop up nails and sawdust and whatever else happened to be there. That stuff would end up in the pies and it became rather hazardous at times.

I asked Larry who was the funniest of the three. Surprisingly, his answer was Shemp. He said Shemp was a natural. He would keep doing funny stuff until the director would holler, "Cut!" The directors would say they never knew when Shemp was finished and didn't know when to say "Cut." Larry thought for a moment and said, "Come to think about it, I don't think that Shemp ever knew when he was through, either."

I must have spent two or three hours with Larry that day. He seemed happy to have me there and patiently answered questions of mine that he must have answered thousands of times during his career.

Later in the day, Larry invited me to come to a rehearsal of the "Ding-a-lings." That was a choir made up of patients and residents of the Motion Picture Hospital. They would get together and sing songs, tell jokes and entertain any visitors at the hospital. They were terrible singers, but they sang out loud and vigorous. Some of them were former actors like Larry and silent film actress Babe London. Others were former stage hands, make-up artists and set designers who just always wanted to get up in front of an audience and entertain. They were funny and corny, but their hearts were into whatever they were doing and it brought a tear to my eye.

I thought to myself, in what industry would you find people who love what they do so much that they never wanted to retire? Shoemakers, truck drivers, doctors and lawyers all look forward to the day they can walk away from their career and sit back and relax. That doesn't happen in show business. At least, not for the people I encountered. I made up my mind that day while watching the "Ding-a-lings" perform, this was the career path I wanted to take. Somehow, I was going to make my living in show business.

When I was leaving, Larry went over to a box near his desk and handed me a book. He said, "Here, take this and read it. It will answer most of your questions for you." It was a book written by

Larry Fine and Joe Carone. It was titled, "A Stroke of Luck." Larry said he named it that because of his stroke. "If I hadn't had this stroke I would never have taken the time to write it," he told me.

In May of 1973, I flew back to New York to get my car. I took Larry's book with me and read it in one sitting on the plane. After reading it, I was amazed at what a life he had. At times I was laughing out loud, at other points in the book I was almost in tears. After meeting Larry, even just that one time, I was saddened whenever he told a melancholy story in the book.

I had originally planned on selling my car in New York and buying a new one in Los Angeles. No one was interested in buying a 1971 Chevy Vega. Most people who had them bought the automatics and had nothing but trouble with them. I bought a three-speed stick shift and totally enjoyed that car. I took it all over the United States. I had no idea how important it was to have a car in Los Angeles. New York had subways and Los Angeles had freeways.

The drive from New York to Los Angeles was an adventure. On any of my long trips across America I had someone with me to talk to and to help share in the driving. I knew the radio reception was pretty bad out on the road, so I brought along some audiotapes. I recorded several hours of one of my favorite radio personalities in New York, Dan Ingram. Ingram had the number one radio show in the Big Apple for many years on WABC-Radio. He had a great sense of humor and would say things like, "This next song is about Ralph Bellamy's mother . . . ," and he would play the song "My Bell Ami."

I also brought along a cassette of "The Best of Buddy Rich" which saved my life several times upon my trek. I would find myself getting hypnotized by the monotony of looking at the road. When I would start playing the Buddy Rich music, I would be boppin' and singin' along with the sounds of his illustrious band—and suddenly I'd be wide awake and the time and miles seemed to fly by quicker.

I purposely left New York at 1:00 a.m. so that by the time the sun came up I was somewhere in Pennsylvania. I had lunch in Ohio and stopped somewhere south of Chicago by the time it got dark. The next day I got up early and made it to Albuquerque before sundown. I pushed myself the third day and breezed into Los Angeles just after 3:00 p.m. No matter how you try to break it up, it takes 48 hours of driving to get from New York to Los Angeles. When there's no one to talk to, all you want to do is drive. I didn't even want to stop for gas or food.

I was wide-awake and full of adrenaline and decided to stop at NBC Studios to see my drum teacher, Ed Shaughnessy, and let him know I was back in town. I wound up staying to watch the show and sat in the audience.

One of the guests on the show that day was "The Amazing Kreskin." Usually when Kreskin did the show he would take a few people from the studio audience to help him do a trick, or whatever Kreskin likes to call what he does. He is a mentalist. I was seated on the band side of the audience, and audience members were almost always chosen from the other side of the grandstand. But this day, when Kreskin asked for a few audience members to participate, he pointed to my side of the gallery, so I got up.

Keep in mind, I had just spent three long days on the road and driven nearly three thousand miles by myself. I hadn't showered or shaved in a day or two. I was also wearing my prescription sunglasses; I left my regular glasses out in my car. So, as I got up from my seat, I realized this and quickly took my glasses off and stashed them in my pocket. I also quickly was reminded of a little mishap I had in my trek across the country. My ball point pen had leaked in my pants pocket and left a rather noticeable stain on the front of my lightly colored jeans. Again, thinking quickly, I pulled my shirt out of my pants to cover the spot. This didn't help much because the stain was too far down the front of the pants and the shirt didn't even come close to covering it up. I was wearing a blue denim shirt that was all wrinkly near the bottom where it had been tucked in. This all happened in a nanosecond as I rose from my seat. As I walked between the cameras toward Kreskin, the thought crossed my mind that I was about to enter into the Land of Oz. I was going to be instantly seen by millions of Americans (well, instantly live on a three-hour tape delay, but close). There I was, one of "those" people, waiting to be one of Kreskin's guinea pigs. Even though I was there just a few days ago, somehow I knew I wasn't in Kansas anymore.

Kreskin's trick had each one of us take a marble out of a bag he held behind his back. One of the marbles was black. When Kreskin asked us who had the black marble, we were all to say we did not have it; even the person who got the black marble was to deny it. After he asked each one of us if we had the black marble, he was able to pick out the one who was lying. And, of course, he was "Amazing" once again and picked the liar. It was thrilling to suddenly be on television and even more thrilling as the stunt was over, because Johnny was standing right along side of us and thanked us for helping out.

I called my family in New York to let them know I not only arrived safely from my trip, but to watch me on the show with Kreskin. Later that night, after the show had aired in New York, I called my mom and asked her if she saw me. "Donald," she said, "couldn't you wear a nicer pair of pants than those you wore with that ink stain on them?" Before I could explain, my sister Arlene was on an extension and said, "What's the matter, you're so vain that you had to take your glasses off?" "And that wrinkly shirt," my mom continued, "You looked like nobody cares about you." They didn't understand the circumstances nor how unpredictable television can be.

It was on that same day in May that I got to meet some important new friends in my life and continue on down the yellow brick road. My plan was to keep on taking drum lessons from Ed Shaughnessy and get a job in television or motion pictures. When I approached Ed about this he said, "Sween-o, it's time for you to get out there and use all I've taught you and get into a band." That day he introduced me to Johnny Carson's son, Cory, and *Tonight Show* trumpeter "Snooky" Young's son, Danny, who were starting their own band. Cory played guitar and Danny played bass. They were both my age and had spent most of their lives in New York. Cory soon introduced me to Shelly Cohen, who was the assistant musical conductor for *The Tonight Show*. Shelly was also a conductor for a one-hundred-voice choir in Woodland Hills. The choir was about to perform one their many concerts and needed a drummer who could read music. I jumped right in and stayed with them for sixteen years. (I also met Catherine Burkhimer, a soprano soloist with that choir, who eventually became my wife. So far, we have been married twenty-four years.)

Cory Carson came over one day to just hang out. It was a Friday and we were trying to find something fun to do for the weekend. Cory suggested that we drive to Las Vegas. Johnny was appearing at

Caesars Palace. Money was tight for me so I asked how much a hotel room was going to cost. He pointed out that whenever his dad played Vegas, the hotel would have a house for him to stay in away from the Vegas Strip. He also had a hotel suite at his disposal and we could stay there. It was very tempting, but it was a long drive to Las Vegas. As we thought it over, Cory offered an alternative. Cory knew what a fan I was of his dad, so he suggested we go see his dad's house in Bel-Air. We decided to stay in town and Cory would take me for a tour of Johnny's house.

It was dark when we got there. You couldn't see his house from the street. Even in daylight, it was completely hidden from view by trees and hedges. We drove over in Cory's car and pulled up to the gate, Cory spoke to the housemaid on the speakerphone and she let us in.

We met Johnny's housekeeper as we entered the house through the kitchen. She was a very warm and friendly person. She was in her sixties and of Danish descent and spoke with a cute accent. She had nothing but good things to tell us about working for Johnny. She told us how he liked to sometimes fix himself something to eat late at night. When she would come in and try to help him, he would tell her it was after hours and she should let him do it for himself.

The kitchen was huge and had two refrigerators. One for breakfast and lunch foods and the other was for dinner foods. After sitting with the housekeeper for a while, enjoying the homemade cookies and milk she fixed for us, Cory took me on a tour of the house.

The house was very modern with floor-to-ceiling windows throughout. The smartly decorated house had little keepsakes and photos that showed that Johnny Carson lived there. The dining room had a black marble floor with a black marble table capable of seating at least twelve. The living room was warmly decorated with earth tones and cushy couches and armchairs. There was a plexiglass paperweight on a coffee table in the living room that seemed to have a stack of $100 bills inside it. I picked it up to have a closer look and found that if I looked at the bills from the side they seemed to be suspended. I asked Cory if the bills were real. He said, "In this house? It's real." Off of the living room was a fully equipped, state-of-the-art projection booth decked out with several types of movie projectors capable of showing 35 mm or 16 mm movies. The projection screen was hidden behind sliding doors that looked like a work of art. The doors would slide apart when electrically triggered by the projectionist. Johnny liked to have viewing parties at his house on a regular basis.

The bathrooms all had telephones near the toilet and even had a telephone in the shower. Apparently Johnny got a lot of telephone calls when he was in the bathroom.

We eventually made our way down a long hallway of hidden storage closets filled with the wardrobes of Johnny and his wife at the time, Joanna. We soon found ourselves in the master bedroom. Off of the bedroom there was a sitting room that resembled an office area with a desk and couch. There also was a closet just for shoes. It was a walk-in closet lined with shelves of shoes laid out similar to the way of shoes on display in a shoe store, except that these were all the same size. Right off of that area was the master bed. The furniture was dark mahogany and in the center of the room was a king size canopy bed.

Cory pointed out a row of push buttons on the night table at the side of the bed. He pushed a button and the television went on. Another button, the stereo began playing. Some of the other buttons triggered the lighting in the room to change. One feature I especially was impressed with was that the entire room could be in darkness but a pin spot would light up one side of the bed to allow for one to sit up and read while the rest of the room was in total darkness.

There was one button that was clearly marked DO NOT TOUCH! Cory and I looked at one another and laughed. What could it be? Cory decided to live on the wild side and hit the button. At first, all we heard was the sound of an electric motor purring. We looked around the room to see if anything had changed and saw nothing. Then Cory drew my attention upward. The canopy above the bed was parting the fabric to reveal a huge overhead mirror. We had a big laugh over our new discovery. We made sure to put everything back as we had found it and got back to the kitchen to bid goodbye to the housekeeper.

I was truly impressed with Johnny's house. I was particularly amazed how we could walk from one room to another throughout the house and never backtrack through the same room. The house was laid out in one big square maze.

Now that I was back in Los Angeles I couldn't wait to get back and see Larry Fine out at the Motion Picture Hospital. It was baseball season and we watched a Dodger game together. Larry was a huge Dodger fan. He knew every player, every statistic and spoke of previous games the way the announcers do. The only thing is that when the announcers remember games and plays they have the help of a statistician. I wished I knew more about baseball to carry on the conversation with Larry.

When the game was over I pointed out that the Three Stooges were on channel 58 (UHF). Larry told me he couldn't watch it because he didn't have a UHF antenna. I couldn't believe it. Larry Fine was on T.V. everyday and he couldn't watch it if he wanted to. I told him I had an extra UHF antenna and I would bring it the following week.

I returned the next weekend and installed the antenna. Larry was very grateful. He kept thanking me the whole time I was there. He announced to me that he had to go to the bathroom. I offered to help him but he said he could make it on his own. He slowly got down off of the bed, took his walker and crept to the bathroom. When he returned he was all flustered and started to cry. He told me he had just peed in his pants. "I'm such a mess. I can't even pee anymore," he said. I told him not to be concerned about it. "Sit back and relax, you're in your retirement years," I said. "After reading all the things you've done in your life, you've done more than three people do in a lifetime." That seemed to relax him and get him out of his funk. I asked him what he would like to do if he could get out for a day. He told me he would like to be able to go to a Dodger game some day. He thanked me again and again for installing the UHF antenna until it was dinnertime and I had to leave.

My car had been rear-ended by a careless driver and neither one of us had auto insurance. So, it had this deep crunch in the rear end of the vehicle. My plan before the accident was to take Larry to a baseball game or even to the racetrack. (He was quite a gambler in his day and I think he would have enjoyed the day out.) But I thought, the people at the Motion Picture Hospital will never let me drive off with Larry in his condition when they saw the condition my car was in.

One thing led to another in the coming weeks and I was unable to go see Larry. Nancy Patano would tell me how Larry was always asking for me and telling people at the hospital how I installed the UHF antenna for him. Then, one week, Nancy told me that Larry had another stroke and things didn't look good for him. She urged me to come and see him again. She said it would mean so much to him. I wanted to go and see him, but I also didn't want to depress him again if he were to get embarrassed about his condition. I fought with myself about it until the day Nancy called and told me Larry died. Being of the Jewish faith, he was buried by the time I heard of his death, so I couldn't even go to his funeral service. I will always regret never going back to see him just one more time.

During the next three years I continued to apply for jobs at NBC, CBS and ABC and continued to deliver office supplies. In August of '73 Cory Carson invited me to stay at his place until I could afford a place of my own. While rooming with Cory, the telephone rang one day when I was alone in the apartment. On the other end of the call was the voice of Johnny Carson. He knew my name and told me he was looking for Cory. I told him I would relay the message and have Cory call him when he got in. After the call, I just sat staring into space trying to realize that I just spoke with Johnny Carson and he knew my name. Cory had introduced me to his dad one day when we were passing in the hallway and the meeting was very informal and matter of fact.

During that time I visited *The Tonight Show* whenever I could take time off from my delivery driver job. Through Cory and Shelly Cohen I met a lot of *The Tonight Show* crew members and hung out with the Tonight Show Band. Sometimes I would help Cory do his job, which was to maintain the music library of the Tonight Show Band. Each day, Cory would take the music books the band used the day before and sort out and re-file the charts. When Doc Severinsen would come in, Cory and Shelly would go over the events for that day's show, Doc would pick the appropriate play-ons and songs for the commercial breaks, and then Cory would put the new books together for the band. I would sometimes help him carry the books into the studio. It wasn't that he needed me there to carry the books, I just enjoyed the pretense of what it would be like to work for a television show.

In the early months of '74, my cousin Merry moved out to Los Angeles and we got an apartment together. Merry worked for an insurance company and I continued to deliver office supplies. One night, about ten o'clock, the phone rang and Merry answered it in her room. She came knocking on my door to tell me that the call was for me. "He said he's Ed Shaughnessy, but I think it's your friend Jerico," she said.

Jerico and I were friends since high school. We went to Bishop Reilly High School in Fresh Meadows, New York. Jerico won first prize in a talent show that I emceed. He did impressions of famous TV and movie stars. He came out to Los Angeles to become a screenwriter. (Jerico eventually did become a screenwriter and wrote "My Stepmother Is an Alien" in 1988 starring Dan Aykroyd and Kim Basinger, directed by Richard Benjamin, and "Matinee" in 1993, directed by Joe Dante and starring John Goodman and Cathy Moriarty.) We would call and do impressions of famous people all the time, but he never would call and simply be himself. Merry thought it was Jerico pulling another prank on us.

I jumped from bed just knowing it was really Ed. He called to tell me he was going to start a big band and wanted to know if I would be interested in working for him as equipment manager (roadie). I was flabbergasted. I told him I would be delighted. After our brief call (Ed never talks on the phone for a long time), I thought it was ironic that Ed was going to pay me to be with him after all the times I paid to have him teach me drums. Since that time I never let the phone ring if I am home because every important moment in my life has happened with a phone call.

Among the many times that I worked as Ed's roadie, I worked with Fred Stites, a percussionist and sound technician. Fred worked with Ed Shaughnessy in Doc Severinsen's road act. Stites was a percussionist first and a sound technician second. Fred started as Doc's percussionist and kept buying amps and speakers to enhance the stage sound for him, and then one day Doc just asked him to do the sound. Fred played congas, bongos, tympani and Latin hand instruments, and he also managed to set levels for the stage monitors for the band and singers. He got so good at it that Ed Shaughnessy asked him to do the sound for him when he started his own band.

I started working for Fred in January of 1975. I was helping Fred do maintenance on his audio equipment. Fred had a storage bin off of Fountain Avenue near Highland in Hollywood. We would take everything out of the garage, look at it, and put it all back into the garage. It seemed we never really worked on the equipment. By the time we would empty out the bin to get to something in the rear, it was time to put everything back before it got dark. Fred kept teasing me with the idea of taking me out on the road with Doc's band. Pat Stites, Fred's wife, worked as Doc's house audio engineer and Fred did fold back monitors on stage. Fred needed someone to help load and unload the equipment from airplane to stage and back again.

From Monday through Friday I worked at Melrose Stationers delivering office supplies to bitchy secretaries. On weekends I worked as equipment manager with Doc Severinsen and the Now Generation Brass featuring Today's Children. With a name like that, Doc's personal manager, Bud Robinson, had to check the size of each theater's marquee to make sure the name of the band would fit before he'd book the group. It was January of '75 when I started touring with Doc Severinsen.

My first trip was to Acapulco, Mexico. The days leading up to our departure were filled with uncertainty. First we were going, then we weren't. One minute I was told to pack for a trip to Mexico, then they were going without me. For several days the trip was called off and the night before we originally were supposed to leave I got a call from Fred Stites. "Do you have a passport?" he asked. I told him I didn't and asked why he wanted to know. He said he would call me right back. A few minutes later he called back and asked if I could get myself over to a photographer's studio in Burbank within the next hour. He explained that we didn't need passports, only work visas, but we needed to have our pictures taken. Then he said, "We're leaving for Acapulco in the morning." And just like that, I was going to Mexico.

The next morning we all hopped aboard a jet to Acapulco. This was a weekend trip, so I didn't have to take any days off from Melrose Stationers. The guys back at the store on Monday would never believe where I went over the weekend.

I didn't realize how far east Acapulco was until we were told to set our watches ahead two hours. Although Acapulco is south, it is as far east as Chicago. When we arrived in Mexico, we were told to form two single lines in alphabetical order and cue up for immigration. "Have your papers ready." they asked. As it worked out, I was second in line and Doc was alphabetically in front of me. When the man from Mexican Immigration took a look at Doc's papers, he very matter of factly asked Doc for his passport. Doc answered something he thought sounded like Spanish, "No gots-o el passport-o." "Passport! Passport!!" the clerk demanded as he started to lose his cool. Doc turned and called out, "Rick?" Rick Olsen was Doc's tour manager, who quickly came to Doc's aid along with a representative from the airlines. The airline representative said a few short phrases in Spanish to the clerk and in moments, everything was O.K. For a second there, I thought we were going to turn right back to Los Angeles.

The trip to Acapulco was a memorable one for all of us. Doc was performing at a Pizza Hut convention. The entire weekend was taken care of, all expenses paid by Pizza Hut. I kind of knew this trip was a bit out of the ordinary because I wasn't the only one impressed with the service we received. Everybody in the band was ooh-ing and ah-ing about the treatment we were getting. I sat and had lunch with guitarist Peter Woodford, Ed Shaughnessy, and Fred and Pat Stites. The waiter brought over a large platter of fresh fruit for us while we waited for our lunches to arrive. Peter Woodford leaned over to me and said, "It's not always going to be like this on the road." This time it was first class all the way.

It was quite a change on weekends from my weekday delivery job. My friends and co-workers at the stationers job didn't believe me for a while. I would sometimes leave work on Fridays, go directly to the airport and fly across the country to work a concert on the East Coast on Saturday and Sunday. Then fly back early Monday morning in time for work at the store once again.

One week we left Los Angeles on a Wednesday night and flew to Missouri, to do a concert at a Ramada Inn outside of St. Louis. We had time to have a nice dinner before the show. Someone had told us about a steak house nearby. It was in a heavily forested area and quite a ride from where we were staying. It was a very elegant restaurant. Every once in a while, we would eat in some very expensive places, and luckily, I didn't have to pay. I was only making $100 a week working at the stationery store and I would barely have enough money with me to eat at a fast food joint. Many times, like this one, I would be asked to join the show members at a fancy restaurant, praying that someone would pick up the tab.

We had the greatest steak dinner that night. I remember looking through the wine list for this place while we were waiting for our dinner to arrive. The wine list was a book. It looked like a Bible. You really had to know your wines in a place like this. One bottle of wine sold for $3,500. Could you imagine ordering that bottle of wine and after drinking it, trying to convince the waiter that you thought it said $35.00 a bottle? I think they would want to see the deed to your house before they would even fetch that bottle. Could you imagine ordering it, taking one sip, and sending it back?

Before the Friday night show in St. Louis, I was to take half of the equipment on ahead to Tampa, Florida. Fred rented sound equipment in St. Louis to get them through the Friday night performance, while I flew on to Tampa. When I got there, I was to start setting up. Doc was playing at a horse jumping championship in a football stadium. I was to set up the stuff I had (in front of an audience of 50,000 spectators, mind you). When Doc and the rest of the band members arrived, Fred had Shaughnessy's drums and percussion gear with them. Fred said they would have a police escort from the airport, because we would be cutting it very close to showtime.

I was all set up and watching the clock and the horse jumping championship simultaneously. Thirty minutes before downbeat time I could hear the sound of sirens wailing. They got the police escort, but it was still going to be a close one. Seconds later I could see a large yellow rental truck pull up to the field entrance gate. They made it. Or did they? The truck was stopped just outside of the gate. I ran over to see what was the matter. I saw Fred, beet red, screaming at an elderly stadium security guard. The guard would not let Fred bring the truck on the field. The 50,000 people awaiting the show thought that this was part of the act! The crowd was reacting to our every move. I felt like we were an act in the Ringling Brothers and Barnum and Bailey Circus, and Fred, the guard and myself were the clowns. The crowd probably expected a team of circus clowns to emerge from the truck at any moment. We could not believe that after flying hundreds of miles from St. Louis and then getting a police escort from the airport to the stadium, everything came to a halt just two hundred feet from the stage because of a misinformed security guard.

While Fred distracted him, I quietly opened the gate behind them. Fred got back into the truck as if to back away, but instead, he gunned it and raced for the stage. The security guard ran after the truck screaming and waving his nightstick. The audience cheered! We came seriously close to upstaging the entire horse show. Someone finally calmed the security guard down and we were able to set up in the nick of time for Doc to hit the show at the time intended.

After each weekend stint on the road, whenever I got back to work at the stationery store, everyone would be talking about what they did with their weekend. One guy worked on his car, another went for a drive in the mountains. When I told them all that had happened on my weekend, they all laughed in disbelief and went on with our day's work. I didn't blame them. I was there and I found it all hard to believe. It wasn't until I returned with a pretty bad sunburn in the middle of an overcast weekend in February that they all started to believe my stories.

In 1975, Doc was doing a show in Seattle, Washington. Before the show I was setting up Ed Shaughnessy's drums when a young man named David Schuur approached me. He asked how he could get Doc to hear his sister Diane sing. He said she had been blind since birth and he was her twin brother. He was wearing two hearing aids. He added that she had a fabulous voice and simply must be heard. I was skeptical because I had seen this happen a few times before. Someone would approach Doc backstage and demand an audition for their young daughter or wife, and the singers were usually terrible. I asked if I could hear her first before I stuck my neck out for her. I thought that he'd give me a tape to take to Doc. He told me she was there in person. He proceeded to take me backstage. All the while, there was music playing; I thought it was a radio. David then opened two huge doors to reveal his sister seated at a piano singing her ass off! She was the radio I thought I'd heard. She was unbelievable. I said, "Oh yeah, Doc has to hear this girl." I went to Fred Stites and told him about this girl and Fred set it up that Diane would audition for Doc immediately following Doc's show. When the show ended, instead of the usual rush to take down the equipment, Diane took a seat at the electric piano and started to noodle a familiar song. By now the theater was empty and the main curtain was open. We were waiting for Doc to change his clothes. As Diane continued to play, I jumped up and started to play along on Shaughnessy's drums. Joel DiBartolo came back on stage and cranked up his bass. This alone was odd; most times band members are out of the theater the minute the show is over. One by one the band members returned to hear Diane sing. Fred quickly got a microphone set up for her and Diane let loose on a gospel style tune. From my vantage point I could see that the ushers of the theater came back into the empty multi-tiered auditorium. Some of the patrons from Doc's show were out in the lobby and returned to the theater when Diane's voice rang out. Even Doc, still wiping the make-up from his face, emerged from his dressing room before he changed his outfit to see where that voice was coming from. It was a phenomenal moment. When the song was over everyone applauded. Ed Shaughnessy came over to me and said, "Get her phone number for me regardless of whether Doc is interested in her." I did.

The next thing I remember was that Diane was to audition for *The Tonight Show*. Bud Robinson (Doc's manager) booked Diane into the Etc. Club on Highland Avenue in Hollywood and had *Tonight Show* talent coordinator Crag Tennis come down to hear her. The word came down simply, "She was not *Tonight Show* material." When I asked Bud what went wrong, he told me that Diane's brother David had come on a little too strong and that also Fred de Cordova and Peter Lassally were afraid that Diane was too much into religion. He said, "That would make Johnny uncomfortable." That was the final word from *The Tonight Show*.

Months later, Diane was flown to Los Angeles by Ed Shaughnessy to sing with his band Energy Force. Ed was debuting his band in concert at El Camino College in Torrance, California. Doc was there to introduce the band. Diane sang an original tune by Tommy Newsom called "Puddintane" and brought down the house.

MacLean Stevenson was in the auditorium that night. He had been a regular guest host for *The Tonight Show* after he left M*A*S*H. He was developing a new show for himself for NBC. After he heard Diane Schuur, MacLean got up and told everyone there that he was going to have a new variety show on NBC and that Diane Schuur was going to be his first guest. We all thought we had witnessed a new star being born.

MacLean Stevenson never got a variety show on NBC or any other network. Instead he starred in a situation comedy called *Hello Larry* that lasted only for one season. Diane did make it to *The Tonight Show* ten years later with no help from Doc, Bud or MacLean. She was "discovered" at the Monterey Jazz Festival with Stan Getz and Dave Grusen. Diane had appeared at the Monterey Jazz Festival around 1978 with Ed Shaughnessy and Energy Force. I wasn't there, but Jerico was and he said she had the audience on their feet. To this day he cannot figure out why that appearance in Monterey didn't launch her career. I guess it just wasn't her time. Diane admitted later, after she had appeared on *The Tonight Show* in 1987, that back in 1977 she wasn't ready for it. She told me she felt she needed those ten more years of experience to develop her voice. When she finally appeared on *The Tonight Show*, she was ready. Once again, she brought the house down.

I grew up listening to the many great comedy albums that Bob Newhart put out in the mid-'60s, such as "The Buttoned Down Mind of Bob Newhart" and "The Buttoned Down Mind Strikes Back," as well as seeing him appear on *The Dean Martin Show* and even *The Tonight Show*. Doc was opening for Newhart at the Frontier Hotel on the Strip. Every time we went to Las Vegas or Lake Tahoe, someone in the band got sick, divorced or fired. We also didn't relish a week in Vegas because everyone got paid less money than usual; we were not being paid on a per show basis but rather a weekly salary. Almost every time we'd go there, Doc would get held over for an extra week. You never brought enough clothes; everyone would get irritable from the heat, the pay, the gambling and having to live with each other for another week. We usually did a lot of one-nighters and weekend jaunts so that Doc could get back in time to do *The Tonight Show*.

Doc and the band would open the show with about half an hour of rousing trumpet solos with a mixture of pop and swing favorites. Doc also had six singers, Today's Children, who sang and danced throughout the show. Even though it was almost the same show night after night, I still enjoyed watching it and hearing Doc's banter between songs and his jokes about the band and *The Tonight Show*, or that his lips were taking a beating. The audience loved it, too.

I had always thought it odd that performers playing Las Vegas were required to shorten their shows. I understand the reasoning behind it: to get the people entertained and back out to the gambling tables. But in most cases, the patrons are paying a higher price to see a show that would cost much less if it were playing near their hometowns. And if they were performing in another area, the show would be longer—an hour and a half for the same price or less. In Doc's case, he always gave audiences their money's worth whether the show was 30 minutes or two hours.

In this instance, Doc was opening for Bob Newhart. So the band played a 30-minute set, the curtain closed and then, from behind the closed curtain, the band would play Bob Newhart's TV theme to bring him out on stage. Once Newhart was on stage, the band could take a break downstairs in the dressing room areas and listen to Newhart's routine on the dressing room speakers. The cue for them to head back up to the stage to play him off was when Bob started to do jokes about the airlines. Each night it worked like clockwork. The band members would slowly start to head to the stage, knowing they had about 10 minutes before they had to play him off. There were two shows a night for seven days, so it got to be fairly routine. The musicians could play his theme song in their sleep, and I think some of them did just that a couple of times.

After his airline jokes he would thank the audience and take a bow while the band played his music from behind the curtain. Then he would wait for the applause to die down and announce that he doesn't do the phony walk-off thing, go backstage and count to 10 and come back out and do an encore. He said: "One night I went off stage and counted to 12. When I came back out, the waiters were putting the chairs up onto the tables." He would say that every show and then do another 10 or 15 minutes while the musicians sat quietly backstage, awaiting his cue for the last joke so they could play him off.

One night, Bob started to do his airlines jokes and the musicians slowly started to make their way to the stage. But this time, for whatever reason, Bob decided to cut his routine short. Half the band wasn't near the stage yet when Bob shouted, "Goodnight, every-body!" The band members who were in the vicinity of the band-stand rushed to their instruments. I was sitting backstage the whole time listening to Newhart's act and noticed that Ed Shaughnessy was nowhere near the stage, so I jumped up to his drum set and we started to play. It was bass, trombone, drums and one saxophone. Newhart, never leaving the stage, pulled the curtain apart in the cen-ter and jokingly said over the microphone, "What the hell was that, an oom-pah-pah band?" It did sound like something one would hear at a beer festival. Bob got a big laugh out of it, so he was OK about the whole thing. He had thought the band was just backstage during his entire show night after night.

I happened to be backstage nearly every show, studying Newhart's approach to comedy. As a young stand-up comic myself, I wanted to see what made him tick. I was amazed to discover that he did exactly the same show every night. Every stutter, every stammer, fell in the same place, night after night. He would have the audience in the palm of his hand. He would not have to finish a sentence. The audience was a beat ahead of him, and he would set them up so that they'd think they got to the punch line before him. He had a style all his own, using his speech pattern to his advantage with a marvelous sense of timing like I've never heard since. No matter how many times I saw his act, I enjoyed it as though I were hearing it for the first time. He was brilliant.

Seeing Bob Newhart in this manner convinced me not to try to become a comedian. Each night, as Bob would do his final joke, take a bow and walk off stage, it seemed very lonely backstage. Sure, Doc's band was there, but they were playing his theme song, and Bob would just give them all a wave of thanks and walk off to his dressing room. The stagehand waiting to bring up the house lights would ask, "Is that about it, Bob?" and Newhart would say yes and head off to his trailer. The Frontier had an oversized mobile home backstage for Bob to use as a dressing room. Looking through the large sliding doors from outside the trailer, you could clearly see Bob's wife sitting and watching the television. I'm sure she had seen his show enough times to be able to recite it along with him. Bob would enter the trailer, quietly fix himself a drink and join his wife on the couch. It made me think: Here is a comedian at the top of his career, a household name, and he has no groupies backstage, no band to hang out afterwards with, and even his wife, although she was there for him, wasn't watching his act. She was watching the Johnny Carson show.

On the last night of his run at the Frontier, as Bob finished his show and was headed for his trailer, I felt that I had to tell him how much I enjoyed listening to him each night. He became very shy when I mentioned how much it meant to me to be able to study his comedy timing, undoubtedly going on longer than I should have. Bob was trying to unlock the door to his dressing room trailer, all the while sheepishly taking my compliments but almost trying to run and hide. He couldn't unlock the door and was nervously fighting the stuck latch to open, still trying to be gracious as he practically kicked the door in to get away. Suddenly I realized that, despite his discomfort, his natural sense of timing had taken hold, and as he went through the pains of trying to get away from me, he seemed to be unconsciously doing a comedy bit with the key and the door. He was a natural comic, even offstage.

Beyond a doubt, Red Skelton was the funniest man in the world. Sorry, Johnny, but he truly was for me. It was 1975, Doc was playing for a convention at the MGM Grand Hotel in Las Vegas, and the headliner act was Red Skelton. My friend Jerico was working with me. He came along to help out, but he really came along to see Red Skelton do his act. Jerico and I were both aspiring comedians back in high school.

Shortly after Doc did his sound check, off in the far corner of the huge ballroom, we could see Red Skelton trying to make his way toward the stage. He couldn't walk more than three or four steps without one of the hotel staff coming up to him to shake hands or ask for an autograph. Red was kind and courteous to everyone.

Red had a trunk backstage with all of his props in it. A young woman was at Red's side and was helping him with his things when Jerico and I approached him. We introduced ourselves to him and told him we were a couple of comics and wanted to ask his advice. We proceeded to ask him questions like, "What makes a joke funny?" "How do you find material for your act?" Red answered all of our questions with sincerity and in a very animated way, always joking but very helpful. When we asked him if he ever gets nervous before a show. He said no, but added when the powers that be call him to do these things he is nervous at first. However, by the time he thinks the show out and gathers his material, he calms down and isn't nervous anymore. He said that some comedians make that nervousness work for them, like Bob Newhart, Woody Allen and even Johnny Carson. Red said he told Johnny not to worry so much when a joke doesn't go over. Just because the four or five hundred people in the studio audience didn't get the joke, there are a couple of million people at home rolling on the floor. He added that Johnny Carson is at his best when a monologue joke doesn't go over because then he has to think quickly on his feet. That's when Johnny's mind goes into high gear and he is at his funniest.

It was getting close to show time and we didn't want to wear out our welcome, so Jerico and I thanked Mister Skelton for talking with us and went up to our room to clean up for the show. While we were getting ready, we were still floating high on the fact that we just had this tremendous conversation with Red Skelton—and then realized we didn't think to have our picture taken with him. As soon as we could, we ran back to the ballroom. Doc and the band were already on stage and wailing away and off in the wings was Red Skelton peeking at the show from the side curtain. We went up to him and asked him if we could have our picture taken with him and he said to us, "Not now, I'm trying to remember my name!" Then he kindly asked us to wait until after he did his show.

Soon Red took the stage and proceeded to perform some of the funniest jokes and routines I had ever heard (and have ever heard since). My cheeks were numb from laughing and at times my eyes would tear up from his hysterical facial expressions and the comedy bits he had perfected over the years. Unlike most performers, he didn't do that phony walk off stage near the end of his act and make the audience applaud until their hands were red and then come out and do another fifteen minutes. Red stayed on stage and after a solid hour and a half, he'd ask the audience if they had enough. Of course they would ask for more and he would do another fifteen minutes and ask them again. More, more, they all cheered until Red had been on stage for two and a half hours. The last time he asked them if they were tired yet and the audience replied "No!" Red said,

"Well, I'm beat to hell and gonna get out of here." He did one last pantomime as the old man and the little boy watching the parade go by. It was one of his classic pieces and a great way to end the show.

As soon as Red came off of the stage, Jerico and I were waiting in the wings to have our picture taken with him. He jokingly ran over to us and shook us both while he said in a panicked frenzy, "I was nervous! I've never been nervous before, but you guys made me think about it and I was nervous as hell out there!" After he dried off and calmed down from his show, he graciously posed for a photo with us. It was a fascinating experience—one I will never forget.

During the rest of 1975 I continued to drive the delivery truck and distribute office supplies, but on weekends I flew all over the United States with Doc Severinsen's road act. The weekends we didn't go out with Doc, I worked with Ed Shaughnessy's band. Eventually I started making enough money as a roadie and left the stationery store job. I felt I was making some headway in the entertainment business and was feeling pretty good about myself until December of '75 when Doc announced that he no longer was going to go on the road with the Now Generation Brass. Suddenly I was out of work and soon, totally out of money.

New Year's Eve of '75 I was feeling low and Jerico and I drove some friends up to San Francisco for the weekend and discussed what my alternatives were. I had no real skills. I was seriously considering enlisting in the Navy. At least in the armed forces I could learn a trade, and I had always liked traveling and being on the ocean.

New Year's Day I was invited to have dinner at Shelly Cohen's house. As was customary at the Cohens, after dinner, Shelly would conduct the conversation in a manner that we referred to as the "Hot Seat." It was almost like a game, similar to a discussion show on television. Sometimes he would single one person out (usually someone having dinner there for the first time) and ask personal and pointed questions. That person was on the spot. The rest of us at the table would encourage them to answer. The game part of it came when we were all invited to ask the "hot seat" person to answer one or two of our own questions. The topic varied from politics to religion, but always seemed to end up on sex. All of us present wanted to know the answers to these questions, but none of us were bold enough to ask about them ourselves.

This night, the after dinner hot seat was no different from the others. It was the first dinner of the New Year, so the questions on hand had to deal more with resolutions and futures. Those at the table that night were Shelly and Leona Cohen, their sons, Robert, Howard and Steven, and composer/musician Jon Charles, a friend of Shelly's. As we went around the table with our questions for the hot seat individual, the tables would often turn. The hot seat victim was able to ask questions of anyone else at the table. Also, when a question was raised to any one individual, the question might be asked of everyone in return. So, when the question, "What are you going to do with your future?" came up, it was my turn to answer. Shelly said, "And how about you, Don? What are you going to do now? You no longer have a job working for Doc on the road. What are your plans?" When I told them all of my plans to join the Navy, Shelly's eyes practically popped out of his head. "You're what?" he said. He begged me to reconsider. He said, "Don't join the Navy. It would be a big mistake." He asked, "What would you want to do if you had your way?" I simply said I wanted to do something in television. I had been trying to get a job at NBC for three years in L.A. and for three more years back in New York. I told him, "I want to work at NBC doing anything, even sweeping the floors if I had to start there." Shelly said, "Don't join the Navy. Something else will come up." I had to promise him I would hold off on my enlistment plans for a while.

January 12th, I got a call from Howard Cohen, Shelly's middle son. He simply said, "Don, would you want to work with my dad at NBC doing Cory's old job?" Of course I would, I said. Cory Carson left the show in 1974 to go to Cal Arts Music College to study classical guitar. Morgan Mason (son of Pamela and James Mason) took the job for a few months and as I was told, left the show when his grandfather died and he inherited a family fortune. Suddenly, there was an opening at NBC. Howard told me to call Fred de Cordova's office immediately and set up an appointment. When I got off the phone with Howard, I took a moment to catch my breath and immediately called NBC. Fred's assistant was Doc's girlfriend (who later became Mrs. Severinsen) Emily Marshall. She knew who I was from some of Doc's tours that she had tagged along on. We set up a meeting for the next day.

January 13th, I walked into Fred de Cordova's office wearing my best powder blue polyester suit (after all, it was the '70s). My conversation went exactly like this. After the usual greetings (Fred and I had met before during my many visits to the show when I used to come in and hang out with Cory), Fred said, "Would you like to work here as Shelly Cohen's assistant?" I said, "Yes sir, very much, sir." He said, "Do you know what the job entails as far as responsibilities and hours?" "I know exactly what needs to be done. I have watched and helped Cory Carson do the job many times," I answered. Fred took a puff of his ever-present cigarette and said, "Good. You can start next Monday." There was a pause for about two seconds and then I eagerly and boldly said, "How about today?" Fred said, "You don't have to start today, but if that's what you want to do, very well then. Go see Emily and she will have you fill out the necessary papers and all." We both stood up and shook hands as Fred said, "Welcome aboard, Don."

I couldn't wait to get to a telephone and call my parents. My folks knew I was going in for the interview, but I still called them as soon as I could. When my Mom got on the phone I jokingly spoke as if I were a reporter covering the big story of the day to his editor, I said, "Today, January 13th, Don Sweeney started work at NBC on THE TONIGHT SHOW STARRING JOHNNY CARSON."

I was barely at the job a week when I found myself at the Tonight Show Band Christmas party. Even though it was January, the band's Christmas party must have been pre-empted until after the holidays. To my good fortune, they waited to have it until after I joined the crew.

The party was in a small Italian restaurant on Cahuenga just north of Sunset Boulevard. We were in a private room on the second floor. The party consisted of Doc, the twenty-five or so members of the band, music supervisor Al Lapin, librarian Shelly Cohen, head carpenter Irv Davis, head of props Jack Grant, Doc's manager Bud Robinson, Doc's road manager Rick Olson, saxophonist Stan Getz, Johnny Carson, and me. Stan Getz just happened to be in town and was friends with a few of the band members, so they asked him to the party. Although the lighting in the restaurant was rather dim (it was nighttime outside), Stan never took off his dark sunglasses. I sat at the small bar talking with Jack Grant. Jack was a very likable character and Johnny had mentioned his appreciation for Jack many times on the air. Johnny would say that Jack was the kind of prop man who when you would ask him to get you a bathtub for a sketch, Jack would ask, "What year?" Jack knew I was the new kid on the block, so he sat with me telling me stories about his job on the show and how great it was to work for Johnny. At one point, Johnny walked over and joined Jack and me at the bar. Jack introduced me to Johnny and Johnny welcomed me aboard. After a few minutes, Jack Grant walked away and it was just Johnny and I sitting at the bar. An awkward silence soon occurred. Even though the party was still going on around us and the band members were laughing and telling stories to one another, the conversation between Johnny and me had ended and we sat there in a vacuum. I was so dumbfounded that two weeks ago I was penniless and at the verge of joining the Navy, and here I was sitting, having a drink with the man I idolized since I was eleven years old, and I couldn't think of a single word to say to him. It's probably just as well that I didn't say something stupid or Johnny would have thought that the new kid was an idiot.

After dinner Johnny got up to make a toast and graced us all with an after-dinner story. It was the story of a young couple who gave birth to their first child. It was a difficult birth and surgery was required. After surgery, the doctor met with the parents and told them that he had some good news and some bad news for them. The parents asked for him to tell them the good news first. The doctor told them that the good news was that they had given birth to a seven-pound baby boy. The couple jumped for joy until they realized that the doctor also had some bad news for them as well. When they asked to hear the bad news the doctor told them that the baby was born without a torso. It was a seven pound head. The parents at first were devastated but soon they learned what a blessing they had. The doctor assured them that perhaps someday a torso would become available for their head and that he would do everything in his power to see that operation happen. Over the years, they learned how to live with the baby's handicap. They would play games with the baby. Their favorite was rolling the baby back and forth to one another. On the head's twelfth birthday the couple received a phone call from the doctor. He called to tell them that a torso had suddenly become available and would be a perfect match for their head. The couple was elated. They couldn't wait to relay this great news to their child and it was especially appropriate that this news would arrive on the head's birthday. They quickly ran to the head's room to tell him the news. "Son," they said with exuberance, "We have the best birthday present a boy like you could ever ask for!" The head looked up at them and said, "Oh yeah? Well, it better not be another fucking hat."

We must have laughed for fifteen minutes. It was funny because it was totally unexpected. It was funny at this part of the evening because most of us had had way too much to drink. But most of all, it was funny to us because Johnny told it. He told it with such poise and class that all of us hung on his every word like children listening to daddy telling us a bedtime story. When the laughter eventually died down, Johnny added that he told this story at a dinner party the other night and when he got to the punch line, one of the guests, Mrs. Bloomingdale, fell face first into her salad plate.

At another Christmas party, Maury Stein was invited to give a toast. Maury owned a popular music store, *Stein's On Vine* across from the Musician's Union Local 47 on Vine Street in Los Angeles that still is there today. If you are a professional musician in Los Angeles you have either been in his store or at least driven by it.

Maury was sitting next to me at the table and he stood up to give a toast. He raised his glass and began to speak and suddenly sneezed into his handkerchief. A white powdery substance emanated from his hankie and a cloud of smoke encircled his head. White powder was all over his dark suit and all over his face. The band members roared with laughter and one or two of them indicated jokingly that Maury just sneezed away a "thousand dollar stash" assuming that the white powder was cocaine. As the laughter continued Maury leaned over to me and said, "A little talcum powder in your handkerchief gets a laugh every time, kid." He was quite a memorable character.

These Christmas parties were stag dinners in fine Italian restaurants. In later years they were held at the Villa Capri in the back room called "The Durante Room." There was a painting on the back wall of Jimmy Durante playing an upright piano. The room was a favorite of Frank Sinatra's where he held many of his private parties. I was usually recruited to draw the invitation for these band parties and the invites always featured a cartoon of all the band members with balloons over their heads making bizarre, silly comments. I had to be sure to include all the band members in the cartoon or I would hear about it. The food was always good and the drinks were free flowing and there were plenty of dirty jokes to go around. It was Doc's way of showing his appreciation to the band.

Some time after I was hired at the show, Cory invited me and the Cohen family to come to hear his guitar recital at Cal Arts and Johnny was there as well. We all arrived early and had some time to kill and someone from the college recommended that we go see the art exhibition the school had in the main lobby. We all quietly walked through the halls looking at the paintings and sculptures the students had on display. Johnny stayed with us or, rather, we followed him wherever he went. Johnny would look at one of the pieces of art and comment in a low voice that only those near him could hear. He had something funny to say for every piece we looked at. It was such a thrill to spend some time with my new boss.

THAT'S A ROOM OF A DIFFERENT COLOR

The greenroom, as it was constantly referred to over the years, was not green. Throughout most of the Johnny Carson years it was a mustard yellow or beige. The greenroom goes back to the early days of Shakespeare and the Globe Theatre. It has always been the waiting room before going on stage. Theories float around as to why they were called greenrooms. I have been in many greenrooms across the United States and they are rarely green. Johnny noted occasionally on the air when someone like Tony Randall, Charles Grodin or George Segal would bring this topic up for a light-hearted argument. Johnny would contend that the term "green" means that you are new to going out on stage. That has been the best explanation for me yet.

If you've ever seen the motion picture "Magnolia," there is a scene where a father brings his young son to be a contestant on a television game show. Director Paul Thomas Anderson creates a wonderful continuous shot of them getting out of a car in the pouring rain and going into the studio. They filmed that scene at NBC Studios. When they get out of the car, they walk right past the spot where Johnny used to park his car. They come in the artist entrance and continue to walk down a long corridor. The little boy is whisked away to make-up while the father continues down the hall and to the left. After going through two doorways, he is in the greenroom at Studio 1. The camera view walks to the end of the greenroom (to the table I used to sit at) and makes an about face and goes out of the room. That was the famous greenroom. (I actually worked on that movie. I contracted the orchestra and recorded the theme song for the fictitious game show heard in the movie. I hired many of the original Tonight Show Band members to record it at the request of Paul Thomas Anderson.)

Besides sharing an office with my direct supervisor, Shelly Cohen, the greenroom was my workplace during the taping of each show. Shelly and I had to watch and listen to the show each night to effectively log the music used onto the cue sheets and we needed to be close at hand in case Doc needed anything during the show. Shelly would remember classical pieces and titles from before my time, and I would identify most of the current pop tunes and some standards.

On occasion, when a show would run short, a guest wasn't as interesting as we thought, a guest didn't show up, or Johnny just wanted to hear the Tonight Show Band play a featured number, the stage manager would come bursting into the greenroom to announce that Doc needed a chart from the library. The band library consisted of well over three thousand charts and was located on the third story above Studio 3. Once I knew what song title Doc needed, I would bolt from the greenroom and run up two flights of stairs and down a long hallway past Johnny and Ed McMahon's dressing rooms. Quite often, my frantic hall running would freak out a security guard along the way. I would find the chart in the library. They were alphabetically listed and kept in cardboard filing boxes on steel reinforced shelving in a room above Johnny's office that used to be a rehearsal hall. Half of the room was filled with musty old costumes from the wardrobe department and the other half of the room was the music library. Among these three thousand charts were about one hundred of Doc's favorite charts spread out on a tabletop that he would choose from on a daily basis. Everything was available within seconds of entering the room.

After obtaining the chart that Doc requested, I would rush back to the stage and the chart would quietly be passed out to the band during the show or during a commercial break. Quite often, this scenario would take place and the band feature would never happen. Suddenly the boring guest got interesting or Johnny would tell a humorous story of his own to fill the segment and, most often, save the show.

Whenever a guest would ad-lib part of a song, we had to immediately identify it. Sometimes a song would be restricted for use on television. Some authors and publishers do not want their work performed on television without prior permission and some don't want their music used on TV at all. To avoid any lawsuits, we would notify Fred de Cordova during the show. We taped from 5:30 p.m. to 6:30 p.m. PST, which gave us three hours to fix anything before the show aired on the East Coast. Fred was always quick-witted. I had to rush to him on stage during the show to tell him that somebody just sang a song that would cost us a lot of money and we should bleep it out before air. On one particular night, the show was rather boring and Fred said to me, "Don't worry, nobody is watching this show, anyway."

Regardless of Fred's reaction, I always typed up a brief memo to him the next day explaining the nature of the concern. Fred would flag that show as a show not to be repeated. Since our show was considered a "live" show (even though we were live to tape) we could play a song once without permission and without having to pay large fees. It was when we would re-air a show that we had to get all the permissions and license fees for any music (even one line) of any recognizable tune. In all the years I was there, we never had a legal problem with music.

Sometimes, friends of ours or of other staff members would come to see the show and we didn't have enough seats for them to sit and watch the show from the audience. So we would let them sit in the greenroom with us. Quite often, that was the better place to watch the show. Sometimes, there was a show within the show going on in the greenroom.

The Tonight Show Band music contractor, Al Lapin, would join us in the greenroom every night. When I started working with him at NBC, Al was the ripe old age of seventy-five. Al had always kept his age a secret and we could only guess how old he was. One time, one of our directors, Bob Ostberg, flat out asked, "Come on Al, how old are you?" Al asked Ostberg, "Can you keep a secret?" When Ostberg said yes, Al said, "Well, so can I."

Another time when we came close to finding out Al's age, he had fallen and cut his knee enough for us to call an ambulance for him. The ambulance attendant asked him to write down his birth date on a slip of paper (probably to see if Al had his wits about him). As I stood above Al, I could see the slip of paper clearly. Soon I was going to find out Al's age. He took the pencil to the paper and prepared to write but instead he kept making circles above the paper without writing anything. He'd look away and think until he finally wrote down, 4/10/90. When Al handed it to the attendant, he read it and said to Al, "I asked you to write down your birth date." Al nodded and said, "That's my birthday." "You're one-hundred years old?" asked the ambulance driver. Al said, "No. You asked for my birthday. That's when my birthday is this year." No doubt about it, Al had his wits about him. Once again, he managed to escape giving his age away.

Anyone playing professionally in this town over the past fifty years has probably worked with Al Lapin. During my sixteen and a half years with the Johnny Carson *Tonight Show*, Al and I had lunch together nearly everyday. As Al once pointed out, despite our vast age difference, we always had something to talk about. I loved to hear him talk about the days of vaudeville, the early days of television and the many celebrity fame scenarios through the eyes of Al Lapin. He sometimes repeated the same stories. He enjoyed telling them and I enjoyed hearing them. As a drummer in vaudeville he taught Buddy Rich how to properly hold the drumsticks when Buddy was just a child. This story was confirmed to me by Buddy during one of his many appearances on *The Tonight Show*. He would always greet Al with a big kiss and a hug.

Al worked with so many legends: Jimmy Durante, Eddie Cantor, Bob Hope and Frank Sinatra (to name just a few). Some of the top artists of today worked with him and would always send their regards.

The list of shows he worked on was longer than any list of variety shows that any network could come up with. He was also the busiest, most respected contractor in the early days of radio. His job was to hire any musicians for a show or pre-recording and keep track of the hours and payroll for the musicians.

Al loved the Tonight Show Band members. He called them "the boys" and they called him "Pappy." (The last time I spoke with him, he was still hoping for Johnny Carson to come back to television, as we all wished. He couldn't wait to work with Doc Severinsen and all "the boys" again.)

A collection of malaprops known as Lapinisms were respectfully collected over the years (unbeknownst to Al). They were photocopied and passed around every major recording session and orchestra pit in the industry. If Al was at a loss for a word, he would invent a new word in its place. Amplifiers became "ample boxes," synthesizers became "sympathizers" and a contrabass was a "contrary bass." The long list of quotes became as legendary as his high pitched whistle calling the finest musicians in the business to the stand.

He taught me so much about the business and how to handle people in a respectful way. Al Lapin was the kindest, most polite person I have ever known. He never had a bad word to say about anyone. He was a diplomat when it came to his adversaries and a gentleman until his last hour. It is with respect and admiration that we list the famous Lapinisms, compiled over the years by the many session players who worked for Al, at the back of this book.

When I was single, it was always a good way to impress my girlfriends by bringing them to the show and letting them sit among their favorite stars in the greenroom. A girl I had been dating for several years had been to the greenroom many times before and should have known to watch what she said. It was during *The Tonight Show* warm-up (Ed McMahon would joke with the audience shortly before the show and Doc and the band would play some dazzling number to get them revved up) and during that time the greenroom was usually empty and quiet. My girlfriend asked to see the rundown of the guests listed for the show that day and saw Monty Hall's name on the sheet. She said, "Monty Hall? He's not going to sing, is he? I hate when people like him come on shows like this and try to be someone they're not." Before I could shoot her or at least gag her with an hors d'oeuvres from backstage, I wasn't able to signal to her that the man sitting in the armchair five feet away was none other than Monty Hall. Luckily, Monty has a tremendous sense of humor. He turned to her and said, "Don't worry, sweetheart, I promise I am not going to sing this evening." She had the sense to excuse herself and left the greenroom until Mr. Hall was well on stage.

Sheena Easton was the new kid in town and had one hit song on the Billboard Top 100 Charts, "Morning Train." She was working on her second, the title theme song to the new James Bond film, "For Your Eyes Only." It became one of a stream of hits that followed. Most artists about to debut their latest hit on live television will find a rehearsal room somewhere within the Hollywood area where they can run through their song or songs until they have reached the level of perfection the artist and the record company have set for themselves. Sheena had wound up using one of the NBC rehearsal halls for the week before she was to appear. She would come into the greenroom and watch the show. One night I got to talk with her and she asked me where she could buy a Beverly Hills type house and still be able to keep horses. I suggested that she take a look at the Hidden Hills area of the West San Fernando Valley. It is a gated community with large properties and zoned for horses.

A man seated nearby overheard our conversation and suddenly chimed in. He was a business manager for someone appearing on the show that night. He handed Sheena his business card and asked her to call him the next day and he would set her up with a realtor friend of his. "He handles some of the best real estate in Beverly Hills," he said. Sheena told him she didn't want a house in Beverly Hills, but the man persisted. Sheena looked at me and rolled her eyes. When the slick businessman finally left us alone to watch the show, Sheena whispered to me, "What was that area? Hidden Hills?" I nodded and she wrote it down.

In one of her appearances on *The Tonight Show*, Sheena professed that she did not want to become a "one-hit wonder." She was determined to have a long lasting career like Barbra Streisand. It was no secret how much she admired Streisand.

A few years later, a friend of mine who is a general contractor was doing some remodeling work at Sheena's house. She was not there when my friend worked there, but he told me he had to go through her bedroom to do the remodel. He noticed that she had a framed photo of Barbra Streisand on her dresser. It all came together when I told him of her admiration for Barbra. And, guess what? Sheena had horses on her property in the gated community of Hidden Hills.

Many people have dispelled the myth about Don Rickles by telling us on and off the air that he really is a nice guy off stage. Beneath that hard eggshell exterior, there is warm-hearted human being. Sure, he might fall into a line or two from his routine and call you a hockey puck, but that is what we expect from him and we are usually honored to have him say something about the way we dress, or talk, or laugh. He will find something to put you down. It is never meant to be harmful.

Don Rickles would always refer to me as "Red." I used to have dark fiery red hair (before it started to fall out). Then I replaced that hair with a series of red wigs. Rickles never remembers me by name; he just calls me Red, even now that I shave my head bald.

He also would refer to me as "Jackson Heights." The reason behind this was that I knew he lived in Jackson Heights, New York, for a period in his career. I used to work for the U.S. Postal Service in Flushing, New York, and pointed out to Rickles one night at *The Tonight Show* that the town of Jackson Heights is one of the narrowest towns in the nation. (It is only four blocks north to south and three miles east to west.) After that, Don thought I was from there, so he would call me "Jackson Heights" from time to time.

My brother Kevin was working for Top Drawer, a company in Los Angeles that lines kitchen drawers and cabinets with a color vinyl. He was always doing some celebrity's house. He told me one day, "I'm going to be doing your friend, Don Rickles' house tomorrow." I told Kevin to say hello if he saw him, but to say the red-headed guy from the Johnny Carson greenroom said to say hello. So my brother sees me a few days later and mockingly says, "I mentioned you to Rickles the other day and he didn't know who you were." I asked if he explained about the red hair and the greenroom, and Kevin said he did mention that to him, but that Rickles didn't know who he was talking about. Kevin said he was going back in a week to do a few touch-ups for him and would give it a second try.

A few days later, Rickles was a guest on *The Tonight Show,* and when he came into the greenroom before the show, I was sitting at my usual spot near the back end of the room. Don walked over and shook my hand and asked, "How ya doin', Red?" As he kept walking to greet a few others in the room I held his hand and said, "Wait a minute. I have something to talk to you about." Rickles asked what was wrong. I proceeded to tell him about my brother talking to him in his kitchen and that Rickles said he didn't know me. Rickles said, "Aw, no, no. He, he, didn't describe you that way . . ." I stopped him in mid-sentence and told him I had an idea for a practical joke if he would help me out. I told him that my brother doesn't believe that we know each other and that he would be back to do some touch-up work in his kitchen in a few days. Rickles told me he and his wife were going out of town for a few days when Kevin would be there. I told it didn't matter. I asked one of my friends to take my picture with Rickles. I told Rickles I would mail the photo of the two of us standing together and I would autograph the photo, "To my pal, Don, from Don." And then I asked Rickles to be sure and tape it onto his refrigerator door so that my brother would see it. Rickles liked the idea and cackled in the way that only he could do.

Weeks later, I saw my brother at a party. As soon as he saw me, the first thing he asked was, "Hey, why did Don Rickles have an autographed photo from you taped to his refrigerator?" I said, "I told you, Rickles and I are good friends!"

Many years later, I went to see Don Rickles perform at the Stardust Hotel in Las Vegas. My friend Peggy March was opening for him there and she and her husband, Arnie Harris, invited me backstage before the show. Rickles' dressing room door was wide open, so I walked in. He was in mid-conversation with his booking agent as he looked up at me. He said, "Hey, I know you. Don't I?" He didn't recognize me because I had stopped wearing my hairpiece and shaved my head. I began to laugh when he saw me and couldn't place where he had seen me. He said, "Wait a minute, you're from the Carson show, right?" I laughed even more and then he said, "Red!" We hugged each other. I hadn't seen him in a few years and suddenly it was just like being back in the greenroom with him again. As the others in the room talked with each other, Rickles quietly asked me if I was okay. He thought that perhaps my hair had fallen out due to a medical treatment and asked, "Where's all of your hair?" I told him it was on a shelf in my closet at home and we laughed. Then he said, "Seriously, Red, is everything okay?" I assured him I simply shaved my head for a new look.

I took out a copy of the photo I kept of Rickles and me in *The Tonight Show* greenroom and asked him to autograph it for me so that I could hang it on my refrigerator. He remembered the gag because he began to laugh about the photo. He called his wife over to show her the picture and he told her about what we did to my brother. His wife, Barbara, looked at the photo and pointed out that Rickles hadn't changed. "Look honey, you look the same today as you did fifteen years ago when the photo was taken," she said. Then they both pointed out how much I had changed. I was wearing my hairpiece in the photo. Don Rickles signed the photo, "To Don, What happened? Love, Don Rickles."

Although Tony Randall, along with Jack Klugman, was star of the successful TV series *The Odd Couple*, some people tended to think of him as a professional talk show guest. Randall was on *The Tonight Show* more than any other personality. The underlying reason for all those visits was simply that Tony was a great guest. He didn't have to have something to plug when he came on. He would tease Johnny Carson about the mispronunciation of a word or a phrase that didn't quite mean what people have always thought it meant. Johnny would pretend to be miffed by Tony's acting as if he were Johnny's grammar school teacher. Eventually Johnny would put an end to the conversation by telling Tony to shut up in a comedic way.

It was always entertaining, and Tony was always available at the drop of a hat to replace a guest who had fallen ill or canceled at the last minute. The talent coordinators loved him because of his ability to ad lib a funny story without an interview beforehand, meaning that the coordinator didn't have to prepare a lot of notes before the show.

There was a long period of time during which Randall did not appear on the show. Tony lived in New York and was not in Los Angeles filming any television show, so sometimes he wouldn't be around.

Then one day Tony was back. He was in the greenroom during the show's warm-up, sitting in one of the armchairs and staring at the color bars on the monitor. As always, he still had the tissue paper sticking out of his neckline, something the make-up department offers to keep the makeup from smudging his shirt collar. When I walked in and saw him there I gave him a warm welcome back and told him how much we missed him. He didn't believe me. He thought I was giving him the "Hollywood insincerity" hype. "Oh, I'm sure you all missed me," he said in a mocking tone. I tried to tell him I wasn't joking around. I, at least, was one of the staff that looked forward to his guest spots. It took a few minutes to convince him, but I think he finally realized that I wasn't feeding him a line.

On every visit to the show, Tony would sit in the greenroom until it was time for his spot. The talent coordinator (usually Shirley Wood) would come into the room to fetch him. Tony would get up and clear his voice all the way to the door and then announce to all in the greenroom, "Wish me luck!" and off he would go for another of his many memorable segments with Johnny.

On one occasion—it may have been an Anniversary Special or just one of those lucky "star-studded" nights at the show—we had Wayne Newton and Bill Cosby guesting on the same night. The greenroom was more packed than usual, and along with Wayne Newton's entourage there was an elderly white-haired man whom everyone seemed to be pampering.

The people associated with Wayne Newton pampered the old man so much that one of them took a chair and placed it directly between where I was sitting with other people and the television monitor, completely blocking our view. They then sat the old guy in front of us. No one said anything because the old-timer seemed to be important, and we weren't about to cause a commotion.

As the show progressed, Bill Cosby emerged into the greenroom and stood in the back near our table. Upon many of Bill's visits to the show, he had often sat with us and joked about us being the working few in the room. Suddenly, out of nowhere, Cosby says to the old man, "That's OK, Pops, we can see the show right through you." The old man turned and struggled to move his chair from where it impaired our view when Cosby recognized him.

Cosby said, "Oh my God, is that Walter Kane?"

Walter Kane was then running second to Howard Hughes when it came to owning Las Vegas property. It seemed as though Kane owned everything in Vegas that Hughes didn't. The old guy could hardly blurt out an acknowledgment to Cosby's line when the comedian went over to him to stop him from trying to move his chair. Cosby then had the attention of everyone in the room as he looked into Kane's face and said in the tone of an old man, "Walter! I thought you died!" Cosby felt secure enough in his own career that he could say something like that, even though he was joking, to Kane and not have it affect his standing in the casino world.

As we continued to watch the interview with Wayne Newton and Johnny Carson, Cosby continued to make comments in jest about everything the two had to say. At one point, Wayne and Johnny were talking about the kind of women they are attracted to, and Johnny asked Wayne what attracts him to women. Wayne's answer was, "Well Johnny, I guess you could say I am a face person." Cosby picked up on that right away and started to echo Wayne's comment in the greenroom. "A face person? Did he just say he was a face person?" Cosby said he was going to get him with that one when he got out there. Luckily for Newton, the singer had to leave immediately after his interview in order to catch a plane back to Las Vegas. By the time Cosby came out, Wayne had already left. Cosby commented on the "face person" line, but never got a chance to tease Newton on the air the way he wanted to.

At the time, the questions were, "Who is she?" and "Where did she come from?" Kirstie Alley was named to be the replacement for Shelley Long on the popular TV series *Cheers*. For anyone who hasn't watched *Cheers*, all five or six of you, Shelley played the part of Diane Chambers, a waitress in the *Cheers* bar. Kirstie was to play the part of Rebecca Howe, playing opposite to Sam Malone, played by Ted Danson. In an effort to save the series, NBC was taking a big risk introducing a new love interest for Sam.

Few knew who Kirstie was. She had not done enough television or film that anyone would remember. However, I recalled her from a summer replacement series she did, costarring with Hugh O'Brien— a show called *Lavender*. Hugh O'Brien played the lead role, a cross between James Bond and the head of a *Mission Impossible* team. The show was filmed entirely on location throughout Europe. Kirstie played the role of tour guide, working undercover for *Lavender* while appearing to work for a bus touring company. I don't remember her getting in on much of the action, but she was the only woman on the team. She would pose as a waitress or tourist at times to distract whoever the *Lavender* team was trying to capture. Not many people watched that show, so I was one of the few who knew of Kirstie Alley.

Kirstie was making her debut on *The Tonight Show*. It was NBC's way of presenting the replacement for Shelley Long. Backstage, everyone was abuzz at her appearance. "Is that the new girl on *Cheers?*" they were saying. "Ew! Her hair is so dark." "She looks like a bitch!" I just wanted to see if she was as pretty and sexy in person as she was on *Lavender*.

Minutes before the band blared "Johnny's Theme," I took my familiar seat in the greenroom, near the back of the room at the round table. I had my usual can of beer and an assortment of crackers from the perpetual array of snacks that Jack Grant would dish out every night. I had just mentioned to all at the table how excited I was that Kirstie Alley was going to be on the show when one of them motioned to me with his eyes, as if to say, "Look out, here she comes." I barely had a chance to turn when Ms. Alley came toward me at full force.

When I'd taken my seat at the table, I hadn't yet turned my chair to face the TV set, so I was facing away from it. She immediately took a seat directly in front of me, facing the TV. She sat so quickly that I was unable to completely move out of her way. My legs were spread wide, and Kirstie managed to sit so that her legs were planted directly between mine. I couldn't change my position to turn around to the TV without causing a lot of commotion. She was nervous and was primping her hair and make-up while puffing away on a cigarette. So there I sat, face to face, knee to knee, while she nervously inhaled her cigarette, blowing her second-hand smoke in my direction. I found myself closer to Kirstie Alley than I ever dreamed possible. I was so close that when she checked her face in the mirror, she stuck her face inches from mine and asked me if she looked OK. My reaction was similar to that of her first appearance on *Cheers*, when she and Sam Malone (Ted Danson) met for the first time. Sam's reaction was akin to mine, "Oooh ah!"

John Candy appeared on *The Tonight Show* when SCTV Network (Second City TV) was still a big hit. I talked to John backstage before the show. He was standing just outside the greenroom, trying to find a good vantage point from which to watch Johnny Carson do his monologue live. At this time, you could no longer see Johnny from the sidelines because some oversized wardrobe cabinets had been strategically placed to prevent large crowds from showing up backstage each night.

You'd be amazed at how many NBC employees would show up on any given night to peek in at the show. They would bring friends and spouses, even small children once in a while, to catch a glimpse of Johnny Carson in action. Who could blame them? But it did get out of hand once in a while and even became a security problem at times. So the cabinets showed up one day and remained until the last day of the show.

I felt compelled to tell Candy how much I had enjoyed a skit he once did as Ben Hur on SCTV. The twist of the skit was, John played the part of Curly Howard of the Three Stooges as Ben Hur. His impression of Curly was impeccable and the skit was hilarious. I told John that I met one of the Stooges, Larry Fine, out at the Motion Picture Hospital. When I said that, I noticed John checking out my receding hairline. I was beginning to lose my hair and was sporting a curly hairdo, so I'm sure he was thinking that I was trying to look like Larry Fine. Believe me, I was not trying to look like Larry, just trying to hide my balding head if I could.

John went on to tell me that the Second City TV shows that were running in Los Angeles were about three years old. He had been finished with that show for almost two years. He said that although he never received any residuals from SCTV, he enjoyed doing sketches on that show, which basically was the key to his early success. "Let's face it," he told me, "without Second City, I wouldn't be standing here talking to you, let alone be a guest on the Johnny Carson show."

He asked me how he could get to watch Johnny live. As *The Tonight Show* theme started up behind us, I told him to follow me through the greenroom, and I ushered him to the spot we referred to as "the well area." This was a place below the audience but directly in front of Carson as he did his monologue. I showed John how to peek over the cameraman's shoulder and try to not let Johnny see him (which was like trying to hide an elephant behind a tree). I told him that Johnny might get distracted if he saw him there. John understood and I left him there to enjoy the monologue.

When the monologue was over and we went into our first commercial, Candy emerged from the well area and came back into the greenroom. His eyes were beaming and he thanked me as he walked by and said, "Man, that was great!" as if he were a young kid who just got to meet Santa Claus for the first time.

At another time, pianist Earl Rose was filling in for the vacationing librarian, Shelly Cohen. Earl is a concert pianist from New York and, at the time, was the daytime drama composer for *Ryan's Hope*. Earl is a phone-a-holic, and there was a telephone on the table where we sat at the back of the greenroom.

When we arrived just prior to show time, there was a young, hip looking man on the phone wearing a nice sport jacket with the sleeves rolled up to his elbows. His shirt collar was up around his neck the way Elvis Presley used to wear his. This guy had on brown loafers without any socks. We figured he was a male model or daytime soap star.

We could hear him talking to whoever was on the other end. He was bragging that he was sitting in the greenroom of *The Tonight Show*. Whether it was his girlfriend or booking agent, we didn't know. But as soon as he hung up the phone, he immediately dialed someone else and began bragging all over again. All the while, Earl was drumming on the table, eager to use the phone himself.

When the show began, the man took a break and listened to Johnny's monologue, as did Earl and I. As soon as we went to commercial break, the guy picked up the phone again. As he went to dial, Earl put a stop to it. He said to the man, "Excuse me, but that phone needs to be available for us to use during the show. We are working here and may need to call the director's booth." The man put the receiver down and asked where the nearest telephone was. (See what pains we went through before cellular phones were invented.)

Earl told him there was a pay phone just outside the studio down the hallway. The guy quickly left the greenroom in search of an outside line.

Our press representative for the show, Joe Bleeden, was sitting at the opposite end of the greenroom and called me from his phone (as he regularly did from time to time) and asked what it was that we said to that guy that made him leave so quickly. When we told him what had happened. Joe chuckled and asked if we knew who that was. I told him we didn't know and asked if he was a guest on the program that night. Joe said, "No, but he's the star of a new NBC show premiering next week, something called *Miami Vice*. That was Don Johnson." Although his show had not aired yet, we knew the name from all the press the new innovative show was getting. Earl just kicked one of NBC's brightest new stars out of the greenroom.

From time to time, we would call Joe Bleeden from one end of the greenroom to the other. As we sat at the round table at the far end of the room, Joe always sat on a short couch near the door and near his own phone. On a night that a particular guest was boring (yes, that happened once in a while), we would call Joe. The calls weren't exactly prank calls. Joe knew it was me or Shelly calling.

Sometimes we would call Joe and say, "This guest is so boring. Why doesn't Johnny bring out the next guest?" Joe would answer, "There is no next guest and we have another half hour to go!"

One night I called Joe when he had a sexy young actress sitting next to him on the couch. I asked, "Joe, who is that lovely woman at your side?" He'd blush and cover the phone as if she could hear me. Heck, I was only twenty-five feet away. If she knew I was the one on the opposite end of the phone, she could read my lips. As Joe continued to fear that the young lady might find out we were talking about her, I added, "Would you tell her to stop breathing so heavily, we can't hear the television."

I looked across the greenroom once and saw a wobbly Milton Berle being escorted in by talent coordinator Shirley Wood. Milton was using a cane and smoking a cigar. He quietly sat on the couch until Shirley returned after Johnny's opening monologue and told Mr. Berle it was time to head backstage because he was the first guest. She slowly helped him to his feet and he gingerly walked off with her. Minutes later, Johnny introduced the legendary Milton Berle. Milton emerged from the rainbow curtain without the cane and sauntered on like a young, spry dancer. He sat in the chair next to Johnny's desk (which we referred to as "the swivel"), crossed his legs, puffed his cigar and came alive like a teenager.

It was remarkable the way the bright lights and applause could do that to someone his age. It was an amazing transition and unexplainable to anyone who has never experienced the roar of the grease paint and the smell of a lion.

Many times I sat in the greenroom and carried on conversations with nervous celebrities and seasoned legends of television, theater and motion pictures—people like Peter Ustinov, Bill Cosby, Larry King, Luciano Pavarotti, Red Adair, Brooke Sheilds, Sally Fields, Robin Williams, and so many more. I once sat and had a wonderful conversation with world explorer Jacques Cousteau. At the end of our conversation I told him how lucky I was to be able to listen to his stories first hand. He answered by saying he was the one who felt honored and privileged and how he felt we at the show had more exciting lives than he and his crew. In a way, we both had to swim with sharks once in a while. The only difference was that I didn't have to wear a wetsuit.

Comedian John Belushi came to *The Tonight Show* along with colleague Chevy Chase. Chase was appearing on the show, and Belushi came along to offer him support. *Saturday Night Live* was only in its second season, and Chase and Belushi were at the height of their careers. I was in the greenroom in my usual place at the round table near the back. That day, my girlfriend, Ilene Finklestein, was with me. She sat next to me and was thrilled to see the two comedians nearby. As the room became quite crowded, Chevy noticed that there was some unoccupied space at the far end of the room, where we were, and motioned for John to follow him.

As they got to our side of the room, Chevy took a chair on the opposite side of the table from us, while John and another man took the bench from an old upright piano, plopped it directly in front of our view of the TV and sat down. Belushi, as if he were doing a bit from *Saturday Night Live*, turned to Ilene and me and said, "Am I in your way? I'm sorry."

"No, that's OK," she said. "We can still see all right." Belushi took the stool and nudged it sideways to block Ilene's view entirely, turned to her and joked "How 'bout now?"

At the end of the show, I caught up with Chevy Chase in the hall and asked him whether he could get my brother, Kevin, into a taping of *Saturday Night Live*. Chevy said he would see what he could do. He told me to have my brother call his assistant and that she would set it up. Well, not only did Kevin get in to see the show, but he also got invited to a party afterwards.

Actor Robert Culp was at the party, and my brother proceeded to make a blunder. Culp was well known as the co-star with Bill Cosby on *I Spy* for so many years, Kevin got their names mixed up. He went up to Culp and said, "Hey, I know who you are. You're Bill, right?"

"No, Bill is the other guy," Culp said. "I'm Bob."

"Yeah, right," Kevin said, "Come on, I know you're Bill Culp. You can't fool me." He continued his gaffe and called Robert Culp "Bill" for the rest of the evening.

Many years later, John Belushi made another appearance at *The Tonight Show*. Doc Severinsen and the band were rehearsing, and the melodious sounds of that fabulous orchestra resounded throughout the halls of NBC. I was standing on the band side of the stage, looking across toward the area where Fred de Cordova would sit during the taping and saw two people standing there. One I didn't know at all and the other I hardly recognized. The latter looked like Belushi but much heavier than I remembered him being, dressed very sloppily and appearing almost dirty. But as I looked closer, it was definitely John Belushi.

As the band blared on, I motioned for John and his friend to come over and get a closer look. Many times celebrities would stop by at rehearsal. They might be taping something in a nearby studio or doing a pre-taped interview for the *Today Show* or some other show. It was not unusual to see him there. He might have been to see the network brass across the way in the administration building and taken his friend on a little guided tour of *The Tonight Show* set. But Belushi gave me a shy wave back and shook his head to say no. I almost walked over to talk to him, but when I saw the condition he was in, I held back. I only wish I'd have gotten a chance to tell him how much I enjoyed his work.

A week later, it was too late to tell him anything. John Belushi had died of an overdose.

Upon one or two occasions, I ventured outside of the greenroom to watch the show and decided to sit up in the director's booth. It was perched one story above the studio on Johnny's side of the stage overlooking the desk, swivel and couch, and had a bird's eye view of the entire stage and audience area. The quarters were cramped up there. There was a long console where our director sat and next to him was his assistant director, the technical director, lighting director, and booth P.A. (production assistant). Behind where they sat there were three or four director type chairs usually occupied by our set designer, unit manager, and various other people associated with the show.

The particular show that I chose to watch from the booth was on a night that our guest host was none other than Kermit the Frog. The show was filled with Muppets and cute comedy bits throughout. One of the guests was Bernadette Peters, and she was going to sing a song from the swivel to Kermit. About midway through the song, Muppets popped up all around her, over her shoulder, behind the couch and at her feet. Our director that night was Bob Ostberg, who asked one of the cameramen to widen his shot to show the cast of characters who surrounded Bernadette. The cameraman kept widening his shot so that the home viewer was seeing the arms of the puppeteers working the characters in front of Bernadette. Upon seeing this, Ostberg began yelling for the cameraman to stop. All hell broke out in the booth as the assistant director and technical director chimed in until we eventually had to stop tape (which was very rare) and start the segment again.

I quietly sneaked out of the booth and went back to my usual spot in the greenroom.

After several months I decided to take a seat up in the director's booth once again. Bob Ostberg was directing, and our guest host was Richard Dawson. One of Richard's guests that evening was singer Della Reese.

When Della was introduced, she came out center stage singing the song "Pieces of Dreams" with the band. She was to "hit her mark" on the floor and stay there during the song so that she would be in focus and Ostberg could plan his camera shots. Halfway into the song, Della started to inch up closer to the cue card man, who was standing just off camera. At first, Ostberg thought she was having trouble seeing the cue cards and asked the lighting director to give her more light. Della continued to squint at the cards even after they were better lit, and she continued to inch up closer to the camera. Ostberg said, "Go with her." Then suddenly Della went crashing down to the stage and hit the floor face first. Her head hit the floor with the sound of a bowling ball dropping on a lane.

Ostberg jumped up from his chair and shouted, "Oh shit! Go to black! Go to commercial! Drop the curtain!" The monitors in the studio went black and a curtain between where Della had fallen and the audience quickly dropped to block their view. Della lay motionless on the floor with blood coming from her head. Within minutes an emergency crew from Saint Joseph's Hospital were there. The hospital is directly next door to NBC. They took her out on a stretcher and out to an ambulance as the staff, crew, and audience sat in silent shock. Ostberg scrapped the show and everyone went home. I never ventured up to the director's booth again.

We found out weeks later that Della Reese had suffered a massive hemorrhagic stroke after an aneurysm burst in her brain during her performance. When she was well enough to come back and sing on the show, the first thing she wanted to know as she entered the studio was where exactly she had hit the floor. When she was shown the spot, she stomped up and down on it and said three times, "Out with you, Satan!" Della was a lucky survivor and continued on with her successful career.

On one of Johnny's anniversaries at NBC, we gathered in Fred de Cordova's office for some champagne with the office staff, a few of the top brass at NBC, and Johnny. As one of the executives raised his glass to toast Johnny's decision to bring the show out from New York to Burbank, Johnny hit him with a curve ball. Johnny said to him, "Is this the wing you promised to build me if I moved the show out here?" referring to the one story pre-fab bungalow we were standing in. The executives were all red in the face and didn't know what to say. Within weeks it was announced that NBC was going to build a brand new wing at the front of NBC Studios to accommodate Johnny Carson's staff. When the job was completed, there were beautiful offices at the front of NBC nearest to Studio 1. They built Johnny a temporary office in the basement during the construction. Johnny liked it so much he decided to stay there when the offices upstairs were completed. The directors' booth and stereo sound booth were also moved downstairs with the latest state-of-the-art equipment.

THE TONIGHT SHOW WARM-UP

If you have ever been lucky enough to attend a taping of *The Tonight Show*, you got to experience the warm-up. That was the period just before the show that got the audience warmed up before the stage manager would give the five-second countdown to start the show.

The audience would start loading in sometime around 4:30 in the afternoon and by 5:00 everyone except for a few VIPs were in their seats staring at the empty set they had seen so many times before on TV. The low murmur from the crowd contained the same phrases night after night. "It looks larger on TV," they'd say, "Gee, why is it so cold in here?" and, "Where's Doc and the band?"

Why did it look bigger on TV? Besides the TV cameras having wide angle lenses, which tend to stretch the picture, we were used to seeing Johnny standing center stage during his monologue, with Ed McMahon off to Johnny's right and Doc and the band off to Johnny's left. But we never saw all three of them in the same shot. Camera one would be over next to where Ed stood, shooting across stage behind Johnny, getting Doc's reaction shots. Camera two was dead center in front of Johnny shooting only Johnny. Camera three was over on the band's side of the stage shooting across to Ed McMahon's reactions. Whenever we saw a reaction shot of Ed or Doc on our TVs at home, we just assumed that we were seeing them from Johnny's point of view. We actually saw them from the opposite side of the stage which made the studio look twice as wide as it actually was. That's part of the magic of television.

The answer to why it was so cold in the studio is due to the hot lights. When the audience is first loaded in, the lights in the studio are barely on. Only a few work lights and a few key spots would be on. But just prior to the opening theme song, the full lighting effect would come on, causing the temperature to rise ten to fifteen degrees. The air conditioning would adjust when the full lights would beam on and keep the studio at a temperature of about 68 degrees.

Where was the band? This question was answered at 5:15, when the orchestra manager, Al Lapin, would let out the sound of a shrieking whistle like he was hailing a taxicab. That was the signal for the band to get onto the bandstand. Not all of the band members would be standing backstage before that whistle. Some would be in the outer hallway or in the greenroom. No matter where they were, they could hear Al's birdcall.

As the band made their way onstage, the lights would come up and the audience would applaud. You'd hear them say, "Look, it's Tommy Newsom," or "There's Ed Shaughnessy." The band members would wave at the crowd and look for friends they may have invited to sit in the audience. Once they were all seated, either Shelly Cohen or I would call out the order of the tunes for the band to have a last-minute chance to get their books in show order. Whenever I did this, I wondered what the audience thought we were doing, because some of the song titles were kind of strange sounding. Often, we would change the names of the songs to make them sound funny. "Ring Dem Bells" would become "Ring My Ding Dong," or "A Foggy Day" might be "A Smoggy Day," and so on. Some of the titles didn't need changing, such as, "Those Bad Bad Boys From Burbank," "Put It Where You Want It," "Legs and Thighs," or "Doc's Flock." I am sure the audience thought we were talking in some secret code.

When the band's books were in order, there would be a slight pause before anything would happen onstage. Off to the opposite side of the stage from the band Fred de Cordova would walk out to his position near the end of the couch on the set. There was a large TV monitor and a clock that kept airtime that would show 11:15 instead of the actual time of 5:15 on it. Fred would set down his folder with the show notes in it on a shelf near to where he would be seated during the show. Next to that folder he would carefully set down his glass with scotch on the rocks that he would sip from time to time.

When Fred was ready, he would simply pick up the microphone on the stand where Ed McMahon would later announce the show and Fred would say, "Let's start this thing!" That was the cue for the band to play a loud and lively vaudeville-type playon. Fred would pretend to lead the band and cut them off. He would then address the audience in his own elegant tone and say something like, "Good evening ladies and gentlemen, my name is Fred de Cordova. What's yours?" The crowd would mumble and laugh at themselves. Fred would continue with, ". . . as you may know, from time to time, due to schedule changes and vacations, our illustrious host needs to take some time off and have someone fill in for him," the crowd would moan. Fred would say, "Fortunately, that is not the case this evening." The audience would breathe a sigh of relief and Fred would say, "The man whose name appears in the opening of this show is actually here tonight!" The band would react along with the audience, as if they didn't know Johnny was hosting that night. Fred would then introduce Doc, who would cross over to the band and kick off a lively tune that would feature several members of the band.

At the end of the band number, Doc would take over the microphone and introduce Ed McMahon. Doc would say something like, "I'm going to bring out this next gentleman who's going to tell a few more things you need to know about the show, that is, unless he's too stoned to remember. I'm talkin' about the one and only, Ed McMahon." Doc would elongate Ed's first name in the same way that Ed would say, " . . . heeeeer's Johnny!" As Ed would walk out and take the microphone from Doc, the band would play two songs simultaneously, "Show Me the Way To Go Home" and "Cocktails For Two." As they reached the end of the playon, Doc would make his way back over to the bandstand where he would gyrate his hips to the last notes of the song, and the band would cut off when he would make one last thrust of his hips in their direction. On the applause, Ed McMahon would say, "You may have noticed that Doc has a strange way of cutting off the band. He does not use a baton."

Ed would continue, "I want to test this crowd and see if they are ready for this show. On the count of three I want to hear everyone give me your best hi-yo. Are you ready? Here we go, on three. One, two, three!" The audience would all gratefully play along and let out with a loud "Hi-yo!"

Depending on time, the various little pieces of schtick that Doc and Ed used would vary. But for many years, night after night, Ed would say to Doc, "I hear one of the members of the band has a special announcement to make." Doc would say, "Yes, Ed Shaughnessy's wife gave birth to a beautiful five pound, three ounce baby boy this afternoon." The crowd would always react with oohs and aahs followed by a round of applause. Ed would ask, "Would the proud father please stand and take a bow?" and on that cue, everyone in the band except Shaughnessy would stand up. The audience loved it. The bit got funnier one night when Doc said the baby weighed nine pounds, five ounces, making it a rather large baby. Each night the weight varied, causing Ed and Doc to find it hard to hold their laughter back. McMahon would add, "If that baby were any bigger it would walk out on its own."

This Shaughnessy baby bit went on every night for at least two or three years. The camera crew and backstage crew were oblivious to it as everyone went about their usual duties to get the show started. But one night, as they did this routine out front, I was walking backstage to get myself a drink. One of the women, who worked on the show for at least the last ten years, pulls me aside to say, "Hey Don, how come you didn't tell us that Ed Shaughnessy's wife had a baby today? I didn't even know she was pregnant." I couldn't believe she was serious. I explained to her that it was just a gag they did night after night. This night she just happened to listen to the warm-up.

All the while that Ed and Doc were doing their pre-show banter, the camera crew and technicians would take their positions. Meanwhile, backstage, Johnny would stroll in and take his usual position near the coffee machine and chat with director Bobby Quinn, Fred de Cordova, Peter Lassally or Jeff Sotzing. No one else was to talk to Johnny at this point unless it was extremely important.

Unknown to the audience, the stage manager would be getting a countdown from the director's booth, and he would signal Ed and Doc, giving them a one-minute or thirty-second cue. Like clockwork, by the time the stage manager shouts, "Here we go, in five, four, three, two . . . " Doc and the band would hit "Johnny's Theme" and seconds later he would cue Ed to say, "From Hollywood, it's *The*

Tonight Show starring Johnny Carson. This is Ed McMahon along with Doc Severinsen and the NBC Orchestra, inviting you to join Johnny and his guests . . . " Backstage, Johnny would walk from the coffee machine position to a mirrored area just behind his rainbow curtain. He would have one last look to see that his tie was straight. Out in front of the curtain, the band was blaring, Ed was listing the guests for the evening. It is all a fabulous build-up to the moment when Ed eventually says, " . . . and now, heeeeeere's Johnny!" No one had to cue the audience each night. Although there was an electric sign above the audience that flickered on and off that read, "AP-PLAUSE," no one was looking at it. All eyes were fixed on the parting rainbow curtain in the center of the stage. There was usually a second or two that seemed like an eternity, just long enough for you to think, "Oh no. He's not here!" But then, Johnny would emerge from behind the parted curtain, much to everyone's relief. It didn't matter who the guests were. It didn't matter that the studio was a little cold or that they had to stand in line for hours to get in. They were one of the many lucky audiences there to see the one and only Johnny Carson.

STUDIO 3, THAT'S NO PLACE LIKE HOME

After a while, *The Tonight Show* set, studio, greenroom and offices were like an extension of my home. I sometimes took that for granted without realizing it.

I was going to take some time off to perform with my band on a cruise ship. I was going to be gone for three months and would have to take a leave of absence. Cory Carson was willing to fill in for me while I was gone. I certainly didn't have to train him for the job and he had no intentions of wanting to come back.

Before going on this cruise I needed to hire a new bass player. My regular bassist, Marty Buttwinick, wasn't able to take that much time away from his many students. The easiest thing for me to do was to schedule these bass players for auditions during my lunch time and have them just bring their bass guitar and plug in to the bass amp on the Tonight Show Band set. It didn't hit me until this poor nervous bassist could hardly talk to me between songs when I realized what was happening. Even though I was clear about auditioning them for this cruise, he came in to Studio 1 and plugged in to the amp and sat in the chair that many bassists had dreams of sitting in one day. He thought he was auditioning to be Doc Severinsen's new bassist for the Tonight Show Band. It was then that I deduced that *The Tonight Show* set was more than a desk, couch and chair. To some, it was the Oval Office, the Paladium, the Taj Mahal of TV, and the Merry Old Land of Oz all rolled into one. I felt sorry for the bass player and auditioned him at another time. But I learned from this that working at that show day in and day out, it had become my home. And, you all know, there's no place like home. There's no place like home.

Studio 1 was where Johnny Carson taped the show for twenty-three years after moving the show out from New York in 1972. Only on rare occasions did we do the show from any other studio at NBC Burbank. Studio 3 was directly across the hall. If you've ever seen the clip when Johnny went across the hall and walked in on the middle of Don Rickles taping *C.P.O. Sharky*, you'd know how close Studio 3 was to Studio 1. Studios 2 and 4 were coupled on the other end of the lot. Studios 2 and 4 eventually became the home of NBC's *Days of Our Lives*. But, prior to that, those studios produced such shows as *The Dean Martin Show, Flip Wilson, The Midnight Special, The Andy Williams Show*, and countless others. Studio 3 had game shows like *Hollywood Squares, The Gong Show*, and *The New Concentration*. Studio 3 also was the home of *Welcome Back Kotter, Sanford and Son, Chico & the Man* and many NBC specials like *The Bob Hope Show, Captain & Tennile* and the forgettable *Dame Edna's Hollywood*.

Many times, on a slow day, I could take an extended lunch break, or if there wasn't a musical guest appearing on the show, I could go and watch what was going on in Studio 3. My favorite show to watch was *Sanford and Son*. I used to watch the show back in New York long before I started working at NBC. Shows like this would rehearse for two or three days on the set and go through camera blocking. Camera blocking is rehearsing where the cameras need to be during the course of a sit-com or soap opera so the director knows where his best shots will be and actors learn what marks to hit so they can get their close-ups.

Redd Foxx, who had been a nightclub stand-up comic for many years, would sometimes ad-lib during rehearsal and many times, if it was clean enough for prime-time TV, his new lines would make it into the finished script. Redd was well known for working blue. If you saw Redd's act live, the language and content was raw and definitely not ready for prime-time TV. Blue.

Redd was rehearsing a scene with La Wanda Page, who played Aunt Esther on the series. Her role was that of a God-fearing Church Lady who was always trying to set Redd (Fred Sanford) straight with the Lord. La Wanda and her other Church Ladies were waiting between takes when Redd impishly took a wine bottle from the set and slipped it down the front of his pant leg. He turned to La Wanda and the others and said in his usual raspy voice, "Hey, Ladies, look at this." The women howled with laughter, but La Wanda Page began to walk off the set, slamming doors and shouting, still in the character of Aunt Esther, "Fred Sanford, when are you going to grow up!" This was rather unusual because La Wanda Page's nightclub act was even more crude than Redd's. The others laughed at Redd. Demond Wilson, who played Fred Sanford's son, Lamont, appeared on the set. Demond took out his car keys and tapped on Redd's pant leg. The chink-chink sound of metal on glass cracked up the cast and camera crew so much that the director called for a ten-minute break until they could all compose themselves.

One night, when I had been working at NBC for only a few days and was collecting the music books from the band at the end of the show, I noticed the band members were scurrying to leave faster than usual. Guitarist Peter Woodford told me I might want to hurry and get out of the way. He quickly explained that Bob Hope was coming in directly after our taping to do his monologue. Hope frequently used *The Tonight Show* audience to pre-tape his monologue for his latest special. His producers would edit these segments into his show so that the opening monologues would be as fresh and current as they could be. The band knew that once the cameras were rolling, they would be stuck in the bandstand area until there was a break in the action.

This was all new to me and I found it a thrill to be able to stick around and watch Bob Hope at work. As the band made their way out of the studio I positioned myself at a seat in the trumpet section so I was to the side and behind Hope. I tried to be as inconspicuous as possible so as to blend in with the scenery. I not only had a great view of Bob Hope, I could see over his shoulder and read his cue cards along with him.

Bob Hope was the first person in television to use cue cards. Barney McNulty, his cue card man, invented the cue card. He was with Hope for many years and set the guidelines still used in cue cards today. There is a certain style in printing letters of the alphabet so that an "L" would be drawn differently from an "I." Dialogue between two people would be drawn in different colors, and so on. McNulty remained with Hope throughout the rest of Bob's career.

As Hope grew older, his eyesight got worse and the letters on the cue cards got bigger, which made it necessary for the cue cards to grow larger as well. I had no trouble reading the cards from where I was perched.

As Bob Hope began to recite his list of topical jokes for me and the studio audience, he would stop himself just short of the punchline if he flubbed a word or got stuck on a pronounciation so that he wouldn't ruin the joke. He'd tell Barney, "Save that joke. We'll go back to it later." Sometimes when he got tongue-tied he would pretend to spit off to his side or he would say something like, "Oh, shit!" and the audience would roar.

I was in awe of being able to watch another comic legend in action. Little did I know that a few weeks later, I would actually be working with him.

Contractor Al Lapin hired me for a Bob Hope special, a tribute to vaudeville, featuring a long list of stars and, of course, Hope himself. I was hired as a rehearsal drummer. For two days, pianist Gil Leib and I practiced with Hope's choreographer in Rehearsal Hall 3 at NBC Studios. The choreographer was taking all the "Hope steps" and mixing them around the musical number we were playing. Bob only knew a certain number of steps, he told us, and didn't have time to learn any new ones. The number was a dance duet with Bob and Sammy Davis Jr.

On the evening of the second rehearsal, in walked Bob Hope and Sammy Davis Jr.; the routine was to be tried out with the principal players. I had my hair in an Afro kind of cut. Sammy took one look at me, walked over, grabbed my face by the cheeks and said in a jokingly jealous tone: "Look at all that hair!" (Years later, I met Sammy on *The Tonight Show* set, reminded him of the Afro incident and told him that ever since that day I'd been losing my hair. "Did you put a spell on me or something?" I asked him. Sammy went into his usual fit of laughter, pounding his heels into the floor as he laughed that heavy smoker's laugh.)

The choreographer demonstrated the number and ended with a "What do you think?" attitude about him. After a moment of silence, Sammy says, "Hey, I've got an idea." He turns to the pianist and me and asked if we knew the song "Mister Bojangles." We proceeded to play the tune as Sammy burst into his elaborate, renowned, classic dance number. When he finished there was an extended silence. It was obvious that if they allowed Sammy to do this number, it clearly would upstage Bob Hope. The show's producer, Paul Keane, spoke up. "That is a fabulous number, Sammy, but it's a soft-shoe number. We already have George Burns doing that style with the sand and everything. Besides, we have pre-recorded all the music for this number and have to stick with that." Upon hearing that explanation, Sammy shrugged his shoulders and agreed without further discussion. It seemed to me that Sammy just wanted to show everyone in the room that he could dance circles around anyone, but he decided to accommodate the needs of the show and not upstage Bob Hope. A sigh of relief filled the room, and we went about perfecting the original dance routine.

The number was a re-enactment of the Olsen and Johnson act where the two would do a light tap dance while telling corny vaudeville-style jokes. Every once in a while they would stop the music and dancing to deliver the punch line. Luckily for me, during the rehearsal, Sammy realized that if all the music were pre-recorded, how were they going to get the rim shots he needed when he performed his Jerry Lewis impression. Everyone agreed they needed live rim shots. The producer quickly turned to me and asked if I would be available the next day for the show taping. Let me check my book. (Of course I could do it.) Do you have a tuxedo, they asked. (Do I have a tuxedo? I borrowed one.) The next day I had to be on camera for the whole show. The show, being all about vaudeville, had an orchestra pit in front of the stage. There I was with my drum set, along with a bunch of extras hired to look like musicians who pretended to play make-believe instruments. I was the only actual musician in the bunch and the only one with a real instrument. However, I had to pretend to play to the recorded music until the time for the rim shots. There were four of them. It was the only time I actually struck my drums all day.

At the end of the taping, Lapin told me I had made out pretty well for the day. Because I hit my drums, I had to be paid as a musician and not an actor. I had to get paid the same money that members of the Les Brown Band got for doing the pre-recording. Not bad, huh? Not only that, but this was one of the few shows that was used later on several times in Bob Hope retrospectives. I ended up being paid residuals for this show for years afterward.

One time I was flying back to L.A. from New York and heard the routine with George Burns and Bob Hope. I looked in the airline magazine to make sure that this was from that same show. It not only was, but tape copies of it were being offered for sale by mail order. When I returned to work, I asked Lapin if a residual was due to me for that. He wasn't sure but said he would investigate it through the musicians union. Apparently I had opened a can of worms, because it took many years to resolve. Al persisted and did get residuals for all the musicians who played on that particular program. It wasn't that it was played on an airline flight that made it pay so well. It was that Bob Hope Enterprises was selling the tape to the general public—that made the big difference and got us all full payment. Not bad for only having to hit my drum four times.

Dame Edna (Barry Humphries) taped one of her specials, *Dame Edna's Hollywood* in Studio 3. The program was a tongue-in-cheek rendition of a Barbara Walters /Oprah Winfrey satire talk show. Some of the questions and answers were legitimate, but much of the dialogue was designed to set up a Dame Edna punch line.

Chevy Chase was one of her guests, and I slipped into the studio to hear some of her interview with him. Almost from the beginning of Chevy's career since starting out on *Saturday Night Live*, there had been a buzz about Chevy being the guy who would one day take Johnny Carson's spot when he stepped down.

Chevy once guest hosted *The Tonight Show* and did not do as well as planned. He seemed extremely nervous and uncomfortable. Dame Edna asked Chevy if he thought he would ever step into

Johnny Carson's shoes. Chevy said he had tried that show once and admitted that it was a disaster. He said he would not make a very good talk show host.

These Dame Edna segments were taped well in advance and would eventually be edited into a series of specials. This Chevy Chase segment was dropped into a show that aired almost a year later. Within that year, Chevy was asked to host his own syndicated talk show that aired in many markets opposite the Jay Leno *Tonight Show*. I don't think that Chevy remembered what he had said on the Dame Edna interview or he might have asked them to pull it from the show. The Dame Edna program aired right around the time that ads started to pop up about Chevy's talk show. It was embarrassing.

Dame Edna had appeared on *The Tonight Show* a couple of times and one time I had to go ask her about an obscure song she uttered during her interview with Johnny. She was already in her dressing room when I tracked her down. She asked me in as we discussed the song. We were well away from the audience, cameras and microphones, yet Dame Edna was still Dame Edna. Barry Humphries stayed in character the whole time. I guess it is some sort of method acting. Lily Tomlin was the same way when she came in to rehearse a song with the band as her nightclub/lounge singer, Tommy Velour. The whole time, Lily was Tommy from when she walked into rehearsal and throughout the taping of the show.

As long as Barry Humphries remained in the wig complete with tiara, make-up and spangled evening gown, he was Dame Edna.

My sister Arlene was visiting from New York one time and she was a big fan of *Hollywood Squares*. It just happened to be taping in Studio 3, so I took her across the hall to let her have a peek. We stood to the side of the audience bleachers so that she could get a good view of the tic-tac-toe set where all of the guest stars sat stacked upon each other. Paul Lynde was the center square and most times the center of attention. All of the stars had comedic answers written by the staff comedy writers on the show. The guest stars could choose the written answers or make up their own. Most times they used the pre-conceived answers. (Come on, you didn't think that all of those actors and celebrities were naturally that funny and quick, did you?)

After Arlene had watched the show for a few minutes, she asked me, "Why isn't the audience laughing?" I took her a few steps forward so that she could see that the audience bleachers were almost completely empty. The only spectators were a handful of other friends of friends of the show and a couple of crewmembers. "Where's the audience?" she asked in astonishment. I explained to her that sometimes the show had to re-arrange the taping schedule to fit the availability of the celebrities and couldn't always quickly assemble a studio audience. Unfortunately, the audience was reduced to a laugh track machine in the audio booth. Everything got a laugh if it was funny or not. Welcome to Hollywood, or in this case, beautiful downtown Burbank.

Many television critics will tell you that variety shows don't work anymore. Network executives cringe when they hear the term used when someone is pitching a new show idea. "Variety shows are a thing of the past," they all say. If the case were given to Perry Mason, he would conclude that variety shows were murdered at the hands of technology.

When producers realized that they could cut costs by having all the music pre-recorded, they saved a lot of money paying a studio orchestra for needle drops instead of having the band sit around getting paid while the production team reset lights or scenery. A needle drop is a term for the starting and stopping of the pre-recorded music. Every time the tape is started and stopped, the orchestra on that recording gets paid another needle drop fee. It is considerably less than paying the band to hang out all day. The artists would sing live to the pre-recorded track, but soon artists and recording companies became protective of their product and wanted the songs to sound exactly like the recorded hit song. Lip-synching was figured into the mix of greedy producers and networks.

Another costly consideration was performing in front of a live audience. Sometimes it was difficult to schedule audiences with the ever-changing schedules of television stars and guest stars. Sit-coms were getting away with canned laughter, letting a producer with a machine decide what was funny and what was not. Soon variety shows were taping without audiences, and canned applause and laughter filled the airwaves.

Home audiences couldn't always decipher what it was they didn't like about certain programs, while others could clearly see that it was all canned laughter, canned applause and canned music—and so they decided to can variety shows.

Some of the highest rated television shows today are variety or musically driven shows. *The Emmy Awards, The Oscars, The American Music Awards* and other shows like them draw large audiences because of the celebrities on them and the fact that they are live.

The reality-based shows with amateur performers competing to be number one are musical variety shows that bring in high ratings. Producers have cut the costs of having to pay professionals to come on and entertain us. The audiences are so starved for live entertainment, they are forced to watch a lot of basically bad entertainment. It's like watching little league baseball when your kid isn't playing.

If you flip around the cable stations today, you will see that British, Hispanic and Country Music stations still feature variety shows. So next time someone tells you that variety is dead, tell them that it's not dead; it just has a social disease.

The Tonight Show always insisted that artists sing live or they didn't perform. Laugh tracks and canned applause were never a consideration. Everything was done in front of a live studio audience.

WHO WRITES THAT STUFF?

Having dealt with writing jokes and doing some stand-up of my own when I first came to Los Angeles, I was curious to know if Johnny Carson was a good comedy writer. Some say that Bob Hope could not write a funny line but he could tell jokes. Others like George Carlin wrote their own material. Johnny had a staff of writers at the show. So I asked one of his writers if Johnny could write his own jokes. He told me that each writer had to come up with ten topical jokes a day for the monologue. So he said your ninth and tenth jokes were sometimes not your best, but in order to fulfill the assignment you would submit it anyway. He said that Johnny would often take those nines and tens and use them in the monologue—and by changing a word or two or adding a facial expression, he'd turn the joke into one of the best jokes in the monologue. Johnny had more than the gift to write jokes; he knew how to turn a mediocre joke into a gem.

I used to see one of Johnny's head writers, Hal Goodman, in the cavernous halls of NBC on his daily delivery of the monologue to Johnny's office. The staff's offices were in a one-story temporary bungalow at the back end of the NBC lot. Johnny's office was at the opposite end of the complex where Studio 1 was. Nearly every day I would see Hal walking down the corridor with the script in his hand. He would stop every ten seconds or so and make a pencil marking, change a word or scratch something out. So I asked him one day why he did that. I thought the writer's assistant was a bad typist or something. He told me that he makes the corrections on the monologue on purpose. He said that Johnny liked to see pencil markings and corrections. It showed him that the writers actually checked what they wrote, and he liked the idea that it was so fresh that they didn't have time to re-type it. (These were the times before computers. If a sketch or script needed corrections, it had to be re-typed.) He said one time he submitted the monologue without any pencil marks and Johnny gave it right back and told him it wasn't ready yet.

Some of Johnny's writers were very protective of their jobs. I once tried my hand at writing a sketch for Johnny. It was mentioned in the news that the character of Superman had turned fifty years old that year. I thought it would be funny to have Johnny be Superman at age fifty, and Ed would interview the old man of steel. So I put together a script and dropped it by Johnny's office. A day or so later, Fred de Cordova came into my office and closed the door. I knew it was something serious or he wouldn't have closed the door. He was asked by Johnny to thank me for submitting the script. Fred said Johnny was genuinely pleased with my writing but it wasn't something he wanted to do at this time. I was a little let down but happy that Johnny actually read it and (even though it was through Fred) had responded to it.

Almost the same day I was making some photocopies in the copy room when one of the writers came in and said, "What's this I hear you submitted a comedy sketch to Johnny?" I told him I took a shot at an idea I had for a comedy skit. He then bluntly said, "Stick to the music department and we'll handle the comedy" and walked out of the room. Apparently word filtered to the writers quickly, and at least one of them wasn't very happy with someone trying to horn in on their territory.

A few weeks later, the Christopher Reeve Superman movie was about to go into the theaters, and Johnny was doing a sketch on Superman. When I read the script, I saw several of the same jokes that I had written in my sketch. I gave the writers the benefit of doubt that the subject of Superman conjures the same images and lines for conjecture. Jokes about being "faster than a speeding bullet" and "the man of steel" lent itself to similar jokes.

I was passing by Johnny's office, as I did every day (the music library was above Johnny's office and the only way for me to get to the studio was to go by Johnny's office), on my way down to rehearsal prior to this Superman sketch. Johnny happened to emerge from his office just as I was passing. He said hello and as we walked down the hall together, he put his arm around me and told me how much he enjoyed my comedy writing and encouraged me to keep up the good work. And then, as if he were apologizing about the sketch, he said the writers had this sketch in the works for a couple of weeks.

I think what happened is that they may have had this Superman sketch in the works but that it wasn't quite ready yet. Then, all of a sudden I came along and submitted my sketch and the writers must have caught hell for it. That would explain the reaction I got from the writer at the photocopier. In any event, despite the words of encouragement from Johnny, I never got in the writers' way again.

One night immediately following the taping of a *Tonight Show*, I was in the production offices getting a few things together before heading home for the evening, when I crossed paths with our associate producer, Jim McCawley.

Jim joined the show in the late '70s, a few years after I started. He started out as a talent coordinator and eventually was elevated to associate producer. Jim's specialty was finding new comedians. Many comedians expressed animosity toward McCawley because he was standing between them and a guest shot on the show. Sometimes McCawley would hear a comic's routine at the Comedy Store or the Improv and tell them they weren't ready yet.

Some of the comics respected his judgment and would hone their craft and take Jim's advice. Others would get bitter when they would clean up their five-minute act for television and be told by Jim that they needed five more minutes of clean material. Jim's way of thinking was if a comedian got a shot on the show and was good enough to be asked back within a month, they would need additional material for the second visit.

As I said good night to Jim I added, "That was a great show tonight!" and Jim replied, "Yeah, and Johnny never used any of my notes."

The coordinators would pre-interview guests for the show and hand in notes, or a script of possible subjects and questions for Johnny to choose from. The notes might say to ask the guest about a recent trip to wherever, or the guest has a story about a new house they bought. An abbreviated set of answers would be there if Johnny wanted to see where the interview would take him if he asked certain questions. Quite often, Johnny would not want to know the answers.

This night Johnny not only chose not to see the answers, he didn't even use Jim's prepared notes. McCawley seemed happy that all of his hard work had gone unnoticed. He explained to me that he could use those same notes the next time that guest was on the show.

Sometimes after the show, I would be heading to my car and would pass by the KNBC local news studio and see our local weatherman Fritz Coleman. Fritz, in addition to being the KNBC weatherman, is also a stand-up comic. He would ask me how the show was that night. I would tell him it was good or great and sometimes say it was the best of the week. Fritz would ask who was on the show that night and even though the show had finished taping less than ten minutes before—many times I would totally draw a blank. I couldn't remember who was on the show, but I just knew it was good.

I once was talking with one of the secretaries on the show about how well the program went the night before and asked her if she had seen it. Her answer was, "No, I don't watch TV. I don't even own a television." I thought to myself, why would somebody even work on a television show and not own a television? I almost wanted to tell her to get out of the way and give someone who really has a passion for television a chance to work on a show.

There should be a test for anyone who gets a job working on a television show. So many shows are hiring students fresh out of college who have no experience nor any knowledge of the history of television. When I started out, I didn't know the likes of Dave Garroway, Edward R. Morrow or Sid Ceasar because they were before my time—but I read books about TV, searched out tapes of old shows, and researched events that took place before I was born.

Producers are cutting corners to save a buck here and there by hiring interns, who work for free in exchange for college credit and a fancy title. This new inexpensive on-the-job training tactic has drastically lowered the standards of television and put a lot of experienced people out of work.

AND YOUR LITTLE TURTLE TOO

From time to time we had animals on the show, usually visits from Joan Embery of the San Diego Zoo or Jim Fowler from *The Mutual of Omaha Wild Kingdom* shows with Marlin Perkins. Embery would have animals with her and a couple of animal handlers who stood just off camera. They would be on hand to help her out if an animal got too frisky or if it seemed frightened by the bright lights and audience. Sometimes the animals were frightened by the sound of the band during the commercial breaks. So much for music soothing the savage breasts—everyone is a music critic.

We were very lucky over the years not to have any animal mishaps. We came close one time when we had on some Bengal tigers. These beasts were the size of a small horse or a Volkswagen. At rehearsal, they were roaming around on stage too much for the comfort of the trainers, and they suggested that we chain them to the floor. Instead of drilling a bolt into the cement floor of the studio, someone came up with the idea to put flat planks of 3/4" plywood down and bolt the chains to the wood. When we were on the air and the curtain went up to reveal these beautiful tigers, either the audience reaction or the sudden bright lights on them caused all of them to want to roam. As they moved, the chains around their necks simply pulled up the plywood. Now we had three Bengal tigers with large pieces of wood chained to them moving about the set.

The trainers quickly bounced into action and managed to get them to retreat backward from the audience. But as the curtain came down, one of them managed to stay on the audience side of it. The trainers still managed to keep it moving backward toward the curtain. The animal must have been as frightened as the audience was, because when it backed into the curtain, it relieved itself, leaving a large wet stain on the rainbow curtain.

All was okay and no one was hurt. The tigers were okay too. However, Johnny's curtain had to be replaced, which cost several thousand dollars. One can't simply call a curtain store and order a fifty-by-thirty-foot rainbow curtain and expect it to be hanging on a rack waiting to be sold.

Jim Fowler once brought on a hawk that was supposed to fly from a perch at one side of the studio set and land on his arm. On one of the attempts, the hawk decided to take a right turn and fly over the heads of the studio audience. The bird perched high above the studio audience on top of one of the lighting poles. Eventually the bird was coaxed into flying back to the stage level and everyone was all right. The hawk even flew from the perch on stage to Johnny's arm before the segment was over.

The next day I was talking with some of our stagehands about how lucky we were that no one in the audience was hurt. Greg Elliot, our head prop man, told me that he thought that Fowler carried a small gun in his pocket just in case things went bad. I don't know what's scarier, a wild bird mauling an innocent audience member or Jim Fowler taking pot shots in their direction trying to save them from an escaped, scared animal.

Animals seem to like to relieve themselves on live television, and it always gets a laugh from the audience. We had a pair of elephants on the show one time when John Davidson was guest hosting. At rehearsal, one of the elephants began to relieve himself center stage. At first, everyone started to laugh. But this pachyderm must have had a lot to drink that day because he kept peeing, and peeing, and peeing. Soon everyone stopped laughing and began to walk away in disgust as the stench from the elephant urine began to fill the stage. It put a halt to rehearsal for a few minutes until the stage crew mopped up the mess and managed to clear the air. They wanted to be in show business.

Eventually we got back to rehearsing and John Davidson was supposed to sit on top of one of the elephants and ride it around the studio. John wasn't paying attention to the trainers and walked between the two elephants to try to climb up one of them. If you've ever watched elephants for any period of time, you may have noticed how they like to sway back and forth. They do that to stay cool. When John walked between the two, one was swaying left and the other was swaying right. Davidson was nearly crushed between the two elephants before a quick thinking trainer saw what was about to happen and managed to move the elephants apart before our guest host became a tattoo on the side of one of these beasts. Davidson wasn't even aware of what could have happened. We were very lucky to never have any serious problems with all of the wild animals we had on the show over the years.

Once in a while, our associate producer at the time, Peter Lassally (Peter eventually became executive producer), would walk through the office halls asking the staff for ideas or assistance for a segment of the show. This particular day, Peter was looking for people who had unusual pets. He wasn't looking for dogs, cats or canaries. We had a woman booked on the show, Beatrice Lydecker, who claimed she could read the minds of animals. She was a well-known animal psychic.

Doc Severinsen told me he had hired her to read the minds of his quarter horses. Doc's horses were racehorses and he thought it would be nice to know what might be going on in their minds. Perhaps this might help to understand why a winning horse stops winning all of a sudden or why some horses have trouble keeping up with the others. Did this experiment work? I don't know. But, I guess if it did work, instead of one of the greatest trumpet players in the world, Doc would be known as one of the richest breeders of race horses.

So, when Lassally searched the staff for unusual house pets, I stepped forward and offered my pet turtle. He was actually a desert tortoise that I acquired through *The Tonight Show*. I grew fascinated with the miniature creatures after visiting my landlord's home, where he had a large collection of turtles roaming around his back yard. Soon after seeing these slow-moving dinosaurs, one of the office assistants was asking the other staffers if anyone would be interested in caring for a broken tortoise. I jumped at the opportunity.

It seems that an old woman, the neighbor of one of our staff members, was being moved to a nursing home. She had a pet tortoise that wandered off her balcony while the movers were relocating this woman. The tortoise fell about three stories and cracked his shell on the pavement below. The old woman was in no position to further care for herself, much less a broken pet. If I paid the veterinarian bill, I could have the tortoise. For a mere $15, I had my very own prehistoric pet. I named him Squiggy.

I used to let him roam free inside my house. He was only about the size of a small toaster and sometimes he would disappear for a day or so, but would always surface whenever he was hungry.

I recall one day, as I was getting ready for work, that Squiggy had managed to perch himself on top of one my cowboy boots. His feet were flapping in mid-air but he wasn't going anywhere because his belly was resting on the boot top. I was about to reach over to help him down to the floor when I suddenly stopped myself. I thought, he got himself up there; he'll find a way to get down.

I had an unusually long day of work and play. After work, I went out with friends and didn't get home until after two in the morning. As I was getting undressed for bed, I glanced over to find Squiggy perched in the same position he was in when I left that morning. I laughed to myself and thought what a traumatic day he must have had. As he tried to free himself for hours by swaying his arms and legs in a swimming manner, he must have thought to himself, "Oh man, it's after four o'clock and I'm still stuck up here!" As he flapped his arms faster he might have thought, "I've got so much I wanted to do today!"

I brought Squiggy into NBC for his premier television appearance. At least, I think it was his premier appearance. Maybe after this animal psychic gets into his head, she might reveal all kinds of stories from Squiggy's sordid past. Squiggy might have all sorts of insight into the lives of animal stars of the past. He might tell us about shady dealings with Mister Ed or his strange relationship with Lassie. There is a whole world of animal star stories that inquiring minds might want to know.

Just prior to showtime, I was introduced backstage to Beatrice Lydecker, the animal psychic. It was obvious that Squiggy had an accident because the veterinarian had wrapped his shell in white tape and sealed the cracks in his shell with some sort of nail mending polish. The veterinarian told me that fingernails and turtle shells are basically the same material. Beatrice began asking me questions about my tortoise, and I was cautious in the way I answered her so as not to tell her too much. I got the feeling she was trying to read my mind as well.

When Beatrice Lydecker was on the show with Johnny, they brought out Squiggy. I was in the greenroom, but when she asked a few on-air questions, Johnny looked to Fred de Cordova for answers and suddenly one of our stage managers burst into the greenroom to tell me Fred wanted me out there. I bolted out to stand next to Fred off camera and answered Ms. Lydecker's queries as best I could.

At first, she kept referring to the sound of an engine. She kept saying, "a lawn mower or car revving sound, and I'm also getting a falling sensation." Well, give me a break. It doesn't take a mind reader to figure out that a turtle all wrapped in gauze had either a lawn mower accident or he fell from somewhere. She added that Squiggy wishes I wouldn't wash the lettuce I have been feeding him; he likes it fresh off the head of lettuce. Again, give me a break. But then, she said something that blew me away. She said, "He especially likes the new home you built for him in the backyard." That very morning, I built a little fenced-in area in my yard so that Squiggy could be outside to dig for worms, eat grass and do whatever tortoises do outside. No one knew about this little project except for Squiggy and me. Even if she was reading my mind instead of Squiggy's, it truly was impressive.

Months later, I'm paying for groceries at my local supermarket and the checkout woman sees my name on the check and says, "Don Sweeney? Where have I heard your name before?" My inflated ego expanded further and I told her she might have heard my name in relationship with the nearby Pierce College Fireworks Show. My band has played there for the last couple of years. "Oh, is that your band?" she says, "No, it wasn't from that." She continued to ponder and I asked her if she liked to read the credits at the end of television shows, I told her where I worked. She immediately remembered, "Hey, are you the guy who had the tortoise a few weeks ago?" You could practically hear the hiss from my ego deflating. My pet turtle was more popular than I was, and he didn't even know it. Or did he?

LIONS AND TIGERS AND BEARS, OH MY!

I think in every job, over a period of ten or twenty years, there would be at least one time that you would have a close call and almost lose your job. There may have been more than one time for me, but the only one I know for sure was this particular one.

From time to time, we had a man on the show who was a professional whistler, Ron McCroby. He had a unique talent of whistling and sounding almost like a flute. McCroby's background was basically jazz, so when he appeared on the show he would whistle out a tune with the Tonight Show Band. This particular visit, I was told at the production meeting a day or so before that he was going to need a pianist to accompany him center stage. That's about all I was told, and I felt no need to ask any further questions. That same day, I told the orchestra manager, Al Lapin, that we needed a pianist for Ron McCroby.

The day of McCroby's appearance, he came in to rehearse his number, and Al Lapin had the *Tonight Show* Band pianist arrive early to run the tune down with him. Normally, Ross Tompkins would have been there. Ross was the regular Tonight Show Band pianist, but for some reason Ross was not there that day and Russ Freedman was filling in for him. Both Ross and Russ were excellent pianists. However, the rehearsal was not going as smoothly as it should have. It seems that McCroby had switched gears on us and no one brought it up in the production meeting that the piece McCroby had chosen was a classical piece. As great a player that Freedman was, it is as difficult for a jazz pianist to play a classical piece as it would be for a classical pianist to play a jazz piece. Russ did the best he could, but they had to scrap the song and do a standard jazz number.

Each day we had two production meetings. One at eleven o'clock in the morning and another was at four-thirty in the afternoon. The second meeting was to check on last minute changes and to briefly talk over what might be in store for the next day. I would normally attend the morning meeting, and Shelly Cohen would attend the afternoon meeting. Shelly and I would discuss anything that was said at the afternoon meeting when he got out.

Shelly came from the four-thirty meeting and informed me that I was getting the blame for this screw-up. My Irish temper flared up, and I could feel steam coming out of my ears when he told me that. I immediately went around to Fred de Cordova's office where he was talking with producer Peter Lassally and director Bobby Quinn. "Excuse me gentlemen," I said, "but there seems to be a problem here that I need to discuss with you." I am sure I took them totally by surprise. "I am not taking the blame for this Ron McCroby misunderstanding." One of them said I should have asked beforehand what kind of pianist we needed to get for him. "Oh, come on," I lashed back, "McCroby has always been a jazz performer. Should I have asked that question if it were Pete Fountain or Tony Bennett? If Luciano Pavarotti were to need a pianist, should I ask if he is going to sing a piece from an opera or a medley of Rolling Stones songs? I would have been laughed out of the meeting or reprimanded for asking such a stupid question. It seems to me that the talent coordinator should have informed all of us that he was going to perform something out of the norm." I should have stopped there, but I was furious. As I left the room, I said, "People are afraid to speak up at these meetings for fear of being ridiculed by the constant sarcastic tone that goes on here." The three heads of the show had no retort. Instead they sat there in silence.

I am sure that when I left the room there were sarcastic remarks that followed. Shelly informed me later that I came very close to getting fired, but Fred de Cordova stuck up for me. After that incident, Fred and I developed a great relationship with each other—one that lasted for many years after we worked at *The Tonight Show.*

I would get an idea for the show and sometimes we would try it and other times it would get shot down. I had an idea for one of our Anniversary Shows and brought it to Jeff Sotzing. Jeff and I are about the same age, and I had an easier time bringing my brainstorms to him rather than Peter Lassally or Fred de Cordova. Jeff rose rather quickly within *The Tonight Show* ranks because he was also Johnny Carson's nephew. I have no problem with nepotism in the world of show business, or any business for that matter, as long as the related person can deliver. Jeff has proved himself many times over. He went from reception to assistant commercial director to associate producer so fast that his title on his business cards was written in pencil, but I never heard anyone claim that Jeff didn't know what he was doing. Jeff runs Carson Productions today, and we are still good friends.

So, I brought an idea to Jeff one day. I thought it would be fun to take all the clips from the moments when Johnny would burst into a spontaneous soft-shoe dance when the joke didn't go over the way he wanted it to. I told Jeff it would be easy for us to find the shows where this happened by looking at the cue sheets I kept. The band would always play the song "Tea For Two" while Johnny ad-libbed his dance. This always brought on a good laugh. We could stream these moments together while the band played "Tea For Two" live, and it would look like a little funny dance number. Any regular viewer to *The Tonight Show* remembers these occasional moments. Jeff's reaction was, "How am I going to sell that to Johnny?" He said, "I'm going to say to Johnny, you know when you tell a joke in the monologue that bombs . . . " Jeff said Johnny would say to him, "Bomb? I don't bomb." I couldn't believe that Jeff was serious about Johnny's reaction, but I added, "Don't say he bombed, say, you know when you tell a joke and the studio audience doesn't get it . . . " Jeff asked if I thought it was worth the risk of getting Johnny upset and said to me, "Do you want to tell him?" I thought for a moment, and answered, "No." We both laughed.

Another Anniversary Show moment was one that actually made it to the air. The producers were looking for some kind of musical idea to feature among the memorable clips on the show. I thought to take a song that had been done by several artists and edit them together to form a musical medley of stars singing one song. I was asked to re-search it. I had drawers full of cue sheets from every show where I logged any song ever sung or played over the years. A task like this would be a lot easier if the cue sheets were done on a computer data-base. This was years before computers were on everyone's desk. We didn't switch over to computers until 1992 after Jay Leno took over *The Tonight Show.*

I came up with several songs that were irritatingly popular at the time. They were irritating only to us on the show because so many artists would come on and sing songs like, "I Write the Songs," "Memory" (from "Cats") and "New York, New York." The producers liked "New York, New York," and I was able to find renditions over the many months of shows by Liza Minnelli, Andy Williams, Steve Lawrence, Sammy Davis Jr., and others. Oddly enough, the very first person to sing that song on the show was Danny Thomas. At the time he did it, the play "New York, New York" was a new show on Broadway, and Liza Minnelli and Frank Sinatra had not done their renditions yet. The Danny Thomas version was not used because Danny had passed away earlier that year and although his version was so hokey it was funny, it never made it to the Anniversary Show. Our producers didn't think it would be appropriate.

Director Bob Ostberg and I spent hours editing the segments together and it was one of the better moments included in our Anniversary Show. Johnny was very pleased with the outcome.

JOHNNY CARSON, BUDDY RICH AND I

Buddy Rich was appearing on one of his numerous *Tonight Show* engagements (Nov. 15, 1984). On this visit, he seemed just like a kid when he started to tell Ed Shaughnessy and me about a set of drums he just bought—a set of Slingerland Radio Kings. He had an endorsement deal to play on Ludwig Drums exclusively, but Buddy would do things to anger or insult the Ludwig people to indicate that he was unhappy with the way they were treating him. Some have said he'd even do such things to people who treated him with the utmost respect.

Buddy told me, "I think I once owned these drums." When I laughed, he said, "No, I'm serious! I think I bought back an old set of drums of mine." Buddy went on to tell us that his Slingerland drum set sported a plaque engraved with the words SLINGERLAND RADIO KINGS 1934. He boasted about the way the set sounded—the tone, the hardware. Buddy had searched his whole life for the perfect snare drum and never found it. I believe he felt he came awfully close this time.

I told Buddy that I had a set of Slingerland drums, a set I, too, was quite proud of. "Everywhere I play with my drums, I get compliments from people who say how shiny they are or how nice they sound." That was a great set of drums. On that, Buddy and I certainly agreed.

That weekend, Buddy was playing at the Universal Amphitheater, opening for Frank Sinatra. He invited me to come see the show Saturday night, but I had a party to play in Anaheim. I asked whether I could come Sunday instead, and Buddy said it was no problem.

Saturday night, after my gig, I made the mistake of leaving my drums in my van overnight while it was parked in the carport of my apartment. On Sunday morning, when I went to move my equipment indoors, I found that everything had been stolen. Someone had broken into my van and taken my sound system and all my drums.

I learned then how it feels to be a burglary victim. You feel so violated. How dare somebody take my hard-earned possessions? My wife, Cathy, and I had started our own band after we married. Cathy was the lead singer in our band and ninety percent of our act. We had bought most of the equipment with money we received as wedding presents from friends and relatives.

All day Sunday I was in shock. I moped around and stared out the window in disbelief half-hoping I would discover it was all just a bad dream. I suddenly realized I was supposed to go see Buddy Rich that night at the Universal Amphitheater. I wasn't going to go, but my wife coaxed me into it. She said it would be good for me to get out and take my mind off our loss. I agreed and went off to see Buddy.

Encountering Buddy backstage, I said, "Remember that drum set I was boasting about the other day? It was stolen from my van last night."

Buddy winced. Just then, a hush enveloped the backstage area. When I was about to ask Buddy why everyone got so quiet, Buddy made a sign for me not to talk. Frank Sinatra had made his way into the backstage area. Whenever Sinatra was backstage, he demanded silence. When he walked over to where Buddy and I were standing, Buddy turned and said: "Hi Frank, what ya say?"

Sinatra replied: "Are you ready to do another one, Buddy?"

"Aw, I think I have another one in me," Buddy said. "How 'bout you, Skinny?" Frank laughed, slapped Buddy on the back and walked off.

In order for us to continue talking, Buddy knew we shouldn't be standing around Sinatra and motioned for me to follow him onto the stage. Buddy asked me to help him try to get a better sound out of his snare drum, which, he said, he was about to give up on. He led me onto the stage, where the curtains were still closed and the bandstand was in place for the concert. While I watched, he climbed behind his drums and played a couple of quick rim shots and rolls on the snare.

"What can you do about that?" he asked. I reached for the adjustment screw on the drum and loosened his snares.

Now any drummer knows that if the snares are too tight, the snare drum will emit a dry, flat sound. I couldn't believe that the "Greatest Drummer in the World" didn't know how to do that. I've heard stories that Buddy never bothered to tune his drums but always had a drum technician do it for him. Either he couldn't be bothered or he actually didn't know how to do it. And if he didn't, it was no wonder he'd never been happy with the sound of his snare and had spent a lifetime searching for the ultimate snare drum.

"Try it now," I said.

Buddy whacked the drum a couple of times, and then a big smile lit up his face. "Yeah," he said, "how'd you do that?"

I gave him the same answer he once gave the Queen of England when she asked him how he could play the drums so fast. "Just lucky, I guess." Buddy recognized the line, pointed his drumstick at me and winked.

I watched the entire concert from the backstage sidelines, a fabulous experience that allowed me to forget, at least for the night, about my stolen drums.

That week at *The Tonight Show*, I bumped into Johnny Carson on his way to work. He said he'd heard about the stolen drums, and I gave him a rundown on what had happened.

To my great surprise, he said: "I have a set of drums out at the beach house. Why don't you make arrangements with Drue Ann Wilson (his assistant) to come out and pick them up?" To this day I don't know if he said, "borrow" or "keep" the drums.

I drove out to his Malibu house that weekend. Drue was there house-sitting. She gave me a quick tour of the house. (It was the house in which Barbara Walters interviewed Johnny on one of her many ABC specials. I believe they still rerun that interview on cable, and this drum set is clearly in some of those shots.)

Dru led me to the beach-level living room, where the drums were set up near a sliding glass door. The salt air had pitted the drums. Every chrome part was marked up, and the cymbals were as green as the Statue of Liberty. A pair of red rubber-handled brushes were sitting on the floor tom-tom where Johnny must have left them the last time he sat at the set. When I lifted the brushes, the rusty tattoo caused by exposure to the damp ocean air remained on the skin of the drum. That stain is still there today.

This drum set had quite a history. The Ludwig Drum Co. brought it to *The Tonight Show* for one of Buddy's appearances. It was a brand-new (just out of the box) drum set that had never been played on. Or tuned, either. Ludwig's executives were on hand to see that the drums were set up for Buddy and that both the Ludwig and Buddy Rich logos were displayed on camera. They tightened the drumheads but didn't bother to fine-tune them. (A new set of drums always needs to be pampered. The heads have to be tightened, played on and re-tightened quite a bit before they are ready to be played on national television.)

When Buddy was presented with his new drum set, he wasn't exactly jumping for joy. He could tell they were not the top-of-the-line set he deserved. Drum companies offer beginner, deluxe and super-deluxe models; this set was their middle model, and Buddy knew it.

After the show, Buddy left the drum set behind as a gift to Johnny Carson, and now those same drums were being passed on to me.

I asked Dru if there were any cases I could use to transport the drums. She said she wasn't sure but asked me to follow her to the storage house next door.

At this time, Johnny was going through the divorce process with his third wife and living at his beach house in Malibu. The paparazzi had paid his neighbors for letting them peer into Johnny's house from next door. Johnny put a quick end to that. He bought his neighbor's house, then used it for storage.

We looked in the garage, where Johnny was storing his famous DeLorean on cinder blocks. Inside the house were stored several drum sets—a Rodgers set, another Ludwig and a Pearl drum set—all in cases. I found the Ludwig cases and packed up the drums.

When I got them home, I scrubbed them clean. The pitted chrome parts looked better after a couple of applications of chrome polish and plenty of elbow grease.

A few weeks later, my band was asked to play at the annual *Tonight Show* anniversary party at the Beverly Hills Hotel. My band played several of these private parties over the years. Each year they became more and more eccentric, because Johnny at random asked eight or ten of the staff members to get up and entertain. The parties were always a lot of fun, each outdoing the previous year's.

When I was able to take a break and talk to Johnny, I mentioned that I was playing the drums he'd loaned to me.

"Those are my drums from the beach house?" he said in amazement. "What did you do to them? They look great."

I told him I'd ordered a new drum set that was to arrive in a few weeks. I offered to return the drums as soon as I got the new ones. Johnny then said, "Why don't you just keep these drums as a second set, as a gift from me?" I accepted gratefully.

From that time on, whenever Buddy Rich played on *The Tonight Show*, I would bring in my drum set and set them up for him. I took pride in knowing exactly how he liked the drums and cymbals placed, and I'd make note of things that Buddy would adjust, so that when he came back the next time, I'd would have the drums exactly the way he liked them.

At a rehearsal for one of Buddy's later *Tonight Show* appearances, Ed Shaughnessy and I were standing off to the side of the bandstand watching Buddy play. While Buddy waited for Doc to count the band into the song, Shaughnessy caught Buddy's attention and said, "Hey, Buddy, those are the drums you gave to Carson and Carson gave them to Sweeney." I thought to myself that Buddy might want them back now that they were all tuned up and broken in. Thankfully, Buddy may have remembered about my drums being stolen. "Oh yeah," he said, pausing for a moment as he looked over the drum set, "Well, he can keep 'em."

I still have those drums under lock and key. Once in a while, on special occasions, I take them out and play them. When I do, I feel that I can play better than usual. I like to think that the spirit of Buddy Rich is still alive in those drums and that some of his drum solos are still echoing through the skins to me.

FOLLOW THE YELLOW BRICK ROAD

Along the way down the yellow brick road I met a scarecrow, a tin man and a lion. There also were a few wicked witches along the way. They were not only the wicked witches of the East, West, North and South, but there were one or two wicked witches of the Midwest as well. But just as in the Land of Oz, there were good witches too. I have chosen not to dwell on the wicked witches for fear they might cast a spell or sic their flying monkeys on me. Some of them are still flying around on their broomsticks. Instead, let's take a look at the people who had a positive effect on my life.

My scarecrow was not in search of a brain. He was a musical wizard. Doc Severinsen never ceased to amaze me. When I first met him and began touring with him on weekend jaunts across the United States and Mexico, I never grew tired of listening to his show. Doc's touring band, the Now Generation Brass featuring Today's Children, was an entourage of twenty-two people. He had an eleven piece band, six singers, a house audio tech, roadie (that would be me), and a road manager, and sometimes his personal manager would come along plus Doc. His show was comprised of popular hits of the day mixed with a few standards from the past. Doc's show was almost identical from town to town, with the same little jokes. After the first two opening songs, Doc would address the audience, "How is everybody out there?" No matter how spontaneously the crowd would react, he would always continue with, "Wait a minute. You sound like an old Merv Griffin crowd. Now, how's everybody out there?" He always would get a bigger reaction every time. At the end of the song "The Way We Were," Doc would build to a big cadenza ending in the highest note he could hit. Doc would add, "Looks like I'm gonna need some more Preparation H for my lips tonight." The crowd always loved it.

I would be listening from the balcony or backstage somewhere, singing along with the tunes or waiting to see if Doc would get the same reaction each night. He would always introduce the band members and singers toward the end of the show. He purposely would change the name of the city and state when he said where they lived. Snooky Young was always from Dayton, Ohio, because that is where he really is from. But most of the band was from New York or Los Angeles, so he would mix it up a little. The band would always get a kick out of it too and play along. What fascinated me was that Doc always managed to say a city that matched the state. For instance, he would say someone was from Peoria, Illinois. He wouldn't mistakenly say Peoria, Tennessee. It doesn't exist. Places like Wenatche, Washington, or Paynesville, Minnesota, and not Paynesville, Montana, were some of the cities he'd mention. One of the singers was of Puerto Rican descent, but lived in New York her whole life. Doc would always say she was from San Juan, Puerto Rico. The audience would always make a sound of "aah!" as if to say, "His group is international." This may sound trite to you, but add the pressure of ten thousand people staring at you and thinking what key your next song is supposed to be in and what tempo it is, you might forget where Wenatche is.

Working with Doc day in and day out for seventeen years was never mundane. Doc is a true leader in every way. Unlike many bandleaders, Doc got a chance to see what it is like from both sides of the baton. Whether it was Tommy Dorsey, Charlie Barnet or even Skitch Henderson, Doc was able to use what knowledge he gained from working under these bandleaders. Besides the brilliant sound that emanates from his trumpet whenever he plays a tune, his sense of humor is what brought him to the attention of the NBC decision makers when it came time to replace Skitch Henderson.

Doc's sense of humor seemed to catch everyone's attention during the "Stump the Band" segments of the early *Tonight Show*. David Letterman attempts to keep this bit alive on his show today, but there is no room for spontaneity there. When the Carson show presented the "Stump the Band" segments, it was usually to replace a comedy bit that was nixed or a guest who may have fallen out of the show. The only contrived part about it was that Peter Lassally and Jim McCawley would go out to the audience waiting in line and ask if any of them had a funny song to sing. They would pick three or four of them and make sure they had an aisle seat where Johnny would do the bit. They would tell Johnny that the guy in the green shirt and shorts had a funny song, or the woman with the flower in her hair would also be a good choice. Letterman calls the audience members out by name and when Paul Shaffer and his band play a comical version of a well-known tune with different lyrics, they have sheet music or cue cards in front of them with the lyrics that the writers on the show wrote for them. Doc, Ed and the band were never tipped off as to what these people were going to sing. Back in the days when Doc was in Skitch Henderson's trumpet section,

Skitch would often call upon Doc to do his rendition of the audience member's song. Doc would always sing something in the upper register of his voice and put a country twang to it. He became a comical favorite whenever they would play "Stump the Band." The personalities of the musicians came out when they would volunteer to make up a song on the spot. Sometimes they flopped, but most times it worked.

Doc's personality on camera carried itself off camera as well. He had some down home roots about him. He grew up in Arlington, Oregon, but sounded like he came from the middle of Texas. There were many times that I had to talk through the bell of a trumpet when talking to him. He had the mouthpiece to his lips eight hours a day, maybe even more. He had a distinctive sound to his warm-up. One time I was over at Studio 2 at NBC where they were taping *The Mac Davis Show*. They had a live band on that show and in the distance I could hear the sounds of a trumpet player warming up. I said to someone working on that show, "Who is that playing over there? He sounds like Doc." "That's because it is Doc," my friend said, "He's a guest on Mac's show today."

Doc's relationship with the band was a complex one. Doc knew from the bands he played with when he was making a name for himself that the bandleader couldn't get too friendly with his sidemen. You may have to fire one of them one day. It makes it kind of difficult to let someone go if your wives are the best of buddies. But Doc was able to maintain an even balance of bandleader and a musical friendship with the band. The band members respected Doc because of that. Doc knew when to joke around with the guys and when they needed to be whipped into shape. He had a knack for getting the band to sound like the best band in the world no matter how bland a chart they might play. On days he thought they needed a boot in the pants to keep them from becoming lazy, Doc would stop the band in mid-phrase and tell them they sounded like a dance band. Well, he might as well have called them a bunch of pansies. Through proper phrasing and dynamics, he'd have them gleaming with grandeur before the rehearsal was over.

Doc would ask the rhythm section to lay out once in a while at rehearsal and just have the horns play. You got a chance to hear the inner voicings of the arrangement and appreciate how tight that band could play without the help of the rhythm section. The bright, crisp sounds emanating from the ensemble were so powerful at times, I could feel my eyeglasses vibrate, and I got to hear this night after night.

Doc also had a gift for taking arrangements that artists would bring with them to *The Tonight Show* and he would perform major surgery on them to make them work for the show. Their charts had been on the road for a few years, so there might be beer stains on them, edges torn, pages missing. What happened quite often, they would have a chart that timed out to over seven minutes and our director, Bobby Quinn would ask them to cut it down to under three minutes. The reason given would be so they would have more time to sit at the panel. The real reason the song had to be shortened is that some survey somewhere in the ratings world determined that when someone sings a song on television, that's when they change the channel or get up to fix a pot of tea. Even if that person is Elton John or Sting. The logic behind it is that songs were the predictable part of the show. The way talk shows today are so predictable, there must be a lot of tea being brewed around the country.

So, here would be Doc with this horrific piece of music that he would have to perform his magic on to get it down to under three minutes. He'd ask the brass to cut from the end of measure forty-five and cut to measure eighty-two. He'd add, "Trombones, you do the same but don't play the pick-ups into eighty-two." "Saxes," as he would pick up his trumpet and toot out a pattern for them to play, "Play that four times at letter 'C' and the fourth time play it up an octave." All the while he is giving out these assignments, the camera men are joking around, the lighting guys are tapping lights into position and at times it seemed like bedlam all around him. Yet, the doctor was able to surgically alter an arrangement into a crowd-pleaser in a matter of minutes.

It is easy to work for someone you admire and respect. I always admired Doc's musical ability and professional demeanor by the way he handled himself with everyone. I respected him because he always gave me respect back. Doc made it possible for me to work in television by giving me my start and for that I will be forever grateful. Indeed, this scarecrow had a brain and he used it night after night without losing any of his straw along the way.

Further on down the yellow brick road, there was a tin man. Many claimed he didn't have a heart. On the surface it may have looked that way to some, but for those who took the time to know him, Fred de Cordova had a very big heart.

Fred liked to play with people, sometimes make them sweat. He had a devilish way about him, and if you showed signs of weakness, he'd lean on you even more. He was a complicated man. He demanded excellence and would go out of his way to compliment you if you achieved a certain goal.

One of the talent coordinators, Bob Dolce, who had been with the show almost the full thirty years, knew how to handle Fred. One day, at a production meeting, Fred asked Bob what was happening with the Bernadette Peters booking. Fred asked, "Is she in for Friday or not?" Rather than giving an answer like, "I don't know," which would have sent Fred through the roof, Bob said, "I have several calls out to her people and they haven't called back." Then Bob got up from his chair and left the meeting saying, "Let me go check again." Brilliant! He totally avoided a confrontation with Fred.

Another time, Dolce was talking to someone in the meeting and had his back towards Fred. Fred was trying to get a particular point across and noticed that he not only didn't have everyone's attention at the meeting, but he was competing with Dolce's conversation. Fred said, "Isn't that right, Mister Dolce?" A quick-thinking Bob Dolce knew exactly what to say, "I'm sorry, Fred. Could you clarify that for me?" He didn't say, "I'm sorry, I wasn't paying attention." Nor did he try to pretend he knew what Fred wanted and risk being made a fool. Fred simply laughed his devilish laugh and jokingly told us all to get out of his office. Bob lasted for many years at *The Tonight Show* because he learned how to handle Fred.

Fred was the principal of our school. He sometimes treated us like children. Some of us acted like children. I went to ask Fred for a raise one time. I had been with the show almost ten years and had received cost of living increases, but somehow the cost of living rose quicker than my paycheck could keep up with. I read somewhere that when you ask your boss for a raise, be sure and let him know how much money you make. Many times, bosses don't bother to look at that. They will mentally think about how much they make in comparison to you and give you the raise out of guilt.

I barely sat down and stated the reason I asked to speak with him was that I needed an increase in pay. I told him what my salary was and Fred thought for a second and said, "Well, you've been here a while and you get the job done well. Okay." It was that simple. I was prepared to give this whole speech about me wanting to move to a better neighborhood and I had a baby on the way. I nervously started to banter when Fred interrupted me and said, "I already approved your raise, now get out of my office before I change my mind." You see, deep down inside, there was a big heart.

For many years, he has been the man behind the man. Fred worked with many of the greats of the business, such as George Burns, Jack Benny and Johnny Carson. He was close friends with Jimmy Stewart, Gregory Peck and Ronald Reagan. Fred was a well-respected individual among many people who walked through *The Tonight Show* curtain. He had a corridor to the elite of old Hollywood and earned respect from any newcomers as well.

Fred ruled the stage and office of *The Tonight Show* with an iron fist, but not in the way that everyone ran and hid when they saw him coming. He expected the best from his staff and would pounce on you if it wasn't done right.

Throughout the seventies and eighties when I was there, smoking inside of buildings was not against the law. That didn't happen until 1992. Fred's office was always permeated with smoke and he always liked to have the room temperature at about 80°, so that it felt like an oven on hot or cold days. He liked to have things written down. If there was a show that contained a song that was restricted or the publisher was going to ask for a lot of money, he asked me to type out the circumstance so he could keep it on file with the show in question.

The writers would always write jokes that included restricted songs. In one case it was "My Way." The publishers just didn't think it was funny when a skit or joke was at the expense of their own property. "My Way" was in a legal dispute between Paul Anka and some other writer who claimed the song was his. At the early morning meeting we discussed the comedy bit that called for the band to play "My Way." I instantly explained to Fred about the problem. He said he would take care of it.

A few hours later, I was walking down the hallway between Studio 1 and Studio 3 and coming from the opposite direction was Fred with Peter Lassally. They were coming from Johnny's office where they must have had a discussion about the use of the song. Fred said, as he saw me approaching, "There's the man we're looking for." He said to me, "I want you to go tell Johnny what you told me this morning." I didn't feel I was in trouble, but I got the feeling it was important enough for Fred to want me to go directly to Johnny about the matter.

When I got to Johnny's office, his assistant Drue was at her desk. I told her Fred sent me to talk to Johnny. Drue always referred to Johnny as Mr. Carson and she said, "Go right in, Mr. Carson is waiting for you." The door to Johnny's office was usually closed, but in this case it was opened, so I peeked my head in and said, "Hello. You wanted to see me?" Johnny was seated on the couch in his office and had a pair of drumsticks in his hands and was drumming on the coffee table in front of him. He looked up at me and casually asked me to come in. He said, "What's all this business about the song 'My Way'?" I answered, "It seems that someone other than Paul Anka is claiming that they wrote the song, so it is in a legal dispute. NBC Music Rights has asked that we not use the song until the Paul Anka suit is settled." All the while I was talking, Johnny continued to tap away with the drumsticks. He tapped a little more and then said, "Oh yeah. Well, the hell with Paul Anka. We won't use the song."

I was a little confused at his reply, but relieved that somehow, as far as Johnny was concerned, it was resolved. I went to tell Fred and Peter the outcome. They were at the NBC commissary at their usual table. Fred and Peter had signs on each of their desks; one on Peter's desk read "Fred Handles That" and the other on Fred's desk read "Peter Handles That." The NBC commissary followed suit with that same joke and had two signs made to reserve their table in the private portion of the commissary. The signs read, "Peter Sits Here" and "Fred Sits Here." Around NBC, everyone knew that Peter and Fred (or Fred and Peter) meant the two producers of *The Tonight Show*. Fred and Peter were easy to find at lunch time, so I brought them the news of what transpired in Johnny's office. They both chuckled at the outcome and Fred said in his own joking tone of voice, "Now, unless you are going to serve us our order, get on your way."

For years, William Holden tried to get Johnny Carson to take a trip with him to Africa. Holden developed an interest in African wildlife preservation, spending much of his private lifetime campaigning and raising funds for the humane treatment of animals. Fred was also a close friend of Holden and eventually took him up on the offer of a safari.

Johnny got word to the staff that he wanted to surprise Fred when he returned by dressing Fred's office up with jungle-like trees while staff members dressed in African animal costumes. Whenever Johnny would have an idea such as this for a practical joke or comedy skit, the staff would jump into action and make sure it happened. This one particular gag turned out to be a lot of fun.

Fred would usually be one of the first to arrive everyday at *The Tonight Show* offices, so we had to beat the early bird to work that day. Fred's office was filled with plants and bamboo baskets; we even hired two musicians to play conga drums. Staff members all donned costumes. We had primitive leopard skin native outfits, an orangutan and an elephant. Johnny and writer Pat McCormick were dressed as safari scouts with pith helmets and all. The front gate informed us that Fred had just driven in so we got into position. We locked ourselves into Fred's office. When Fred came in, his assistant, Barbara Meltzer (who was not in costume), sat at her desk and welcomed him back from his vacation in a very "matter of fact" way. It was not unusual for Fred's office door to be locked. As soon as he turned the key in the doorknob, the conga players began playing a jungle beat and Fred opened the door. He was immediately greeted by our safari leader, Johnny.

Johnny was known for practical jokes over the years from back in his college and early days in radio and television. Occasionally he did little stunts like this on the show. He once had Ed McMahon stopped at the NBC gate as he left one night and had the security guards check Ed's car trunk. Inside the trunk were several items like typewriters and boxes of office supplies planted there by our props department to make it look like Ed was stealing from NBC. This stunt was all captured on hidden cameras and the joke was revealed as a prank when Johnny showed up dressed as an NBC security guard. It was stunts such as this one that sparked the beginning of the NBC show *Bloopers and Practical Jokes*, which was hosted by Dick Clark and Ed McMahon.

Fred was genuinely surprised and honored that Johnny took the time and effort to welcome him back from safari. We spent the next hour posing for photos in our silly costumes.

Fred came from an era where he could refer to the women in the office as "sweetie," "honey" or "darling" and no one took offense. He used the puff of his ever-present cigarette to set the comedic timing, something I am sure he learned from George Burns, or for that matter, Bette Davis. As far as I know, Jack Benny didn't smoke, but his way of letting the crowd linger before he hit the punch line was also part of Fred's make-up. Fred's humor was usually very biting, but he was quick-witted.

Not much further down the road was the cowardly lion who thought he needed courage. He was more like a big teddy bear than a lion. Each night, he let out a roar: "Heeeeeeeere's Johnny!" to bring out the Wizard—and that took a lot of courage. Ed McMahon is like an uncle to me. He always had time to talk or listen if I stuck my head in his office doorway. With his resounding tone, he always had your attention. I always admired the way he would walk into a room full of people and say hello over the crowd. He didn't single one or two people out; he towered over most, so his voice was aimed over the masses, yet you felt he was saying hello to only you.

My mom has always been a fan of Ed. Whenever I watched the show with my parents when I was in high school and some comic would tell an "off-color" joke, I would be suppressing my laughter because my parents were in the room. My mom would not think the blue joke was appropriate for TV and she would say, "Look, Ed McMahon's not laughing." Madeline Kelly, who was Ed's assistant for many years, told me during Johnny's final weeks of the show, "I have never heard Ed utter a swear word in all the time I have worked for him," she said.

I used to watch him many afternoons pre-recording commercials for Alpo, Budweiser or the countless top name sponsors we had over the years. They all wanted Ed to do their commercials or pre-record something they would air at a convention. Ed became known among the crew as "One Take Ed." He had a knack for getting exactly what the sponsors needed on the first run through. He would show up totally prepared, either memorizing the script or looking at it once before the cameras would roll and get it on the first try. He once revealed one of his secrets to me when I asked how he was able to get everything needed to be said in the 30 seconds or 60 seconds he had to say it in. Ed told me the trick is, say all you need to say in the time allotted but save the last few words at the end of the script so when the stage manager counts down the last few seconds you can relax and end on time.

One day, when *The Tonight Show* was still ninety minutes long, I was making a trip to the restroom during one of the half hour station breaks and was stopped from entering the men's room by a sign that read OUT OF SERVICE. I knew that there was another men's room in the floor below the studio level so I went down there. When I got into the lower corridor I saw Ed McMahon wandering aimlessly. He was beginning to panic. The show was on a three-minute commercial break, but it was definitely still in progress. Although Ed's participation in the show dwindled during the last half hour—he was usually pushed to the end of the couch—he still thought it was his duty to return to the show before we came back on the air. It seems that Ed McMahon was on a liquid diet—a diet about which he had spoken with Johnny on the air—and he would be very embarrassed if they were to return without Ed at the end of the couch. Johnny might notice and let America know that Ed had to go relieve himself during one of our beloved sponsors' commercial spots.

As soon as Ed saw me, he frantically asked, "Where in hell is the men's room down here? I have to get back up there before the break is over." He was looking at each door in the hallway trying desperately to find the lucky door that read GENTLEMEN on it. He looked pretty distraught, so I quickly showed him where it was. He thanked me and continued to mumble about using the bathroom before me because he had to get back upstairs to the show.

One time early in my career at the show, I crossed paths with Ed McMahon in the men's room back in the bungalow offices at NBC. I walked in one day to find our distinguished announcer dressed in a sweat suit but barefoot, washing out his socks in the little sink. I didn't say anything more than hello. Ed was embarrassed that anyone would see him doing what he was doing, so I guess that's why he chose to explain to me why he was doing his laundry in the men's room sink. Ed told me that he was having a house built in Bel-Air according to his design. He decided to stop off on his way to NBC to see if the recent rains had damaged any of the new construction on his place. When he stepped out of his limousine his feet sank into about a foot of mud. The ground was so saturated it was like quicksand. He didn't have another pair of socks with him, so there he was. I thought that it was funny that this multi-million dollar celebrity, the most recognizable face in the industry, had to hand wash his socks in the office men's room.

Ed does have an infectious laugh, but his laugh is genuine. He would laugh when something caught his funny bone and he would laugh whole-heartedly. After all, he was Johnny's sidekick. A good sidekick would always be there to support the top banana. And sometimes, that took a lot of courage.

Back in the sixties, AFTRA (American Federation of Television and Radio Artists) called a strike and Johnny, who was an AFTRA member, went on strike with them. Johnny's contract was up for re-negotiation, and NBC was not seeing eye to eye with him. Parts of his demands were about money and parts of his terms were over more control of the show. *The Tonight Show* was a huge money machine for NBC and many knew that it was due to Johnny Carson. He continued to not show up for work for several weeks.

In those days, the show would open with Ed saying, "From New York, it's *The Tonight Show*, starring Johnny Carson. Johnny's guest host tonight is . . . ." And Ed would read off the person filling in and the list of people on the show that night. He then would say, " . . . Skitch Henderson and the NBC Orchestra, and me, I'm Ed McMahon." Each night that Johnny didn't show up for work made it tougher for Ed to be there every night. The newspapers wrote how difficult it was for Johnny's sidekick to have to carry on without the main attraction. When Ed would say, ". . . and me, I'm Ed McMahon," each night the applause got bigger and bigger. Before Ed brought out the guest host for the night, he would have to do a live dog food commercial or beer ad. It took a lot of courage to get through those weeks.

During this contract dispute, many replacement hosts were mentioned to take over for Johnny if he did not return. Bob Newhart was one of them, but another person who was doing a fairly good job of it and getting considerable ratings was Jimmy Dean (of the pork sausage fame). He was also well-known as a country act at the time and for singing the popular song, "Big Bad John."

When Johnny's contract was resolved, he got a huge boost in salary and NBC met every one of his demands. Johnny emerged from the month long walk-out with a considerably higher salary, a better dressing room (that was part of it) and more control over the content of the show. Eventually, the Best of Carson Shows (re-runs of *Tonight Shows*) began to air on Monday nights giving Johnny a four-day work week and more money. As contracts were penned over the years, the Best of Carson moved to Tuesday nights and Monday nights became guest host nights giving Johnny a three-day work-week and more money. The popularity of the show grew even more with each year and pretty soon the network executives began to think that the term seen on the commercial slides going in and out of commercial breaks reading, "More to come," was possibly a fore-shadowing of Johnny's next contract demands.

Many things changed on the show. The show used to go on the air at 11:15 p.m. in many markets and Skitch Henderson and Ed McMahon would fill the fifteen minutes before Johnny would come on. The extra fifteen minutes was there so that the affiliated stations across America could sell ad time for themselves. In later years, the network managed to squeeze five minutes for the local stations by starting the show at 11:35 p.m. as it does today. Johnny's new contract did away with the pre-show at 11:15 p.m. One of the many changes was the way the show opened. The new opening had Ed announce, "From New York, *The Tonight Show* starring Johnny Carson. This is Ed McMahon along with Skitch Henderson inviting you to join Johnny and his guests . . ." After the list of guests he'd say, ". . . Ladies and gentlemen, Heeeeeere's Johnny!" and Johnny would come out and do his monologue before the first commercial and it stayed that way until Johnny's retirement in 1992.

A MOMENT WITH THE KING

One time, Tommy Newsom and the Tonight Show Band were performing at the Beverly Hilton Hotel for a benefit honoring Ed McMahon as Man Of The Year. A cast of Beverly Hills celebrities was on hand. I was there to set up the band and be their librarian. All the band members were ready to go and seated in their chairs on the bandstand except for one. Ed Shaughnessy, who was never late and never missed a downbeat in his life, was not there. The contractor, Al Lapin, asked me to jump into Ed's chair and get his book in order. Tommy was calling out the order of songs. I quickly jumped into position and got Ed's book in order for him. We all expected Ed to walk through the door any minute. He never did make it to the gig. We found out later that Shaughnessy had had a car accident, but was okay.

Newsom may or may not have noticed that I was in Ed's seat as he proceeded to set the tempo for the first song. It was 1984, the year the Olympics were in Los Angeles, and it seemed the "in" thing to do was to start every function with the national anthem. So that was the first tune of the evening. Realizing that Tommy was about to forge on ahead with or without a drummer, I figured I'd better be ready to play. But then I noticed there were no drumsticks. I darted off the stage and over to a nearby table and grabbed a couple of knives. I jumped back to the drum set just as the national anthem started. I managed to play a drum roll with the handle ends of my butter knives and made it through the "Star Spangled Banner." Newsom started to count off the next tune. It was a tune of Louie Bellson's called "Let Me Walk My Own Walk." It was a light song with a two feel. The only cymbals I had were the ones on the high hat, but I could play the standard ding, ding-a-ding with my knives. Somewhere in the intro of this song, Snooky Young saw what was happening and stated loud enough for the band to here, "Damn, look at that. Sweeney's playin' the drums with a pair of butter knives." A lady in the front row must have overheard that remark. She had apparently had quite a bit to drink. She picked up a rather large ladle, hurled it at the stage, and slurred, "Here, let's see if he can play with this." The ladle whizzed past my head, missing me by inches. I thought, give me a break, I'm only trying to fill in for the regular drummer! Tony Bennett was also scheduled to perform a few songs with the Tonight Show Band that evening. Luckily, a few songs later, Tony Bennett's drummer Joe LaBarbara showed up with sticks, cymbals and a tuxedo. He finished the night out for us.

After LaBarbara took my place, there was little for me to do but to wait for the show to finish so that I could pack everything up. To pass the time, I went off to the band dressing room to read a book and nibble at their platters of food. Ed McMahon would soon be receiving his award.

I had this rather large room all to myself until the door at the far end opened and a few of the people running the event, in a whispered commotion, ushered in the surprise guest. They were hiding him until the appropriate time in the evening, and this was the room they chose to hide him in. They practically shoved him through the door and closed it on him, locking him in with me. As I looked across the room, the tuxedoed surprise guest turned toward me—and we were both amazed. He was shocked to find that he wasn't the only person there, and I was pleasantly astonished to discover that the surprise guest for the evening was Johnny Carson. Johnny's reaction went from puzzlement and nearly apologizing for barging in on me to a calmer state when he recognized me. He walked over to where I was, said hello and sat down. He explained to me that he was to surprise Ed McMahon.

So suddenly here I was, face to face and all alone with Johnny Carson. Before I worked on the show, before I graduated high school, I used to imagine what it would be like to sit with and interview Johnny Carson. The newspaper articles on him, magazine interviews and even the rare one-on-one interviews that Johnny had over the years never asked the questions I would have wanted to hear answered by him. I would have asked him if he were happy doing what he was doing. Did he ever wish he were someone else? What was his ultimate goal? Questions like these were touched on from time to time, and Johnny would spar with the interviewer and ultimately avoid the answer with a witty remark or evasive reply. I felt that I would persevere more than these previous interviewers and not relent until I got an answer from him. This was my big chance, the moment I had been waiting for—and suddenly I was eye to eye with my boss, my idol.

At that moment I wanted to be Mike Wallace or David Frost, but unlike those reporters, I had no staff of writers to think up questions, no research team, no notes, no microphone. I had to wing it. I could see that Johnny was nervous. He always seemed to have his nervous twitches and various tics, but he was out of his element tonight, knowing that in a few minutes he was to go out and surprise Ed

McMahon and about a thousand dinner guests. I am sure he had every joke well planned out ahead of time. Nonetheless, he seemed a little more twitchy than usual. I thought to try to put him at ease and engaged in light conversation. I knew that Johnny and his wife had just been in Europe on vacation in Italy. I had been to Italy about a year prior to this, so I started to ask him how his trip went. Instantly he began to talk of some of the places he went, and we each compared stories about our trips abroad.

It was a veritable conversation, very much like Johnny would have with his guests night after night. He was charming and witty in his knowledge of the Italian culture. I think I was able to calm him down a little by taking his mind away from the party going on just outside the dressing room. Unfortunately it was soon time for Johnny to make his surprise entrance at the gala outside. He politely excused himself and went off to entertain.

Although I never got the courage to get to my "in depth" questions, that night I learned a lot more about Johnny Carson than I ever learned from any interview before. He was genuine. His persona off camera was similar to his persona on camera. What you see is what you get. I got to chat with the man I had been in awe of for more than half my life. Life is good sometimes.

A COMMAND PERFORMANCE FOR THE KING

In 1981 Johnny formed Carson Productions and gained full control of *The Tonight Show*. His deal was to produce the show for NBC as well as produce other shows for the network. The staff of the show as well as the staff of Carson Productions were invited to a big private party each year to celebrate the anniversary of *The Tonight Show*.

The first year the party was held at the Bistro in Beverly Hills in a small banquet room on the second floor. This was the first chance to meet and greet the Carson Productions staff, made up mostly of accountants and attorneys. It was an elegant night out and we all had a great time.

The second year our anniversary party was held in a tent in Chasen's parking lot. Chasen's used to be a legendary restaurant on the corner of Doheny and Beverly Boulevard. Johnny's plan was to have the party inside, however Elizabeth Taylor had beat him to the punch and booked the main room for the wrap party from her off-Broadway production of *Little Foxes*. Johnny announced that there were only two reasons the city of Beverly Hills would allow a tent to be erected. One was if there was a circus in town, and the other was if you were having a bar miztvah. Johnny said, "Luckily we worked things out with the fire marshall. So, I want to welcome you all to my bar miztvah."

The following year the party was held at the Beverly Hills Hotel in a ballroom directly off the main lobby on the first floor. Johnny had attended a party given by Frank Sinatra at the opening of the new Universal Amphitheatre in which my newly formed SRO Band had played. Johnny asked us to play at his party. He then got the idea, why bother to go out and hire outside talent to entertain at the party? Talented people surrounded him on his staff. Why not let them be the entertainment? So he recruited staff members to get up and amuse us all. He would hand pick ten staffers weeks before the party and ask them to prepare some sort of talent for five or ten minutes each. They could sing, tell jokes, recite poetry, or give a speech. Anything except to be laudatory. The results each year were staggering.

The first year one of the staff members lip-synched a song pre-recorded by a well-known opera singer who asked to remain nameless. Some of the lyrics contained language that would never have been allowed on television. One of the writers on staff brought a small cassette player and placed it on a stool, hit the play button and vanished from view. The audio on the tape was his voice talking about how much he hated talking in public. This kind of amusement went on until the wee hours of the morning as each performer presented themselves, and nobody wanted it to end.

The following year the party was moved downstairs at the Beverly Hills Hotel to the Crystal Ballroom. Weeks before the party, Johnny picked his ten entertainers, only now they had all these demands. They wanted my band to accompany them, they needed special musical arrangements made up for their acts, they needed a follow spot, they wanted to know where they would be placed in the show, and they wanted a chance to rehearse their pieces before the room filled up.

The performances were more outrageous than before. The wardrobe department helped by supplying feather boas, break-a-way clothing—or whatever they needed to enhance their acts. Our assistant director, Jim Kantrowe, completely fooled the crowd. He sat at the piano and played a beautiful tune for everyone, except that he wasn't really playing. I cued up a tape and played it through the sound system. Everyone just assumed they were hearing the stage piano, but instead they were listening to a piece especially recorded for the evening by a professional musician. It was days later that we let the secret out.

Thus the tradition of the Tonight Show anniversary parties began. Each year got better and better. The performances got more and more elaborate and racy. Each year the staff members waited to see if they would be asked to perform, and it was something we looked forward to every year and talked about all year until the next one.

GOOD DAYS AND BAD DAYS

People sometimes ask me, "What was your best day at *The Tonight Show* and what was your worst day?" I can honestly say that there were so many "best days" working on that show, it is difficult to pick out one. Most of the contents of this book are about my best days. I guess if I had to pick one day as the best day, that would be the day I was hired.

There were bad days, as there would be in any job that lasts twenty years, but we try to forget the bad days. At least, it is healthier that we do. There is no reason to dwell on the negative. But, to answer the question, one of the worst days for me was when one of the Tonight Show Band members passed away.

Everyday the band would arrive at 3:15 in the afternoon to rehearse any musical numbers for the show. That is when artists like Steve Lawrence and Edie Gorme, Celine Dion, Kenny Rodgers and the long list of musical celebrities who walked through *The Tonight Show* doors would rehearse their songs with the band. If there wasn't a musical guest on the show, Doc would use this time to get the bugs out of a chart from the musical library of more than 3,000 arrangements—the ones I maintained for the show. Doc also would run new arrangements that a small army of top arrangers in the business would bring in. Some of them were commissioned by Doc to write something and others like Tommy Newsom, John Bambridge, Mike Barone, Bill Holman and Dick Lieb didn't need an invitation.

The band would break from rehearsal sometime around 4:15 or 4:30 p.m. and take a break until shortly before the show taping. Usually the orchestra manager, who would be meticulously watching the clock to keep track of the hours the band worked every day, would tell the band what time they needed to report back to the bandstand. The show had become so routine, everyone knew when to return, so Doc would point to trumpeter Conte Candoli, who we all referred to as "The Count," to say a few words to the band before we broke. Count always had something funny to say. He would refer to Doc as the "Old Man" with Doc standing right there, even though Count had a few years on Doc. Sometimes he would jokingly scold the saxophones and tell them that the "Old Man" wasn't happy with the way they played a particular piece. Count would tell them to stay after rehearsal and work it out. The band members loved his routine. Count would always end his daily banter with a loud and lively "5:15!" which was the call time for them to return to the show after the break.

The band members would hang out at the NBC commissary or in the greenroom where they could watch the news or sports shows until the guests started to arrive. A few of the guys were known to go across the street to Chadney's Restaurant to enjoy a cocktail or two before the show. This was okay with Doc as long as it didn't affect their playing. I don't remember anyone ever having problems with a drink or two before the show.

The call time to return for the show was strict. This gave the band ample time to get on the bandstand and play the show's warm-up. As the band stood backstage, the orchestra manager, Al Lapin, would summon them all to get on to the bandstand. There was no excuse for lateness. The show was run like clockwork every night.

One early afternoon, I received a call from Fred de Cordova telling me that one of the guys in the band had passed away. Trumpeter John Audino had had a massive heart attack and died. I continued to pass the sad news on to everyone. By the time the band came in for rehearsal, everyone had heard about Audino.

No one ever had anything bad to say about Johnny Audino. He clearly loved his job of being the first trumpet in the Tonight Show Band. John was also proud to have been asked to play with Frank Sinatra on several of his albums, television shows and live concerts.

He was one of those trumpet players who was a perfectionist when he played. He was a strong lead player no matter if he was backing a well-known performer or if he was playing for a comedy tag to one of Johnny Carson's skits. He was a strong voice among many that made the roar of music nightly on *The Tonight Show.*

John Audino was one of the nicest guys you would ever want to meet. He made a sound like "Gying, gying" whenever a pretty woman would walk into the studio. When the band heard that noise, they would all look around to see what Johnny had detected. He was a short balding guy with a heart of gold. He had developed an on-air friendship with actress Angie Dickinson who would usually wave to Audino from the panel as she sat talking to Johnny Carson. "Where's my friend Johnny Audino?" she'd say as she would find him in the band and flirt with him as if to make Carson jealous. Anyone who has seen her appearances on the show knows how she liked to flirt with Johnny.

One time, a guest conductor was running a number at rehearsal before the star singer arrived. When the band played the chart down, there was a fermata at the end (meaning the band needed to hold that note until the conductor cut them off). The conductor was pre-occupied with making a correction on something that occurred earlier in the chart and forgot to cut the band off at the end. Johnny, being the perfectionist he was, played out the note until he turned beet red and even started to turn a little blue, until he finally took the horn from his mouth and shouted at the conductor, "You gotta cut us off, man!" The conductor apologized profusely. Although Audino sounded angry, he was never arrogant.

There was no musical guest on the day Audino had died, so there was nothing to rehearse. Instead, we all shook our heads in disbelief that he was no longer with us. Doc was too overcome to even speak. He merely pointed to the Count. Count stood up with tears in his eyes and could barely get the words out. He simply whispered, "5:15." The band sat in silence and one by one, the guys left the stage without looking at one another or speaking a word. It was at that moment that it all hit us that Johnny Audino was not coming back.

John Audino was one of the first band members to pass away. Nick DiMaio, a trombonist in the band for many years, had died

Glued to the TV. Friends would be invited to Nana's house to watch the new fad of the '60s, color TV.

Long before Don was affiliated with The Tonight Show, *Ed McMahon obliges a pose with Don at the Auto Show in New York City (circa 1970).*

Backstage at the MGM Grand Hotel in Las Vegas, comedian Red Skelton gives some advice to a young comic (1975).

Contractor Al Lapin worked for NBC before television came along and was exclusive to The Tonight Show *from 1972 to 1991.*

"Okay, I'm ready to guest host," as Don sits at Johnny Carson's desk playing with the double eraser pencils and drumming near the ever-present cigar box, lighter and coffee mug. (Courtesy of Carson Productions.)

The drum set Buddy Rich gave to Johnny Carson and Johnny gave to Don.

Ray Charles backstage at the Century Plaza Hotel in Los Angeles prior to performing with Don's SRO Big Band.

Conducting for Ray Charles, Don had to constantly remind himself that it was not a dream and that the "real deal" was sitting at the other end of the piano from him.

As a practical joke, Jungle John greets Fred de Cordova back from an African safari with an office filled with co-workers garbed in jungle attire and animal costumes. (Courtesy of Carson Productions.)

Don Rickles posed for a photo in the greenroom and later signed it "To Don, what happened?" referring to Sweeney's shaven head.

Backstage at the Stardust Hotel in Las Vegas, Don Rickles and Don reminisce about the "old days" on Johnny Carson's Tonight Show.

Charo, the "cuchi cuchi" girl, backstage with Don at the Madrid Theatre in Canoga Park (2004) after she performed a free children's concert for the Valley Cultural Center.

Johnny Carson and most of the Tonight Show Band (top row l. to r.):
Bill Perkins, Maurie Harris, Ernie Tack, Gil Falco, Eugene "Snooky"
Young, Peter Woodford, Joel DiBartolo, Don Ashworth, Bruce Paul-
son, Ernie Watts; (middle row l. to r.): Conte Candoli, Chuck Findley,
Don Sweeney, Ed Shaughnessy, Johnny Carson, Ross Tompkins,
Shelly Cohen; (sitting l. to r.): Pete Christlieb, Tommy Newsom.
(Courtesy of Carson Productions.)

Photo by Earl Rose

The Tonight Show Band music
library, in a former rehearsal
room above the production
offices, housed well over 3,000
big band charts.

Courtesy of Don Sweeney

Tonight Show Band musicians John Audino and Conte "The Count"
Candoli relax in the greenroom between rehearsal and show time.

Drummer Ed Shaughnessy with former drum student and friend for over thirty years.

OIL!
THIS WAY
←
CHEAP

Ed McMahon is beside himself as he jokes for a photo at one of the many office parties.

Still friends after all these years, Cory Carson and Don in 2005.

Don poses with The Tonight Show *producers, Peter Lassally (left) and Fred de Cordova (right), in front of the empty booking board prior to the taping of Johnny Carson's last show.*

prior to Johnny, but he had been sick for a long time and his death was expected. Drummer Nick Cerroli, who was a substitute drummer from time to time, died suddenly and way too soon. We saw Cerroli at the show maybe three or four times a year. I think Audino's death hit us all so hard because we saw him every day.

We all went to Audino's funeral, and I felt honored to be asked to be one of the pallbearers. When we got to the cemetery plot where everyone was to gather to give their final respects, there was a huge arrangement of red, white and yellow roses that Doc had sent over in the name of the Tonight Show Band members. It stood on an easel about four feet high and five feet wide. The roses simply spelled out, "5:15."

The other saddest day was one of the saddest days in *Tonight Show* history, the day that Johnny Carson retired. He gave us a year to absorb the fact that he was no longer going to be entertaining us. In television, if you lasted three years on a show without getting cancelled, you could consider yourself a success. Most people I came in contact with were thrilled to be with a show for five years. So, at *The Tonight Show*, there were some people who moved out to Los Angeles from New York to remain with the show. Others, like me joined up with the show along the way. I worked with Johnny Carson for sixteen and a half years. He was on for thirty years, so, the way I figure it, I worked more than half the shows. My batting average goes up even higher if you take into consideration that several years of shows from the '60s were destroyed thanks to someone at NBC who thought it would be better to toss those shows without asking anyone. They dumped those reels of precious videotape just to make more shelf space in a warehouse.

I had always thought that Johnny would have just one too many bimbo actresses to deal with one night and stand up, take his cigarette lighter, cigarette box, a few of those double eraser pencils he'd always drum on the desk with, turn to Ed McMahon and say, "Why don't you lock up for me?," walk off the set and never come back. Instead, he took the classy way out. He had the chance to say goodbye to all of his friends and have them on the show one more time. He gave America the chance to say goodbye to him, and he had a chance to bid farewell to us at his own pace.

I was happy for Johnny and deeply saddened at the same time. He certainly earned a good retirement after being there night after night for us. I think a lot of us took him for granted. You'd be home watching TV after the nightly news and start watching Johnny's monologue. He would take some of the topics presented by the news media and make us laugh about the absurdity of it all. In the '60s, when Kennedys were being assassinated, Martin Luther King was gunned down, war protesters were rioting in the streets and it seemed that all hell was breaking loose, you'd have Johnny joking about the hippie movement, Liz Taylor's latest marriage or his own marriage problems. Somehow, for that moment, he made us all feel good.

He never went after someone with vengeance. Even if Johnny joked about someone in the monologue or in a sketch, he never tried to kick anyone when they were down.

He once did one too many jokes about Wayne Newton. He would joke about Wayne's voice being so high pitched and joked about his manhood. Wayne called Fred de Cordova and asked that it stop immediately. When the jokes continued to occur, Wayne took the matter into his own hands. He flew in from Las Vegas and got through NBC security because they recognized him and thought he was a guest on the show. Wayne marched right up to Johnny's office, and Johnny happened to be standing in the outer office talking to his assistant. Suddenly Newton was right in Johnny's face. He more or less told Johnny to stop the jokes immediately or he would take defensive action against him. Johnny was clearly ambushed and apologized to Wayne. There were no more Wayne Newton jokes after that.

It was difficult to consider that toward the end of Johnny's run that we would do "the last" Aunt Blabby routine, "the last" Carnac, "the last" Tea Time Movie. We all became so sentimental about so many aspects of the show. The staff members were like extensions of our families. Things would never be the same. I was torn with emotions. I had been asked to stay on with Jay Leno's *Tonight Show* a year before Jay was to begin, so I didn't have that element of fear about finding life after the show. I was certainly happy to be staying on, but depressed that my idol since the early years of high school was no longer going to be there.

The transition into the Jay Leno crew was somewhat of a distraction for me. I didn't have time to really grieve about Johnny's retirement. Not only was I still working at NBC Studios and still in television, I had to make new friends with the entire new staff that Jay and his manager, Helen Kushnick, had assembled. On Friday, May 22, 1992, I went from being the young kid on the show to Monday, May 25, 1992, being the old guy on the show. Most of Jay Leno's staff were fresh out of college and most had never worked on a television show before. A few of them had never watched the Johnny Carson shows because they weren't old enough to stay up that late.

Johnny's last week of shows went fast for me. I would work all day on the Johnny Carson *Tonight Show* and stay after work to do test shows for the Jay Leno *Tonight Show*. We taped test shows after Johnny's show because some of technical crew from Johnny's show were also going to be working on Jay's show. We taped the beginning weeks of Jay's shows in Studio 3. It was convenient to be right across the hall from Johnny's show, but I can't tell you how many times during Johnny's final week that I would walk down the hallway between Studio 1 and Studio 3 and not know which way to turn.

I had permission from Fred de Cordova and director Bobby Quinn to shoot video behind the scenes of the final two Johnny Carson *Tonight Show*s. Our receptionist, Mike Beron, also was allowed to videotape behind the scenes. We both interviewed various members of the staff and crew and got some rarely seen views in that significant time for us all. (I later took our footage and edited it together and made a keepsake out of it.)

Technically, the final *Tonight Show* was on May 21, 1992, when Johnny had on Robin Williams and Bette Midler. The emotions ran high as the staff started to empty out their desks, dismantle wall hangings, and box up their personal things while still performing their everyday staff functions. The members of the band were equally emotional. They were losing the greatest gig in television. My home video camera captured the reaction from the band when the studio cameras shut down and we were off the air. Doc stood in front of a silent, speechless band. The audience continued to applaud long after Johnny, Ed and Doc left the studio. Doc was the last to leave. He turned to the audience and the applause grew louder. He simply motioned toward the band for the audience to acknowledge them, and then he quietly walked off the stage.

The next day, the staff had planned to give Johnny a gift from all of us. What do you get a guy who has given us so much? He gave me a fabulous way of life for sixteen and a half years and entertained me and the rest of America for most of our lives. It was hard for the staff to let go. We gave him a nautical clock from Tiffany's, something he could use in retirement on his yacht. Johnny joked and reminisced about the show the night before and how everyone was talking about it on every television news station around the dial. He was flattered how there were signs hanging on the freeway overpasses on his way in to work. Fans knew he had to drive past on his way in from Malibu.

As Johnny looked to the corkboard behind Fred de Cordova's desk, he lost his breath for a moment. The board that once was cluttered with the names of the who's who of the entertainment industry had one card on it. It simply was the date, Friday, May 22, with nothing more than a series of push-pins and staple marks. "Oh, my God, what a long summer it's going to be," he said as he joked about how he could remember the days when we needed anybody to fill some of those spots. Yes, there were occasions when guests would fall out at the last minute or it was seasonally a dry time in Hollywood when no one was in town and no one had anything to plug.

It was time for Johnny to get ready for the show. Johnny joked one more time before leaving the room. He said, "It just worked last night," referring to the Bette Midler and Robin Williams show, "We should have just stayed home today." He joked about putting on a re-run instead and added, "Somehow, I don't think that NBC would take too kindly to that." Johnny left the room with a wave and told us he would see us all later at the party. For some of the staff members, this was one of the few times they spoke to Johnny on a one-to-one basis. They were also high-strung that day, not only because it was the last hurrah, but also because Johnny invited the entire staff and their spouses out to his home in Malibu for one last anniversary party.

The program that aired on May 22, 1992, was Johnny Carson's last television show for NBC, but was considered a special. There were no guests; it was a clip show with a look back over the full thirty years. It was also Johnny's network goodbye. The audience consisted of staff members and their spouses and invited guests. I was just starting to get to know my new bandleader, Branford Marsalis. I got him a seat in the audience; he sat with my wife while I was seated in the greenroom. Branford was thrilled to witness the final bow from Johnny, Ed and Doc.

The last hour went all too quickly. Johnny simply sat on a stool center stage and introduced clips from the past thirty years. During a commercial break, Johnny admitted to the staff and studio guests that he was nervous. He joked with Doc and the band off camera and joked about going on tour with the band as an opening comic. Being such a class act right up until the very end, Johnny carried off the remaining segments with poise and panache. Although his hair had turned white and his face was creased with laugh lines, he still had the same innocent "boy from Nebraska" look about him.

A nervous feeling came upon me deep within my stomach when I looked at my watch and realized that we barely had five minutes left in the show. In just a few moments the ride was going to be over.

We thought we shed all of our tears the night before when Bette Midler sang "One More For The Road" to Johnny. Fighting back his emotions as he always did in the past, Johnny managed to compose himself until the credits rolled soon after he bid us all, ". . . a very heartfelt goodnight" for the last time. Millions of viewers across the nation went to bed that night saddened to see the King of Late Night turn out their night light for the last time.

After the show, everyone on the staff headed out to Johnny's house in Malibu. Valet parking attendants met us at the entrance to his home. The entryway into the house and living room area had marble floors, glass walls, a sunken couch area and a tree that grew right up through an opening in the glass ceiling. It was very industrial looking at first. Don Rickles once was noted to have said upon the first time he entered Johnny's house, "Where's the gift shop?" I had seen pictures of this house before Johnny moved into it in the early eighties. It was in an *Architectural Digest* someone had shown me. The pictures didn't do it justice. As you made your way to the back of the house, there was a magnificent view of the ocean from his cliff-topped patio. On a lower level there was a swimming pool with the ocean as a backdrop, and across from the pool there was another terraced patio and the rest of the living quarters of the house.

The main house was for the cocktail portion of the party. After a while we were all asked to join the Carsons across the street on the tennis court, where dinner would be served. Johnny's house was at the end of a cul-de-sac. The road actually looped around his tennis court. You couldn't see it from the road due to a high wall that encircled it. There was an underground walkway that Johnny would use when he played tennis there. We all walked across the roadway.

Covering the tennis court was a large white tent, and inside it, a live big band emanated, Les Brown and His Band of Renown. There was no need for a talent show at this party. Johnny wanted his guests to sit back and enjoy the evening. The tent was elegantly decorated with white tables and chairs and twinkle lights throughout. At one side of the tennis court there was a building with bathrooms and changing rooms (for visiting tennis players to freshen up if you were ever invited to play tennis with Johnny). Along the inside wall of the pavilion was a long credenza where there were photos of Johnny with Jack Benny, George Burns, Lucille Ball, Jimmy Stewart and other icons of the business.

At the end of the evening, I went to say goodnight to Johnny and his wife, Alex, and thank them for a wonderful time. Johnny was as gracious as any host could be. I managed to tell him how much I appreciated working for him over the years. I said, "It was an honor and a privilege to work for one of the legends of the industry." And just like Johnny reacted many years ago when I first introduced myself to him at Barney Googles in New York, he couldn't take the compliment. He said to me, "Oh come on," and I said to him, "Like it or not, you are a living legend."

We shook hands and said goodnight.

I continued to work for Johnny after he retired. I cleared the music and supervised the musician payments for the Carson Home Videos that continue to sell well today. I never really spoke to Johnny after the farewell party at his house. I sent him a couple of homemade greeting cards when he had his heart attack and for most of his birthdays. Johnny would send me handwritten thank you notes. We communicated through Jeff Sotzing, who continues to run Carson Productions.

Many people would say they were surprised how Johnny never returned to television after his last *Tonight Show*. Johnny did a couple of cameo appearances on *The Late Show with David Letterman*. He was on *The Kennedy Center Honors* at the end of 1992 when he received the Medal of Freedom, the highest accolade a civilian can ever receive. Who better to get that medal? But he never did a TV show again. It didn't surprise me. He deserved his retirement. If you listen closely to the last thing he said before walking off *The Tonight Show* stage for the last time, he said, ". . . I can only tell you, that it has been an honor and a privilege to come into your homes all these years and entertain you. And I hope when I find something I want to do, and think you will like, and come back, that you will be as gracious in inviting me into your homes as you have been. I bid you a very heartfelt goodnight."

I guess he never found something he wanted to do that he thought you would like. He went out on top. He knew when to come out on stage, and more importantly, he knew when to leave. He left with the crowd cheering for more, and they continued to cheer for more for the rest of his life. We still cheer for more even after he is gone. Luckily, for us, he left us with his greatest work, thirty wonderful years of *Tonight Show*s to remember him by.

2

Doc Severinsen and the Tonight Show Band

Although they played together on national television every night in unison and perfect harmony, this was a band of individual characters, tremendous personalities, and extraordinary musicians.

Viewers who tuned in nightly to hear the Tonight Show Band perform saw seventeen musicians on the bandstand. There was a rotation of players from night to night like a baseball team. There were about twenty-five players in the Tonight Show Band dugout. This gave ample time for the regular players to take outside gigs either in town or around the country. The main core players were called domestic regulars and the guys who filled in for them were called subs. But it got rather confusing to find that some of the subs were there more often than the domestic regulars. It was contractor Al Lapin's job to keep track of who was there and who was not so that the seats were occupied with seventeen competent musicians every day. It was about this daily routine of musical chairs that Al once asked, "Who's sitting in that empty chair?"

An on-going conflict with the band and NBC Studios was parking. The studio did not have to supply parking for the band other than the general parking lot a block away from NBC. Some of the sax players had to carry several horns to work every day and Al would negotiate a minimum of five spots for the sax section closer to the studio.

I managed to have some fun with the guys one day by playing a practical joke on them. The five spots were up for negotiation again because NBC had built a new studio on the lot where the spaces were and one day the places were marked for someone else instead of the Tonight Show Band. Don Ashworth who played baritone sax in the band was the most vocal about the mess-up because he had to bring a baritone sax, clarinet, flute, and sometimes an oboe or bass clarinet every day. Al Lapin would take an executive out to dinner or lunch and get them to approve five spots for the guys elsewhere near the studio. Whenever anyone parked in the wrong spot at NBC, security would post a ticket on the windshield warning that you would be towed away if you continued to park illegally. I printed up a mock version of this NBC ticket on my own and put it on Ashworth's car windshield one afternoon while he was in rehearsal. After the show I was sure to get out to my car before Ashworth could pack up his horns and get to his car. My car was parked about fifty feet from his, so he couldn't see me looking with binoculars at his reaction to my prank. I wish I had a video camera, but this was in the late '70s and video cameras were expensive.

I sat there for quite some time until I could see Don Ashworth and tenor saxophonist Ernie Watts approaching their cars. They carried on a conversation for what seemed to be forever. Finally, Don bid goodnight to Ernie and got into his car. He immediately jumped out to retrieve what had been left on his windshield. He quickly read the notice and called Ernie back to show him what he had found. All of this was done in pantomime like a Red Skelton comedy routine. The body language told it all. Ashworth was outraged as he motioned by pounding his fist on his other hand and kept looking at the mock-summons. Ernie kept shaking his head in disgust but I am sure he wondered why he hadn't received a ticket on his car. He was parked two spaces from Don's. I chuckled quietly in my car and wished I had a hidden microphone to eavesdrop on this silent movie.

Ashworth finally unfurled the folded ticket that was one of my best works of art. Outside it looked like an NBC warning, inside I clearly printed in large letters, "YOU DIDN'T BELIEVE THIS WAS REAL, DID YOU?" I could clearly read Ashworth's lips as he uttered several obscenities but with a smile on his face when he realized he had been had. Both Ernie and Don looked around to see if they were being watched but neither one of them spied my car in the distance. We all had a great laugh over the whole thing the next day when I revealed that I was the wise guy who had pulled the harmless prank on them.

When I started to work at *The Tonight Show* I was twenty-four years old. Most of the guys in the band were in their fifties, so the band members considered me to be a kid. It was like working with a bunch of my uncles every day. A few of the guys were just slightly older than I by five to eight years; those guys were like cousins to me.

The trumpet section consisted of John Audino, Eugene "Snooky" Young, Conte "The Count" Candoli and Marrie Harris. When I first started working there, Jimmy Zito was on trumpet and when John Audino passed on, Chuck Findley became a regular and Pete Candoli (Conte's brother) would fill in. Whenever the band would rehearse I liked to stand over next to Maurie Harris, who was the trumpet chair furthest to the end. I would stand next to him and read his trumpet part to hone my reading skills.

Trombones were originally Gil Falco, Nick DiMaio and Ernie "The Flea" Tack. When Nick passed away Bruce Paulson became a regular and Kenny Shroyer and Randy Aldcroft subbed on a regular basis. Bass trombonist Ernie Tack was known as "The Flea" from all of the "Stump the Band" segments over the years. Ernie would jump out from his position on the bandstand and perform a spastic dance he called "The Flea."

Saxophones were Tommy Newsom, John Bambridge, Ernie Watts, Pete Christlieb and Don Ashworth. Early on in the '70s there was Lou Tabackin, Don Menza and Dick Spencer. Others who were there more regularly than the rest were Tom Peterson, Bill Perkins, Bob Cooper, Brian Scanlon, Bob Holloway and Terry Harrington. Tom Peterson and Bill Perkins were there five days a week filling in for someone because Tom and Bill played alto, baritone and tenor sax. Sometimes with the musical chairs arrangement of subs and regulars, they would bring the wrong horns forgetting whom they were filling in for and have to run back out to their car to make a switch of instruments.

My usual place to stand and listen to the band when I wasn't looking on with the trumpet section was over at the end of the row of saxophones. Pete Christlieb was always muttering jokes out of the side of his mouth, Tommy Newsom would come out with a gem once in a while. After playing a bossa nova arrangement one day, someone asked who wrote that piece. When they were told it was written by Jobim, Tommy interjected, "I knew his brother, Jim Beam!" Christlieb added, "Wasn't his cousin Jack Daniels?" This kind of frivolity went on daily.

Ernie Watts was playing a difficult Bill Holman piece one time and hit a rare wrong note. Ernie seemed to be unusually upset with himself even though it was just a rehearsal. I got the feeling he was trying to get through the year without making a musical mistake and this was November.

I can't say enough about drummer Ed Shaughnessy. He was a fabulous teacher and fun to watch and listen to as he roared through the most difficult band arrangements on a regular basis and on all the arrangements that visiting performers brought to the show. Ed had to sight read many charts, as did the rest of the band. Where horn players have to play exactly what's written on the page, drummers deal with suggested beats and improvisation. Some arrangers do not always know how to write for drums and they leave a lot to the imagination and creativeness of the drummer. Ed knew how to adapt to the many styles of music he was challenged with every day and he created grooves and feelings from parts mostly filled with nothing more than hash marks and repeat signs.

One night after the show, Ed was packing up his cymbals while a woman reporter from a local music periodical threw some questions his way. As she finished up she thanked Ed for his time and asked how to spell his name. It was obvious that Ed was preoccupied with getting out the door in a rush that night. He quickly spelled out his name but the reporter asked, "Is that S-H-A-W?" "No, no," Ed interrupted, "S-H-A-U . . ." He then realized she was standing in front of his drums and pointed out to her, "It's on the drum heads, lady."

When Ed formed his own band and named it "Energy Force" he asked me to come up with some sort of logo for the band. I dabbled with a few ideas but was only happy with the first two I drew. The first was the name "Energy Force" drawn to look as if it were racing across the page with animated lines of movement trailing off the letters. The second thing I drew was Ed's initials "ES" rounded so as to fit within a circle. I tried a few other drawings but was never happy with any of the others. I just drew them so that Ed would have a choice of logos. The next day when I showed him my sketches he liked the "Energy Force" in motion as I drew it. But then he said to me, "Sweeno, you must be psychic." He was referring to the circular "ES" design I made. Ed told me that he and his father had the same initials and had a ring with the "ES" on it in the same way that I drew for him. Ed used both of my drawings for the band logo and continues to have the "ES" on his drumheads today.

Other drummers who filled in for Ed whenever he had to take time off were Colin Bailey, Nick Cerillo, Jeff Hamilton, and the great Louie Bellson. Louie was always fun to listen to and watch. Louie plays with such perfection and he plays the drums in a musical way. By this I mean that he is not just keeping time or showing off how technical and fast he can play, he uses the tone of the drums to complement the other instruments in the band. Louie's brother-in-law, Nick DiMaio, played trombone in the Tonight Show Band and had had a heart attack while playing golf with Louie one day. Nick survived the heart attack and was okay, but the next time Louie filled in for Shaughnessy, the band members were asking Louie about the ordeal. Louie joked about how difficult it was being out in the middle of a golf course when Nick had the attack; "It was tough. I had to hit the ball—drag Nick, hit the ball—drag Nick."

John B. Williams had played bass in the Tonight Show Band the year before I joined the show. John was also playing with Doc's road show and quit the road gig just prior to a performance in Lake Tahoe. He had had a confrontation with someone in the band and told Doc, "Either he goes or I go," and Doc let him go. Doc announced John's departure from the band by coming out on stage to the awaiting band and asking, "Does anyone know of a bass player who can do the show tonight?" Several of the guys piped up that a new guy in town, Joel DiBartolo, could do it. Joel used to play in Buddy Rich's band and had just come into town to try and make a mark on the L.A. music scene. I first saw Joel play in a rehearsal band in Hollywood led by trombonist Bill Broughton. Joel had also become a regular in Ed Shaughnessy's band. I knew Joel was having a tough time financially and would jump at the opportunity to play in Doc's band. Some guys who played in the Tonight Show Band had to play in the road band. So John B. Williams walked away from both gigs and Joel lucked out. When I heard that Joel was on his way up to Tahoe to join the band, I knew if he couldn't get a airplane ride up there, he would be running down the highway with his bass guitar and amp on his back to make this gig. Joel remained as the Tonight Show Band bassist until Johnny Carson retired. From time to time when Joel would take off, Jeff d'Angelo played on the show.

Guitarists Bobby Bain and Peter Woodford shared that chair in the band for many years. Mitch Holder also played in the band in the mid-'70s but left when he no longer wanted to tour with Doc's road act. Peter also played in Ed Shaughnessy's band over the years and was such a good player that Ed did not have a keyboard player in his band. Peter's guitar playing filled out the rhythm section where a pianist was not needed.

Bobby Bain was the guy who played guitar on Henry Mancini's classic recording, "The Pink Panther." Those ever-familiar opening guitar notes along with the saxophone renderings of Plas Johnson are forever etched into that unforgettable tune of our pop culture.

Pianist Ross "The Phantom" Tompkins was in the Tonight Show Band the entire time I was with the show, with Russ Friedman, Biff Hanna and Bob Alberti filling in on his days off. Ross became known as "The Phantom" for several reasons, one was that he never needed to look at his music. Somehow "The Phantom" knew what to play. Vocalists who came to sing on *The Tonight Show* were treated to Ross' expert ability to accompany anyone. Although he was an excellent sight-reader he played by ear a lot of the time. One time I recopied a chart that was falling apart from age and the band ran the song to check that I got all the notes written down correctly. The band was halfway through the chart when I realized that Ross was playing it without looking at his chart. I had to remind him why we were running the piece and asked him to check that the part was correct.

The other reason he was known as "The Phantom" was that Doc's band was playing in Cleveland and Ross was stuck in Philadelphia. There was a big blizzard on the East Coast and no planes were allowed to fly out of Philly. Doc and the band realized they were going to have to do the gig without a piano player. There wasn't enough time for Ross to drive to Cleveland. Moments before Doc counted off the first tune, he looked over and saw Ross seated behind the piano ready to play. Doc said he didn't know how Ross got there and didn't want to know. Doc said it would ruin the mystique.

Another one of Al Lapin's Lapinisms stemmed from a day when the band was on a break and Al called everyone back to play. Everyone showed up except Ross. Al ran all over the studio and most of NBC to find him but came up empty-handed. Upon Al's return to the studio he said, "It figures, he's 'The Phantom' until you need him."

The only time I ever saw Doc lose his cool was on a night the Tonight Show Band was doing a personal appearance in Kansas City, Missouri. Doc's tour manager at the time was Marc Savalle, and Marc's wife was due any day to have their first child. I had just been through the same blessing of fatherhood earlier that year and knew how important it was for Marc to be there when his child was born. I offered to take his place on a three-day weekend with Doc and the band.

We flew to Allentown, Pennsylvania, for one night at a theater there and flew to Kansas City to close out the last night of a week-long music festival. Comedian Pete Barbutti opened for Doc. Pete is a jazz comic. He likes to tell jokes about musicians and comes across like a hip Vegas musician who is too cool for the room. We always looked forward to Pete's many visits to *The Tonight Show*, especially when he would come and tell a few jokes to the band that he couldn't possibly tell on television. The band loved him.

In Kansas City, Barbutti was telling a few jokes to a small group of us talking with him before he went on stage. He told me he wanted to introduce the band. I told him that it wouldn't work because the band had a special piece to open with that had Doc's intro built into it. Having Pete out there introducing Doc would be redundant. He shrugged it off and said okay, and he went out on stage and proceeded to do his act.

Doc was in his dressing room all the while being interviewed by the local Kansas City television station. As it got near showtime, I quietly got the band on stage. Pete was out in front of the curtain doing his routine. The band was ready to play whenever the curtain would fly open. I signaled Doc that the band was set in place and that it was time to go. He wrapped up the end of his interview with the reporter, and I escorted Doc to the stage.

Once Doc was in place, I was to go to the opposite side of the stage to do a voice-over on an off-stage microphone once the band started playing. Unbeknownst to me, to Doc and to the entire Tonight Show Band, Pete Barbutti decided by himself to introduce the band from in front of the curtain. It seemed as if it happened in slow motion: I remember stepping on stage with Doc just as we heard Pete say, "Ladies and gentlemen, Doc Severinsen and the Tonight Show Band . . ." The curtain started to open as I darted behind the bandstand to get to the other side of the stage. Pianist Ross Tompkins thought that he should cue the band and off we were into a shabby opening. As I made my off-stage announcement to bring Doc on to the stage I felt all the blood rush from my head to my toes. All this time Doc's music stand was on the outside of the curtain from us and I never had the chance to put Doc's music in order before Barbutti went onstage.

For the opening number, Doc didn't need music. He had it memorized. But the second number was buried deep in his folder and he didn't realize it until he had already announced the song and counted the band off into playing it. He hastily tried to search for it with one hand while he played the trumpet with the other. He signaled Ross Tompkins to find it, and Ross put his book in order. But I could see from the look on Doc's face that he was seething in anger. This was one of those things that looked bad from backstage, but the people in the audience didn't know there were any problems at all. They were too busy enjoying the music to notice.

As soon as the curtain closed after the last encore, Doc ordered the entire band into his dressing room. When we all tried to piece together what had happened and how, it all came down to Barbutti taking it upon himself to bring on the band. Doc asked me to bring Pete Barbutti into his dressing room and dismissed the band. I don't know what Pete told Doc, but luckily for me, Doc dismissed the whole thing as a big misunderstanding. I thought I was going to lose my job, but on the plane flight home, Doc and I sat together and he didn't blame me at all. He told me the situation was out of my control and not to worry about it.

3

Brushes with Celebrity

It was 1977, and I had been working at *The Tonight Show* for a little more than a year when producer Fred de Cordova called me to his office. He said that a friend of his, actor Paul Burke, had someone he thought *The Tonight Show* might be interested in booking. Fred asked me to phone Burke and set up an audition. I did so and arranged for Paul and his performer to show up at rehearsal time.

His discovery was a nine-year-old boy from New Orleans, a piano player. I informed Doc of this audition, and he said he would listen to the kid after rehearsal.

When that time came, I introduced Burke to Doc, and the young boy, very nicely dressed in a blue suit and tie, took his position at the grand piano, replacing Tonight Show Band pianist Ross Tompkins. The young boy played the Duke Ellington tune "Sophisticated Lady," then continued with a second number in which he vocally impersonated Louie Armstrong. I thought that for a nine-year-old he played and sang very well.

Peter Lassally and Fred de Cordova were on hand to hear the youngster play, and when it was over and Paul Burke and the boy had left, the producers approached Doc for his expert opinion.

"Leave the kid alone," Doc told them. "Let him lead a normal childhood and keep him away from show business." The word to Paul Burke was later conveyed by de Cordova: "The kid doesn't have what it takes to be on *The Tonight Show*."

Who was this little boy? Harry Connick Jr.

Fifteen years later, someone pointed out to me that Harry Connick stated in a *Downbeat* magazine interview that he held a grudge toward Doc for having kept him from playing *The Tonight Show*. This incident triggered my memory of the little boy.

After putting the pieces together, I met Connick just prior to his appearance on *The Tonight Show*. I was working a double shift: one for Johnny Carson, who was winding down the last weeks of his 30-year reign, and the second for Jay Leno, doing test shows in preparation for taking Johnny's place. Connick is a good friend of Branford Marsalis, soon to become the new bandleader of the Jay Leno *Tonight Show*, and Branford introduced Harry to me in his dressing room. I asked Connick if he was indeed that little boy who auditioned back in 1977 (I didn't remember the kid's name). He not only confirmed that story to me, but also, that night on *The Tonight Show*, proceeded to tell the whole story on the air to Johnny.

Johnny asked Doc whether he remembered the incident. Doc said, "Yeah, I remember Harry, and I also recall I was the only person who said we should book him on the show."

Johnny, aware of the real story and Doc's attempt to cover his ass, said, "Quick thinking, Doc!"

This encounter with the very young Harry Connick Jr. inspired me to start writing down all the encounters I had with the many celebrities who crossed my path. The following vignettes are a compilation of some of my brushes with celebrities while working on *The Tonight Show* from 1976 through 1995. I wasn't an autograph seeker. I found it much more gratifying to introduce myself to the artists and engage in conversation with them, even if it were for only a brief moment in time. I have tried to capture some of those moments and offer them to you to show what some of those celebrities were like.

Sometime in the mid-'80s, my wife Cathy and I were invited to a party at the home of composer/arranger Henry Mancini. He was giving a dinner party for flutist James Galway. Galway and Mancini were starting a national tour together, and this party was to be the tour send-off.

We arrived at the Mancini mansion on time and took advantage of the valet parking out front. I remember commenting on how much his home looked like a Hollywood set or something out of

Disneyland. It just didn't look real. The house was ornately decorated with high-backed chairs, sculptures, paintings and much Italian artwork. When we entered the house, Hank's wife Ginny greeted us and asked us to sign a guest book in the living room. We then were drawn to the back patio by the sound of guests out by the pool, but before going outdoors, I glanced to my left where, at a complete bar in front of a mirrored wall, a man, who appeared to be a midget, was serving drinks. It turned out that he was actually about six feet tall, but the floor behind the bar was sunken, which gave me the impression that the bartender was only three feet tall.

Standing in the doorway to the yard, Ginny asked us if the music was too loud. I didn't hear any music, only the sound of someone switching from one radio station to another. The sound was coming from yard speakers, hidden among the beautifully landscaped hill beyond the pool. I started to say, "Oh, you have speakers hidden out there in the wee . . ."—I caught myself from saying weeds, realizing at the moment that people in Beverly Hills don't have weeds. And if they did, they would find some fancy name for them. Ginny's expression went from a smile to a look of puzzlement. In trying to desperately find a way to cover up my slip of the tongue, I began to babble on about how good the music sounded. In doing so I started to nervously wave my hands in gestures (which I never do). Ginny's expression started to change to almost a chuckle when suddenly I bumped something from behind with my hand. It was Henry Mancini—I had bumped his wine glass, filled with red wine. The red wine was dripping down his face, onto his shirt, and his pants, and his brown suede shoes. Ginny Mancini, upon seeing what had happened, burst into laughter. Mancini was, at first, motionless, but when I offered him my napkin to dry off with, he waved me off. He was being a good sport about it. After all, he was the one who had sort of sneaked up behind me. I don't think I'd ever been so embarrassed in my life. After Mancini changed his clothes, he remained good-natured about the accident, and we joked about it all night. I had always thought him to be a shy, quiet kind of person, but that night he proved to be the opposite—the life of the party.

Dinner tables had been set up on the back patio alongside the pool. We sat with saxophonist Don Menza and his wife. In addition to Galway, composer Lalo Shifrin and flutist James Walker of the group Free Flight were on hand. Henry bounced from one table to another, checking to see that everyone had enough to eat and drink and that we all were having a good time. He would joke about his musical success. A song would emerge from speakers (hidden in the "weeds") and Hank would say, "That's a good song. Did I write that?"

After dinner, everyone was free to roam about the house. At one point I was admiring Mancini's Grammy Awards, which were perched on square shelves surrounding a large-screen television set that was built into a wall unit. As Cathy and I stood there, we both sensed someone standing behind us. This time without waving my arms, I turned slowly and jokingly advised Mancini that one of his statues was missing. There was one empty square shelf in the group. Henry said that was done on purpose so that there would always be room for one more.

Later in the evening, everyone was asked to gather around the living room for a concert. Galway, Walker, Mancini and one of the flutists from the Los Angeles Philharmonic Orchestra gathered to perform a piece written by Mancini for four flutes. It was the first time it had ever been performed and perhaps the only time it was ever to be performed. I couldn't get over the fact that I was sitting in Henry Mancini's living room, next to Lalo Shifrin, listening to James Galway and Henry Mancini present a private concert. I thought: "If my friends could see me now."

Band contractor Al Lapin would get many calls in any given week asking for the Tonight Show Band to appear at the wedding of some executive's daughter's or the bar mitzvah of a son. Al would either graciously talk his way out of it or he would recommend my orchestra, the SRO Band, for the occasion. He'd always talk us up the way any good agent or manager would, and we'd usually get the job.

On one of those occasions, Al got a call from Ray Charles's publicist, Bob Abrams, who happened to be a nervous, heavy-set, sweaty type of guy. He seemed to be totally intimidated by Charles and avoided any kind of confrontation with him. Bob needed a good band to play for Ray's birthday bash at the Beverly Hills Hotel.

Ray Charles was spokesman for an organization called E.A.R. International. In addition to having been blind since he was a young boy, Ray recently had been developing a loss of hearing. The doctors at E.A.R. performed a delicate operation on Ray's ears and did improve his hearing. Ray happily became their spokesman. Ray once spoke at one of their fundraisers and said, "I can live without my eyesight, but if I lose my hearing, I'd have nothing."

Every year E.A.R. International would throw a big fundraising dinner on the occasion of Ray's birthday, and our SRO Band became the dance band for the party as well as the back-up for Ray Charles if he decided to perform a few songs. But when Bob Abrams first hired us, I asked him what song or songs Ray would be playing, and how many was he likely to do. Bob's answer was that no one knew.

"Can you ask him?" I inquired. The reply was negative.

"We don't know what song he's going to want to do that night. He likes to surprise people."

Everyone around Ray Charles seemed reluctant to approach him. And his manager, Joe Adams, took the attitude, "Don't bother me with detailed questions."

So, I managed to obtain every Ray Charles record I could find and made cassette copies for the band members. Maybe we'd get lucky. I even took one of Ray's recordings to *Tonight Show* drummer Ed Shaughnessy to listen to. It was a song done in 3/4 time. Most drummers would play a waltz tempo with accents on two and three in kind of a boom-chick-chick feel, even if it was a jazz waltz. Some country drummers play a country waltz with the accent on the second beat, creating a distinctive boom-*click*-chick sound. Ray's drummer played everything on the first beat and nothing on the second and third beats. I'd never heard anything like that before.

When I played it for Ed, he admitted that he would never think to do that, even if it had been written that way on his music. He called it playing "ignorant." Now Shaughnessy didn't mean that in a disrespectful way. He explained that when you play for an artist like Ray Charles, you have to think like an unschooled musician, someone who was self-taught, who would feel perfectly comfortable playing bass drum, snare and cymbal on the down beat and play nothing at all on three and four. I knew exactly what he meant. When I first started to play drums before I took any lessons I didn't know the difference between 4/4 and 3/4. All I knew was that 3/4 was a little harder to play than 4/4 and sounded different. Once again Ed

Shaughnessy was able to solve my drumming problem with a simple one sentence explanation as always. With that in mind I was ready to tackle Ray Charles.

That night was a big press night for Ray, E.A.R. International and the California Raisin Growers Association. The Raisin Growers had used Ray's likeness and voice in one of its award-winning commercials. Ray was animated by way of Claymation, and the ad literally put raisins and Ray Charles back on the map. The Raisin Growers had a new follow-up commercial with Ray and the Raisinettes singing "I Heard It Through the Grapevine," and they chose Ray's birthday bash to debut the ad to the press. The 60-second film clip was such a hit that they ran the film a second and third time for the Beverly Hills Hotel crowd of charitable elites. We played "I Heard It Through the Grapevine" live while six people dressed as raisins danced around the room and posed with Ray for the array of newspaper and video news-media crews that seemed to be everywhere. It was now time that Ray got up and sang a tune for everyone.

Now Ray was not known for being easy on musicians. On more than one occasion at *The Tonight Show*, I had seen him rip Ed Shaughnessy apart in front of everyone for dragging the beat or not playing the chart exactly as it was written. It was an impossible situation for Ed. Sometimes the drum parts were written exactly as Ray wanted the drums to be, and other times there would be nothing but empty measures and the blind pianist wanted a specific thing done in that spot but he couldn't explain what he wanted in words. Such moments became awkward, tense and embarrassing for Shaughnessy—so much so that Ed told Doc Severinsen that he never again wanted to work with Ray Charles. He said next time, tell Charles to bring his own drummer. Doc agreed and said that no one should be subjected to that kind of harassment.

The next time Ray was to appear on the show, he was supposed to bring his rhythm section. That's what we all believed right until the moment that Ray and his entourage walked into the studio without his drummer or rhythm section. We were told they missed their plane, a lame-sounding excuse, and we had to put up with "the wrath of Ray" once again.

With this kind of history with Ray and drummers, I was fully expecting a tongue lashing from Ray that night at his birthday bash.

Instead, as Ray sat at the piano, he never tipped us off one bit about what he was going to play. He just started to play the old standard "There'll Be Some Changes Made." Not even two measures into the song, he shouted, "Half notes, son, half notes." He couldn't have been talking to me because I hadn't touched my drums yet. I had my brushes ready to play, knowing he was going to do something soft. I couldn't find where "one" was, so I hadn't started to play. I figured that if I laid out, he wouldn't say anything. What the heck, he wasn't able to see. Maybe he'd think the drummer took a break and wasn't even in the room. My bass player Marty Buttwinick, was the only one playing at the top of the song, so he got the brunt of the static.

When it was all over, Bob told us that Ray was happy with the band. In fact, he asked to meet my pianist, Kathy Craig. Ray liked what she was doing and just wanted to let her know. He must have liked us, because we continued to do his birthday parties for the next couple of years, and each year it was the same story. We never knew what he was going to play until he got there.

A few years later, I got a call from a producer named Walter Hoeflin. He was producing a dinner concert/show for the Los Angeles Open Golf Tournament. Ray Charles was scheduled to perform and needed a big band. He obviously was referred to me by Al Lapin once again.

The evening was supposed to feature the SRO 17-piece big band for half an hour in front of Ray Charles, and then Ray was to perform for about an hour. I was told he would bring his rhythm section. This time they actually showed up.

Bruce Paulson, one of *The Tonight Show* trombone players, remembered that Ray's book called for four trombones. When he told me that, I immediately called Bob Abrams, who told me to go with three. I still wasn't satisfied with the way he brushed it off without checking with Ray, so I called the producer, Hoeflin, who was footing the bill for all of this. If he wanted to play it safe and have me hire the fourth trombone, I'd do it, but he, too, said to just go with three. So I did.

When the day finally arrived, I figured, great, I'll get the few things out of the way that I needed to run through with the band for my portion of the show, and then I could sit back, relax and watch Ray Charles rehearse his portion. When Ray arrived, Bob Abrams brought me backstage. Bob was sweating (as always) and nervously introduced me to Charles. Ray just about finished shaking my hand when he started to go on to me about what tempo his opening number was and how it segues into the second song. I said to Ray, "So, you want me to just kick off the first tune and get out of the way?" It was at that moment that I started to realize that Ray wanted me to conduct his entire show for him.

Trying to get out of this as best as I knew how I asked, "Ray, wouldn't it be easier for you to kick off each tune yourself? You know your arrangements better than I do." Ray was determined for me to handle this task. "It's only music," Ray said in one of those unforgettable moments in my life. I gave it my best effort. Then, Charles gave me one of his quotable quotes to live by. He said, "Life's too short to count 1-2-3-4, just count off 3-4." I'll never forget that.

I never had to conduct from out in front of the band before. I had done a little conducting in front of the Tonight Show Band before for a short play-on, but never for an entire song, let alone an entire concert. And we all knew Ray Charles's record for intolerance of musicians. I must say, I was surprised. Ray was quite cooperative and things were going smoothly until we got to one particular song. Ray stopped the band and asked the trombones to play a certain section of the arrangement for him. It didn't sound full enough for him. When they played it for him he said to me, "Don, how many trombone players do we have here today?" I told him we had three and he said, "How many am I supposed to have?" I didn't want to go into a long discussion in front of the band about the run-around I got from his publicist and the producer of the show, so I just said, "How many do you need, Ray? I will have however many we need to make you happy by showtime." There were a few tense moments of silence, and then Ray said, "OK, then, let's move on."

When the rehearsal was over and Charles was being escorted off to his dressing room, I ran after Ray. I said I'd called Abrams, who told me to go with three trombones, and Hoeflin, who also said three would do. Then I said to Ray, "If you wanted 76 trombones I would have had them there for you. It's no skin off my nose." Ray realized there was a communications breakdown somewhere, but that at least I had made an effort to set things straight. He told me not to worry about it and let's just have a good show. And then he repeated that memorable quote: "It's only music."

He may have been right. It was only music, but it was Ray Charles's music, and if the show had suddenly come crashing to a halt, I'd have had a blind pianist and several angry bodyguards chasing me out of the Century Plaza Hotel. I called over to *The Tonight Show* while it was in progress and asked Al Lapin to have any one of the three trombonists at the show to help me out and come over to the hotel. Luckily, Gil Falco was able to get over there and he sight-read the entire show.

I couldn't believe that I was about to conduct my first concert, and that it was going to be with the infamous Ray Charles. I remember going to my dressing room and calling my friend Jerico. We laughed uncontrollably about the whole situation.

The show went off without a hitch. I kept hearing all of these songs go by sounding just like they do on the radio and then looking over at Ray and realizing that this wasn't somebody doing an impression of Ray Charles—this was the legendary Ray Charles. His drummer let me in on a little secret and offered a good piece of advice. He told me not to follow Ray's head movements for the tempos. Many pianists will nod their head in time with the music to set tempos and cue the band for entrances and cut-offs. Ray, like many blind people, moves his head uncontrollably, and the motions have nothing to do with the tempo of the song. His drummer said to follow his foot, which would set the tempo. From where I was standing, I couldn't see his foot. The drummer said that he would watch Ray's foot and that I could look to him for the tempos. It worked out well. Ray and everyone involved were happy with everything. We were even asked back to play Charles's birthday party again later that year.

The next time that Ray Charles came on *The Tonight Show*, I told Doc Severinsen about this little secret. Doc thanked me at the end of the show; it made things flow much easier that day.

When Ray turned 60, there was a big TV show in his honor in which my SRO Band and I were not involved. Soon after that, the tax laws changed quite a bit as far as write-offs for fund-raisers were concerned, and there were few such events anywhere, therefore the E.A.R. International people didn't have many large parties after that.

In later years I'm sure that Ray still celebrated his birthday some-where, somehow, but with some band other than mine. I can't help but think that when he did he was probably shouting at some unsus-pecting, scared-stiff musician: "Half notes, son, half notes!"

The seemingly endless parade of musicians and singers who passed through *The Tonight Show* was virtually a "Who's Who" of the en-tertainment industry. One person who perhaps stands tallest among all of them is Tony Bennett.

Whenever a musical artist would appear on the show and not uti-lize the Tonight Show Band, the band members would take a break and rarely stay to see the performance. Especially in the later years of the show, we seemed to have more and more rock bands that were self-contained. Many times *The Tonight Show* musicians would run out of the studio because the music was too loud for them to en-joy. But when Tony Bennett was a guest, whether he was singing with the full big band or he brought his trio to back him up, the band musicians stuck around to enjoy Tony's interpretation of what-ever song he was rehearsing. They particularly enjoyed shows with Tony because he sings the way a musician would play a musical in-strument. His voice was his instrument.

One time, Tony was rehearsing a song with the Tonight Show Band and standing in front of the brass section using a hand-held microphone. This was long before there were wireless microphones. While the orchestra was playing an instrumental interlude in Tony's arrangement, the singer, enjoying the sound emanating from the band and smiling from ear to ear, spun himself around in the excite-ment of the moment. The movement caused the microphone cord to wrap around Tony's ankles, and he nearly fell over into the trom-bone section. Tony managed to keep himself upright and came in singing his part right on cue.

Tony Bennett, in addition to his phenomenal musical talents, is a well-known and respected painter and artist. He came to *The Tonight Show* every day for a week and just hung around the studio, sketching workers, musicians and all the surroundings of the show's crew. The plan was for him to be a guest at the end of that week and display his sketches and other examples of his artwork. I found it es-pecially interesting to watch him draw since I am an artist as well. (I drew cartoons and sketches whenever someone on the show had a birthday, and I'd draw comical invitations to parties and other events.) But I only wish I could draw in Tony's style. He could capture the faces of the people he drew with partial strokes of the pencil. Peter Falk was a guest that week, and Tony managed to capture his character by drawing only a portion of his face. There was no doubt in anyone's mind that the sketch was Peter Falk.

Friday of that week, Tony was our musical guest, and when he sat at the panel, he displayed and described the sketches he did that week. When the show was over, I went to Tony's dressing room to ask him if I could keep one of his sketches. He said to take whatever I wanted. When I got backstage to where the art was, I found the crew members already scooping up everything before I could get near it. I didn't get a thing, and I'd been the only one who had asked permission.

It brought to mind the old story about the motorist who needed a parking space near the courthouse. Although the signs clearly read "No Parking," cars were parked in every space except one. In a rush to get into the courthouse, the driver asked a nearby police officer whether it was OK to park there. The officer said that if he did park there, he'd have to give him a ticket.

"But, what about all these other cars?" the motorist inquired.

The policeman replied, "They didn't ask."

During the many years I was working at *The Tonight Show*, there were few people I "had to meet." But, because I grew up in the era of the Beatles, when Ringo Starr was booked to do the show, I "had to meet" him. I made a big mistake when Paul McCartney was on the show a few years prior to Ringo's visit. I asked if I could meet him. Shirley Wood, known as "Crazy Shirley," lived up to her name and told me not to go near him. Security for McCartney was tighter than usual. Everyone with the show had to wear their badges and anyone else who belonged backstage needed a special backstage pass. I had both passes but didn't go near him as Shirley requested. Meanwhile, album covers, books, posters, photos and anything else that could be signed by the former Beatle were being passed into his dressing room before the show. I just wanted to shake his hand and say hello, but I listened to "Crazy Shirley." When McCartney was to go from his dressing room to the stage, the security guards cleared the hallways and the backstage areas so that you couldn't even catch a glimpse of him passing by.

When he did make it to the stage, I was able to stand in a recessed area of the studio audience bleachers and stand about fifteen feet from where McCartney sat as he spoke with Johnny. I had a front row seat, so to speak.

It must have been part of the booking that Paul would not sing a song. Johnny Carson tried to shame him into doing something. McCartney persisted even when the moans and groans came from the studio audience. It wasn't until the final segment of the program that Paul fiddled with an acoustic guitar that just happened to be backstage and in tune for him just in case he felt a song come on. As I remember, he barely noodled out a tune by show's end. What would have been the big deal for him to sing us a song?

When the show was over all hell broke loose. The strict care that was taken to keep the public and the staff away from McCartney had all been for naught. The simple fact that no one had arranged for the security guards to work a half-hour or so after the show was overlooked. All of the security personnel were off the clock at 6:30 when the show was finished. There was no one to escort Paul out to his car in the midway. As was the case at the end of all of *The Tonight Show*s, friends and relatives in the studio audience came down onto the stage. Although security held everyone back until Johnny Carson and Paul were safely off the stage, Paul still had to get from his dressing room to his car. My friend Jerico was with me backstage that day. At the end of the program he came on stage to meet up with me. He said, "Come here. You gotta see this." He wanted to point out to me how poor the security around Paul was. As we went down the hall to the larger section of the hall, there was McCartney surrounded by about a hundred or so fans, staff members and crew members hounding him for a signature or a hand shake. I could have joined the crowd, but I stood back, amazed at the sight of Paul very politely trying to accommodate all who approached him. Paul was barely able to move his hands to sign an autograph for the people pushing and putting books and things in his face to sign. McCartney continued through the madness to ask the people things like, "How do you spell that?" "What name did you say, dear?" all the while slowly making his way nearer to the doorway with no help from security. Jerico managed to get close enough to touch Paul's shoulder. He came away to say jokingly, "I touched him. I touched him." He proceeded to show me the hand that touched him (like I could see a visual difference in his hand since he touched Paul McCartney).

Years later when Ringo Starr came to the show, I had learned my lesson. I didn't ask if it was okay to meet Ringo. I just decided to go knock on his dressing room door and give it a try.

Fifteen minutes before we started taping the show, I knocked on his door and a young woman opened it and asked who I was. I told her I was Doc Severinsen's assistant and wanted to say hello to Ringo. After she turned and asked if it was okay, she let me in. There I was face to face with Ringo, who was on a chair next to a few of his friends, who were seated on the couch. Among the people with him was his wife, Barbara Bach. Ringo was seated when I came in but somewhere along the line he stood up and carried on a very casual conversation with me. "I have been a fan of yours since I was a kid and became a drummer as a result of that. I have always wanted to meet you," I said as I shook his hand and introduced myself to him. I asked him a few drummer-to-drummer questions.

I realized how sensitive he had been lately about claims that he did not play on some of the Beatle recordings. So I purposely asked him questions about how he did certain beats or how he came up with ideas for certain drum fills. One thing I remember asking him was how he kept his hi hat cymbals separated. In a film clip from *A Hard Days Night* his hi hat cymbals were not touching one another but they seemed to be so rigid. He proceeded to tell me that he pushed the pedal all the way down and then adjusted the cymbals to where he wanted them to be so that he would not have worry about it during the song. He also said that most times the drum sets were not his own, and he didn't have time to adjust them, so he had to go with whatever was there. He told me that he has been accused of playing double bass drums when he never has or that he used a certain brand name drums when he didn't. About that time, a stagehand came in to have Ringo sign a photo taken backstage at *The Ed Sullivan Show* in 1964. Ringo pointed out in the picture how it must have been doctored for some reason. "Here you go," he said to me as he pointed out in the photo, "These were not the drums I played on the Sullivan Show. This is a white set of drums, and my drums were gray pearl. I've never played a white set of drums yet there they are."

Soon after our exchange, Johnny Carson entered the room. Johnny welcomed Ringo to the show and made some comment about Ringo and I trading drum secrets with one another. Suddenly I realized that I was standing in conversation with a former Beatle and Johnny Carson. Fred de Cordova was standing nearby and was concerned with the show starting on time. I certainly did not want to be blamed for holding up our host, so I quickly excused myself by saying, "Excuse me gentlemen, but I've got to go. There are way too many legends in this room." Johnny looked at me and then at Ringo in the typical Carson-like take as if he didn't know what I was talking about. And so I left. I finally had my moment with one of the Beatles without going through "Crazy Shirley." Like the story of the man and the policeman outside of the court house . . . I didn't ask.

Whenever a guest host suddenly was unable to fill in for Johnny (due to illness or scheduling problems), we could always count on Steve Allen to jump in at the last minute. Steve was able to fall right in and ad-lib an entire show. After all, he's the guy who perfected the talk show long before Johnny and Paar. Steve was always well respected by the staff, musicians and production crew.

I always enjoyed the nights when he would play a number with vibraphonist Terry Gibbs along with the Tonight Show Band. Steve and Terry had a number where they both played on the same set of vibes that was very musical, comical and very well choreographed.

Steve would sit at the piano center stage instead of doing a stand-up monologue. He would play off the audience members and usually welcomed impromptu questions from the crowd. He would then take their comments or questions and turn them into hilarious moments. He often would sing their names or put a silly melody to the name of the town they were from. If an audience member said they were from Biloxi, Mississippi, Steve would sing something like, "Biloxi, Biloxi, I just met a girl from Biloxi . . ." The next day I would always get a call from his assistant who would tell me that Mr. Allen wrote that song, "I Just Met A Girl From Biloxi," and that it is published under Rosemeadow Music (Steve's publishing company). I think Steve Allen taught comedian Steve Landesburg to do the same. Whenever Landesburg was on the show, he would call me and say, "Last night I sang a song that I wrote . . ."

Steve Allen wrote many books during his illustrious career, I read one of them, "Schmock, Schmock!" It was hysterical, I admired Steve's ability to twist words and expressions to mean other things than their original intention. For instance, a studio member once said, "Mr. Allen, I have a quarter that says you don't know how to play the song 'After You've Gone.'" Steve replied, "What do you know about that, a guy with a talking quarter!"

On a day that Steve was guest hosting, I brought the book in for him to sign, and I knew he would twist whatever I said to him out of context to make a joke. So, I simply approached him and asked him to sign my book. Steve said, "That's not your book, that's my book, it already has my name on it." He got me.

Comedian Garry Shandling made his leap into stardom when he made his very first appearance on *The Tonight Show*. The expression among comics when your act overwhelm an audience is that you "killed." Garry "killed" on his first appearance on the show. We were all talking about him in the office for days.

Around this time it was announced that Joan Rivers was to become the permanent guest host for the show. Until then there was a merry-go-round of stars who had their shot at guest hosting. MacLean Stevenson, John Davidson, Rich Little, Roy Clark, and Bob Newhart all were there on a regular basis.

I always felt that Bob Newhart was better at it when he had a full week of guest hosting. On Monday and Tuesday he would be uncomfortable and nervous (more than usual). As the week would go on Bob would get cocky and seem more at ease, so that by the time Friday arrived, I was disappointed to see him go.

When it was announced that Joan Rivers was going to be the permanent guest host, I was rather saddened. I liked the variety. As good and as bad as some of them were, it made us appreciate Johnny's return even more.

Roy Clark was scheduled to be the final guest host before Joan Rivers was to begin her new contract. The day of that show we learned early in the morning that Roy was sick, and the production staff were making calls to find someone to take Roy's place. A guest host for the guest host. When it came back to us that Joan Rivers was unable to do the show that night because she was entertaining out of town and couldn't get back in time, it was announced throughout the office that we were going to cancel the taping that day and put on a re-run, a "Best of Carson."

I was talking to the staff members outside of my office as we did everyday. It was common practice for us to gather around and joke about the previous night's show or talk about guests or skits, or whatever was happening in the news, for that matter. This day was no different. I was talking with Joyce Estrin, assistant to talent coordinator Jim McCawley. The people who booked talent for the show were always called talent coordinators. Now-a-days they are called segment producers. Joyce and I were thinking of who could come in and do the show, and we both started to talk about that comedian who "killed" recently on his first appearance. We hardly remembered his name. As we were talking about him, Jim McCawley came around the corner echoing the announcement that we were going to put on a re-run. Immediately, Joyce and I mentioned the possibility of that comic, what's-his-name. McCawley dismissed it immediately. "Garry Shandling?" he said, "He's a funny guy but he has never hosted a talk show." So, I told Jim that we had nothing to lose. The staff, cameramen, and stage crew all had to get paid for the day anyway. Why not give Shandling the chance? If he was awful, we could put on a re-run. McCawley thought for a moment and said, "You're right." He immediately marched around to Fred de Cordova and Peter Lassally to tell them of our idea. Moments later, Jim came back at us all excited and said, "We're going to try this. Get Garry's manager on the line."

Flash ahead in time, twenty years. Joyce and I were attending the funeral of Fred de Cordova, and Garry Shandling was there. Joyce and I went over to say hello to Garry and we proceeded to tell him this story. Garry had never gotten the full story before, and he was fascinated to hear how it all went down. He told us that a comedian works at his act, hones it, perfects it in hopes of getting the call to appear on *The Tonight Show.* He continued to say that he was lucky enough to get a shot at it and never thought he would go over as well as he did. "And Johnny gave me one-of-these," Garry said as he raised his hand and made the okay sign, "Comedians dream of that moment." Garry continued to tell us that after the show, he was on a high for days. And then, he said that he got a call from his manager telling him that *The Tonight Show* called and wanted him to guest host. Shandling hung up on him, thinking it was a gag. His manager called right back and convinced Garry that it was no joke.

Garry went on that night and "killed" again. He was a natural. He surpassed many of the previous guest hosts in so many ways. We were so happy for him, and it was so exciting to see a new comic make it right before our eyes and to feel that we had something to do with it all. Pretty soon, reality set in, and we realized what a shame it was, that as good as Garry was, he wouldn't be back. Joan Rivers was just named as permanent guest host. She remained there for six years until she jumped ship to start her own short-lived talk show on the Fox network. When Rivers left, Garry finally was asked back and replaced Rivers as the new permanent guest host.

On one of Garry's many visits as a guest host, I was in the green-room preparing my clipboard for the show. Part of my job was to log any and all music used on the show and submit that to A.S.C.A.P. and B.M.I., so that the writers and publishers would get proper credit for their work. At the top of the cue sheet I would fill in the date of the show, the guest names, Ed McMahon as announcer, and Doc Severinsen for bandleader and I proceeded to fill in Garry's name where the spot for host was, and I spelled it "Gary Shandling." A man was watching what I was doing and without hesitation he told me I misspelled Garry's name. I asked him how to spell "Shandling," and he said it was Garry's first name that was spelled wrong. "Garry spells his name with two Rs," he said. So I said to him, "Look, just 'cause Garry spells his name wrong doesn't mean that I have to spell it wrong too." I don't know who that man was, but I hope he knew I was joking.

By then, Garry had made quite a name for himself. *It's the Garry Shandling Show* was already running on HBO. Soon after he followed with the successful *Larry Sanders Show* which was a satire of all talk shows. He went on to host *The Emmy Awards Show* in 2000. You see what happens if you start your television career with Johnny giving you "one-of-these" on your first guest shot.

Charlton Heston made several visits to *The Tonight Show,* usually to promote a film or a political cause. Johnny Carson would not allow many performers to use the show for a political platform or soapbox, but Heston was one of the few exceptions. On one occasion, Heston was on hand to plug the re-release in theaters of *The Ten Commandments.*

Everyone was standing listening to Johnny's monologue. I made my nightly trip to get myself a cold drink at the backstage bar, which Jack Grant, our head prop man, always kept fully stocked with whiskey, vodka, gin and plenty of beer. Jack would always have a platter of hors d'oeuvres for the guests to munch on. I waited for the monologue to be over, and when we went to a commercial break I walked over to Charlton Heston.

I usually avoided approaching celebrities before their TV appearance in case they were nursing a case of nerves. Heston actually turned and started talking with me about Johnny's monologue. He couldn't believe how Johnny could keep it so fresh and so new night after night. I turned the conversation to the topic of *The Ten Commandments* and told him I'd heard that in addition to portraying Moses in the film, he also was the voice of God. Heston smiled and said that the voice of God was that of the great Cecil B. DeMille. His smile grew wider as he added: "DeMille wanted to play the voice of God because he really thought he was God." As I laughed at his comment, he added, "And sometimes we believed he was God, too."

In addition to Orson Welles being a frequent guest on *The Tonight Show,* there was one time that he hosted the show.

Jerico came by that day to watch Orson Welles rehearse his illusion. When the two of us walked into the studio, it was empty except for one mountain-sized man, Orson Welles. He was seated in the audience section over near the band area. We approached him and I introduced myself to him and then informed him that the band didn't arrive until 3:15 (it was about 2:45). Jerico and I started to ask him questions about the illusion he was about to perform. A few moments later Fred de Cordova strolled into the studio. Fred walked over and stood in front of Mr. Welles and Jerico and me. Fred puffed his cigarette as he eavesdropped on the story that Orson was finishing as Fred approached. When Orson finished his tale he said, "Hello, Freddy." There was a long pause as Fred drew another drag from his cigarette and he said to Orson, "Are these two gentlemen bothering you?" Orson said, "To the contrary, my dear Mister de Cordova. These gentlemen were kind enough to keep me company while I awaited the arrival of your crew." As Fred and Orson continued with idle chatter, the crew began to emerge on the set, and within moments the place was buzzing with a flurry of activity.

He was planning a majestic illusion. He had a woman handcuffed and gagged, wrapped her in a canvas sack and locked her inside a trunk. Within seconds of locking the trunk, two people rolled out a red king's throne, which Mr. Welles wrapped in cloth and spun around three times. The third time, the cloth was pulled away to reveal the woman from the trunk, out of the sack, seated on the throne and no longer handcuffed. He then opened the trunk to show that it was empty. The throne and the trunk were never closer than fifteen feet from one another. The studio floor was solid concrete, so there were no trap doors. I was amazed to see this trick until our contract person, Sue Dewey, gave me a hint. She said there were two women on the contract. Twins! What a rip-off, I thought. When the trick was rehearsed a second time, I decided to watch from the wings. The trick was so simple, I was almost angry. The girl who appears on the throne was simply hiding in the base of the chair until the cloth was unwrapped. The girl who was handcuffed and locked in the trunk remained there for the entire trick. Orson opened the trunk, which had a false bottom. When they leaned the trunk forward to show it empty, the girl was crunched down below the false bottom and concealed from view by the rest of the trunk.

Not being a standup comic, he did not do an opening monologue as Johnny did. Instead, he was to perform a magic trick (he was a magician). At the top of the show he was to throw ping pong balls out to audience members. The ones who were lucky enough to catch one of them were asked to call out a five-digit number. Orson had two young men in the audience (unbeknownst to the studio and home audience they were students of Mr. Welles, amateur magicians no doubt). One of them had a calculator hidden between his legs, and as the audience members shouted out the numbers, he was adding them all up. Welles was sweating plentifully (he sweated a lot and breathed heavily from his enormity; he also could not stand for long periods of time). He was taking the numbers the audience gave him. He would write them out on a blackboard on stage. The trick was, through using the calculator, the young boys were to give the final five digit number that would make all the other numbers add up to the predetermined number that Orson was going to write on the board, thus making it look as if Orson was calculating all of these large numbers in his head to arrive at the precise answer. Needless to say, his answer was way off. Something went wrong with the boys and the calculator. His trick bombed terribly and by the end of the first commercial the two boys had left the studio audience; they were probably half way out of California by the time the broadcast was over.

Another trick or illusion that Orson Welles had in store for the show involved a large cake of ice. In the center of the ice was a booklet that Orson told us contained the "secrets of the universe," which he would reveal to us by the end of the show—without breaking the ice. Michael Landon, who was a guest on Orson's show, told us that he knew the answer to the ice cube illusion and told the audience that they were going to be amazed when Orson revealed the trick to them. Well, the show ran long and he was never able to perform the ice trick. Years later, when Orson Welles and Michael Landon had both passed away, I noted that now we would never know the "secrets of the universe" that could have been revealed from the ice cube illusion.

When working at *The Tonight Show*, one gets to meet many famous people. After a while, they don't seem to be as special as you might imagine. You get used to seeing stars and you realize they are no different from you or me except for the salaries they get and that they are recognized by most people. Some even cause near riots and traffic jams, but, other than that, they're just people. But every once in a while someone comes along who is bigger than life. Usually they were stars from my childhood (Buffalo Bob, Desi Arnaz, Roy Rogers, etc.). Frank Sinatra was one of those people I just had to meet. The legend that follows him and the persona of "Mafioso" made him the "Celebrity Godfather." Once when Frank was a guest on *The Tonight Show* he was going to sing a few songs. It was my job to get the singers' signature on a form that stated that their arrangements had been paid for before use on television. If an artist sang a song that was paid for live performance, the arranger and copyist were paid again for its use on TV. Usually the artist's conductor could sign this paper. So, I went to Sinatra's dressing room and found the door wide open. Several rough looking guys were all standing around, catering to Frank's every wish and laughing at his jokes and jumping when he snapped. I walked in and went directly to his conductor and ask him to sign the form for me. He looked at it for a moment and said Mr. Sinatra would have to sign this because it says "artist" where the signature should be. I turned to Sinatra and asked him to put his John Hancock on the paper for me. He said he didn't have his glasses but he'd trust me. He said, "A nice looking Irishman like you isn't gonna rip me off, right?" Just as he took the pen from my hand we heard a voice from out in the hallway. It was Don Rickles. His show *C.P.O. Sharkey* was taping in Studio 3 next to *The Tonight Show*. Rickles stuck his head in the doorway and said, "Hi ya, Frank. You look terrible. Your face is all wrinkled. You look old and your wig is crooked." Sinatra looked up with a startled look on his face. It seemed as if twenty minutes went by before his expression changed, but it was actually only a few seconds. A silence fell upon the room where moments ago it had been filled with laughter. Very slowly, Sinatra laughs, "eh huh, eh huh, eh huh, eh huh . . ." until the rest of us laughed nervously along with him. Sinatra then got up and gave Don Rickles a big hug and said, "How you doin,' ya fat Jew?" and everyone laughed a sigh of relief. I thought to myself, "Just sign the paper and let me out of here." He signed the paper and I was out of there.

Al Lapin worked with Frank whenever Sinatra worked in Los Angeles. Al told me one time that he felt Frank hired him because his people (staff) thought that Al was Italian. James Petrillo, the alleged mafia-connected president of The American Federation of Musicians throughout the '50s, also thought Al was Italian. Al said, "They thought it was shortened from Lapinino or something." For whatever reasons (most likely because Al knew the best musicians in town), Sinatra's organization hired Al Lapin to contract his Los Angeles engagements.

Al would constantly be giving me advice on how to sell my band and how to eventually be a contractor when he retired. I once had a gig at the Beverly Wilshire Hotel and Al asked me what room it was going to be in. I couldn't remember the name of the room and Al pounced on me. "You, as a bandleader or a contractor, should learn the names of these rooms at the different hotels. It is very important that you know this. It is your business to know this and to know the names of the food and beverage managers of these places." I agreed with him and from that moment on I made it my business to remember the names of the many banquet rooms throughout Beverly Hills and Los Angeles.

Keeping this in mind, the Tonight Show Band was to perform with Frank Sinatra for the NBC affiliates show in May of 1982. As usual, Al Lapin hired me to bring the drums, music stands, music and amplifiers and told me to be at the Bonaventure Hotel at 9:00 a.m. to set up in the Los Angeles Room. At 8:30 a.m. I arrived and started to unload the equipment onto my cartage wagon and wheeled my way into the Bonaventure Hotel in downtown Los Angeles. The main ballroom, the Los Angeles Room, happened to be packed with IBM employees who were deep into some kind of slide presentation when I walked in. I proceeded over to where the slide projectors were and asked one of the guys running it what time they would be finished. He said they would be finishing up shortly after lunchtime and asked me why I needed to know. When I told him the Tonight Show Band was supposed to rehearse for that evening's show with Frank Sinatra, he became puzzled, but cautious. Secretly, he tells me that the guests entertaining in that room that night were the Beach Boys, which was to be kept a secret from the IBM employees. It was supposed to be a surprise. He heard nothing about Sinatra. When I pointed out that my show was a show for the NBC affiliates, we both realized something was wrong. Could Al Lapin have had the wrong date?

I went outside the ballroom to make a phone call and soon came across a few of the Tonight Show Band members, who were starting to arrive. They were asking me where they should hang out and why all those IBM people were in the ballroom. After about twenty minutes of confusion and dismay, we learned what had happened. We were not supposed to be in the Los Angeles Room at the Bonaventure, we were supposed to be in the California Room at the Century Plaza Hotel clear across town in Century City. I quickly threw everything back into my van and everyone scurried to their respective cars and headed for the Century Plaza, ten miles west of Downtown L.A. I'm sure Al was embarrassed about giving us the wrong name, but at least he never again gave me a hard time about knowing ballroom names and hotel employees.

After much confusion and haste, we all soon assembled in a banquet room at the Century Plaza Hotel where the NBC executives had decided the band could rehearse, leaving the main ballroom (the California Room) for them to set lights and rehearse other things. These affiliate conventions were run like television shows, with the same professionalism and madness of a live T.V. special.

The Band was soon ready for rehearsal, and we were assigned a stage manager, Ted Baker, who had on a radio headset so he could be in constant touch with the director of this gala. He would convey to the booth how the band was progressing. I knew Ted from seeing him around NBC Studios. He usually worked across the hall from us on *Chico and the Man, C.P.O. Sharkey* and any other show that came into NBC. He was a very good stage manager and he would occasionally work for *The Tonight Show* whenever our staff stage managers, Kevin Quinn or Dan Ford, took a day off. Ted was sharp and friendly.

Mr. Sinatra was not at the rehearsal, but his conductor, Vinnie Falcone, was there along with Frank's drummer, Irving Cottler, and a bass player, Gene Cherico. I provided my own drum set for Irving to play on. At the time I had a beautiful set of Slingerland drums that I knew Irving would feel comfortable playing. Irving was from the Big Band Era and was perfect to play Sinatra's style of music.

During the morning rehearsal, it was great to be able to sit there and enjoy the sounds of the band playing Sinatra's arrangements to all of his memorable tunes. It was like one of those karaoke machines only a thousand times better. It was nearly impossible to sit there and not sing along. When the band began to play the notable version of "The Theme from New York, New York" I found it difficult not to get up and start doing the Rockettes' high kicks along with the music. During that song, Vinnie Falcone needed to stop the band to tell them about a tempo change or something. He gave the conductor's signal for the band to stop playing. Being the best musicians in show business, they stopped playing immediately. The only person in the room who did not see Vinnie's cut off was our stage manager, Ted Baker. As the music stopped all we could hear was Ted singing the lyrics of the song at the top of his lungs. He was so into his Sinatra impression that even he didn't realize we could hear him as he finished out the lyric, ". . . Come one, come true, New Yor— . . ." The whole band looked at Ted and laughed for about ten minutes. Ted was very embarrassed, but luckily could also laugh at the situation. For a moment, Ted thought he was Frank Sinatra, and we all caught him trying to pretend.

The concert later that evening was a huge success. I was so proud that I was able to provide my drums for Frank Sinatra's drummer. I felt like I was really part of the show. I sat at one of the tables up front, to the right of the stage. Technically I shouldn't have been there. It was strictly a private surprise performance given for the Affiliate Station Representatives of NBC.

Although I did not get to meet Sinatra that evening, I did get to hang out with Frank's assistant, Larry "Nifty" Victorson. I am sure that Sinatra must have given him the nickname Nifty. I could hear Sinatra say, "I can't have someone named Larry working for me." Nifty was not supposed to be a replacement for "Jilly," Frank's former bodyguard. He was more like a personal valet. It was a kick to sit and talk with him about what it was like to be with Frank Sinatra. Nifty and I were about the same age and had had similar experiences. Without telling me anything I could read in the papers, he basically said that no matter how moody Sinatra would get, Nifty was in awe of Frank. "After all," he said, "the man is a legend and I am proud to just be around him. It is an experience I will carry with me for the rest of my life, long after Frank Sinatra is gone."

Another time, the Tonight Show Band was doing a benefit at the Beverly Hilton Hotel for myasthenia gravis, and Frank Sinatra was performing. Tony Randall was the master of ceremonies and told a funny story at the top of the evening. He jokingly admitted that before that evening, he knew nothing about myasthenia gravis. His agent, Abby Greshler, simply called him and told him, "Tony, you need a disease. Your career is taking a nose dive and the only thing that is going to save you is to latch on to some organization and become their spokesperson. Look what it has done for Jerry Lewis!" Then Randall said, "So here I am."

It was the usual Tonight Show Band with about another fifteen or so strings and percussion added. During Sinatra's performance, he introduced a new song by Peter Allen. The correct title of the song was "Lovers Once Again." In the introduction Sinatra said he didn't like that title, so he decided to call it "You and Me." Frank stated that this was the first time he had ever performed this song in public, so he didn't know how it was going to come out, ". . . but, here goes," he said. He also apologized for having to read the song off of the sheet music. He hadn't memorized the lyrics yet.

Halfway through the song, the music on the music stand began to slip off. The pages began to unravel from the accordion format in which music is usually folded, and in a very short time the music began to fall out of control in the middle of this very soft, romantic ballad. Frank turned to the conductor and told him to stop. Frank's musical director, Vincent Falcone, couldn't believe that Sinatra was stopping in mid-song, and Frank had to summon him twice. The orchestra stopped, and there was an awkward silence. Having been there to set up the band and do the library for the show, I felt I should go out there and help him. I turned to my friend Jerico, who was backstage with me also helping out. I asked him if we should go on stage and help him with the music. He said, "Sure, I'll cover you while I stay here and watch the horses, Kimosabe." I decided to let Frank handle it himself.

Sinatra apologized for the mishap and asked them if they wouldn't mind him starting the song from the top. The audience was very forgiving and urged him to start again. Only Sinatra could make a moment like that work in his favor. When he composed himself and sang through the song with ease the second time, the crowd was with him all they way. By the time he hit the last note of the song, the audience was on their feet. One reason for this was he really did sing the song well. But the other reason was that they felt they had witnessed a side of Frank that most audiences never get to see. Even though it was a star-studded audience, they were thrilled to be able to forgive Frank Sinatra and let him know it was all right to make a mistake once in a while.

As Sinatra left the stage, I was standing with Al Lapin. Frank hugged Al and said, "Send me the bill." Frank picked up the tab for the whole night, which was about $10,000.

For a moment after his performance, Sinatra assembled his crew in a greenroom backstage until his wife Barbara could be escorted from the ballroom and brought backstage. His party consisted of his assistant, Nifty Victorson, his conductor, Vinnie Falcone, and eventually, his wife Barbara. When she emerged backstage, his entourage left in a hurry. Jerico signaled me to follow Frank and friends out the back door. Jerico said, "Come here, you gotta see this." Not knowing what he meant until I followed, we witnessed a typical "Hollywood" ending to the Frank Sinatra story. Frank and his friends went out the back door of the Hilton, which opens to a long narrow staircase that empties out to a small private parking area off of Santa Monica Boulevard. We stayed at the top of the stairs as Frank, Barbara, Nifty and Vinnie got into a black stretch limo with blackened windows. Four bodyguards walking at each corner of the limo escorted the car out of the lot. The bright fluorescent lights beamed off the jet-black finish of the highly polished limousine. As the car slowly made its way onto Santa Monica Boulevard and into the night, Jerico, who was standing behind me, said in an announcer-like voice, ". . . and so ends the Frank Sinatra Story. Roll credits and fade to black."

If you've ever been at the scene of a crime or accident, you know how two or three people can witness the same incident and come up with three different points of view, much like the cameras do on a television show. Usually at least three cameras are all focused on the same point; yet if you isolate each camera and play them back after a scene takes place, you are likely to find three different views on the same subject. I especially enjoy this phenomenon when it actually happens to me in real life. I would witness something from my point of view and then hear someone else relate what he or she saw from their position. This is exactly what happened when I encountered talk show host Regis Philbin.

It was mid-morning in Studio 1. Usually at that time of day, the studio was empty, except for an occasional NBC tour coming through or perhaps a single stagehand or two repairing a broken light or polishing the floor. This day, it was quite empty. I was the only one around, trying to retrieve a piece of music I was looking for under the piano in the band area of the set. Suddenly, I heard the voices of two men coming from the opposite side of the stage. They didn't see me, but I could see them and almost could discern what they were saying. In this case, actions spoke louder than words. The one man did not look familiar to me, but I recognized the other as Regis Philbin.

I became aware of Regis from having watched his local ABC morning show, *A.M. Los Angeles.* That show was much like his subsequent national ABC show, *Live with Regis and Kelly.* Every weekday morning, I'd watch his show while I was getting ready to go to work. Although Regis started out on *The Joey Bishop Show* as Joey's announcer, I never paid much attention to that show because, after all, it was opposite *The Tonight Show.* When Regis started hosting *A.M. Los Angeles,* I became a big fan.

Apparently, Regis was at NBC to negotiate a new deal. I later found out that NBC wanted Regis to host a morning talk show and broadcast it live across the nation. The man with Regis was probably his agent or close friend.

As I tried to be inconspicuous, I could see Regis standing in front of the set of Johnny's desk saying to his friend, "Look, this is where it all happens. There's Johnny's desk and the guest chair." Regis looked around and thought the studio was empty. Upon the coaxing from his friend, he went around to the back of Johnny's desk and sat in the chair. I had to keep from laughing out loud, seeing Regis acting like a little kid in Daddy's chair. He was rubbing the fabric on the arm rests and began stroking the leather-topped desk when suddenly a voice came over the P.A. system in the studio. I recognized that it was the voice of our assistant director, Jim Kantrowe. Our director's booth was situated above the studio where anyone in there had a bird's-eye view of the entire stage. Kantrowe simply said in a loud and commanding voice, "Get out of the chair, Regis." Regis bolted out of the chair, and he and his friend quickly left the studio, giggling all the way like a couple of school kids.

The very next day on *A.M. Los Angeles,* Regis told this same story, but it was from his point of view. His rendition helped to fill in some of the gaps in my point of view because I couldn't hear what was being said; I could only go by hand gestures and body language. As Regis conveyed his story to the television audience, it matched what I saw except for the last part. Regis said: "Johnny Carson must have a surveillance camera fixed on his desk. Because as soon as I sat behind the desk, like the voice of God from heaven above, Johnny's voice came over the loudspeaker and told me to get out of the chair!" It drew a big laugh from Regis' studio audience, and whether Regis really believed it was Johnny's voice or not, it made the story a very funny one.

The third point of view of this same scenario is that of Jim Kantrowe. Jim later told me that at first he didn't know who it was—that it was just someone who managed to escape from the NBC tour. Jim was watching them to make sure they didn't take any souvenirs. It wasn't until Regis sat in Johnny's chair that Kantrowe recognized who he was. Kantrowe got a kick out of scaring the pants off Regis.

It was Christmas time and Cindy Williams (Shirley of *Laverne and Shirley*) was a guest on *The Tonight Show*. I had had a crush on her ever since *Laverne and Shirley* came on the air. I met her in the greenroom, and she was very friendly. I told her about the staff Christmas party we were having backstage immediately following the show and asked her if she would like to come with me. She said it sounded like it might be fun and said she would see how she felt at the end of the show.

When the show was finished taping, prop man Jack Grant had a saloon setting backstage with plenty of Budweiser and other assorted booze. The audio department played some disco music over the sound system, and the lighting department put up a mirror ball and some flashing lights to give the atmosphere of a discotheque. Some of the staff members got together to take a group shot with a couple of Inst-o-matic Cameras on the set at Johnny's desk. We pulled the protective sheets off of the furniture, and one by one, we took pictures of each of us sitting at Johnny's desk. Some of them sprawled out on the couch or pretended to play the role of a guest sitting in the swivel chair. We all had too much to drink.

I almost forgot about Cindy Williams. She went to her dressing room after the show and told me she would meet me backstage. It had been almost a half hour since the show finished taping, so I went to her dressing room to see what was keeping her. She was still there, but she was talking to someone on the telephone and told me she would be out shortly. I was getting drunker by the minute, and I'm sure she could hear it in my voice. She finally came to the door and told me she wasn't going to go to the party. She explained that it was a staff party and she would feel funny going. I tried to assure her that it was a very informal party and that she should try to loosen up and come out and join me. It became obvious to me that she did not want to come to the party, so I asked her if she would at least give me kiss for the holidays. Much to my surprise she said, "Oh, okay." She came out and gave me a kiss on the lips and wished me a Merry Christmas. I was so drunk I just wished her a Merry Christmas in return and went back to the Christmas party. So there. Now you have it, my exclusive "lurid affair" with Laverne's best friend, Shirley Feeney. Lenny and Squiggy, eat your hearts out.

I was on the road with Doc Severinsen in 1975 in Beckley, West Virginia. Some kind of big week long celebration was going on, and Doc was one of many acts that were flown in that week. Roy Rogers and Dale Evans were in a parade the day we arrived, and I said I would love to meet Roy if I could. When we got to our hotel, we barely had time to check in, but Doc's soundman, Fred Stites, needed to run up to his room for a minute. I waited in the lobby for him. Suddenly, the elevator doors opened and out stepped Roy and Dale. I went over and introduced myself to them, and Roy said he remembered meeting me backstage at *The Tonight Show* one time. I think I would have remembered if I had met him before. I went along with it rather than contradicting him.

A few years later, I really did meet him backstage at *The Tonight Show*. He came across the hall from Studio 3 to watch some of our rehearsal. Roy was taping a segment for a summer replacement show. He and his stepson were there to perform the song "Happy Trails" as a duet.

I asked Roy how his ranch and museum were doing. He had a museum in Apple Valley, north of Los Angeles. He asked me if I rode horses and I told him I had a little riding experience, but I would much rather sketch horses. Roy invited me up to his ranch. It was an open invitation that I unfortunately never took him up on.

It was Thanksgiving Day in the late '70s, and Olivia Newton-John was one of the guests on *The Tonight Show*. When she entered the studio she said hello to everyone. I remember vividly when she came over to where I was standing; she reached out her hand to shake mine and said, "Hello, I'm Olivia. What's your name?" I had quite a crush on her too.

Later that same day, I went to her dressing room before the show to get her to sign the paper concerning the use of her arrangements on TV. When I knocked on the door, a young girl as beautiful as Olivia answered (I found out later it was Olivia's younger sister). When I told her I needed Olivia's signature, she said, "Livi's in the shower at the moment. Could you come back?" Just then, Olivia's voice in the distance said, "Let him in, I'm just finishing up." I entered, and I could see Olivia Newton-John emerging from the shower stall, wrapped only in a towel. She was soaking wet.

"Come on in," she said, "What do you need me to sign?" Stuttering and stammering, I managed to get her to sign the paper. Olivia's sister and another girl were giggling from the other side of the room as they watched everything.

Of course, I left as soon as the signature was completed. I got the feeling that Olivia enjoyed embarrassing guys in situations like this one.

It was near the end of Johnny Carson's reign as host of *The Tonight Show* when Stevie Wonder made an appearance to say farewell to Johnny. Stevie was to perform a song center stage with his own group and then, when he sat at the panel, he would sing the song, "I'll Be Seeing You" to Johnny. This was one of Johnny Carson's favorite songs, but it seemed inappropriate for a blind man to be singing it to anyone. In any event, Stevie was unsure of the lyrics. Most people would use cue cards to get through an unfamiliar song, but a blind man may find cue cards ineffective. So, Stevie must have had this problem worked out in his head beforehand. He wore these earpieces for monitors so that he could hear his band or himself better whenever he was on stage, thus eliminating the cumbersome floor speakers that any blind person, as well as a seeing person, could easily trip over. Now-a-days, almost every major act uses these earpieces. They are called ear molds.

Stevie said he would have his assistant off stage on an isolated microphone reading the lyrics to him. He would hear her through his earpieces and would sing the song. He assured everyone that this had been done before, so everyone seemed comfortable with it. All went reasonably well at rehearsal. However, I thought it was odd that his assistant was a young Asian woman who had a very heavy accent. To make matters worse, she didn't know the song either, so her timing was a little off. I almost volunteered my services, but thought to myself, no, stay out of the way. And so, the show went on.

Stevie sang his latest hit center stage without a hitch and was escorted to the panel where he joked with Johnny and complimented Carson on his many years as host of *The Tonight Show*. Stevie said, "I've watched you all my life." Johnny was embarrassed and humbled by Stevie's remarks. Then came the moment for Stevie to sing one of Johnny's favorite songs to him. Stevie began, "I'll be seeing you in all the old familiar places . . ." Offstage was his assistant on the isolated microphone saying, "I be seeing you en aw dee all famew-ya pwaces . . ." Tension was upon Stevie's face while he sang. He was sweating a little too much as he fumbled through the song. He almost made it through the song until he got to the line, ". . . I'll be looking at the moon, but I'll be seeing you." Stevie sang, ". . . I'll be looking at the SUN, but I'll be seeing you." It was an awkward moment for all, but Johnny helped Stevie out by feeding him the word "moon" in Stevie's moment of hesitation, and I doubt if the home audience or studio audience knew what had happened. It became a memorable moment in spite of the technical problems.

The movie "10" was about to open in theaters, and I went to a special advance screening the week before it opened. The memory of Bo Derek was still etched in my mind the next day at work. Actually, the image of her running along the beach with her braided, beaded blond hair and the French-cut tan swimsuit is still etched in my mind more than 25 years later.

When I got into work the morning after the screening, I told everyone who would listen about the beautiful woman in the movie. While we all sipped our morning coffee, trading jokes and stories, I wandered to the reception area and proceeded to tell receptionist Mike Beron about the movie. Mike just sat there listening and grinning like the Cheshire cat. When I started to rave about the beauty of the new star of the film, Mike tried to stop me with a hand motion. He quickly jotted down a message on a slip of paper. He wrote "Bo Derek" with an arrow pointing to left. As I looked to my left, I saw a young woman sitting in a chair next to the desk of Ramey Warren, assistant to *Tonight Show* talent coordinator Bob Dolce. It was indeed Bo Derek, awaiting a pre-interview for the show, but neither Bob nor Ramey were there yet. After a brief walk back to my office, I created several "reasons" to return to the reception area for another glimpse of Bo.

She was dressed in gray sweat pants and matching top, and she wore a red baseball cap that made it difficult to see her face. I activated one of my lame excuses to walk by Bo, and she looked up from the magazine she was reading and smiled at me. I smiled back and managed to utter a good morning to her. She simply said, "Hi." I nearly fainted, but managed to get myself back to my office. Back in 1978, Bo Derek became the ultimate sex symbol for many years to follow.

In the late '70s, David Letterman used to substitute as host for *The Tonight Show* when Johnny Carson took vacations. I had noticed that Letterman behaved in a peculiar manner prior to the start of each show. He'd be in full make-up and fully dressed for the show, but he would walk or pace around outside of the studio. It made me wonder what was he thinking.

Sometimes he would walk down the hall and over to the vending machine area (which was rather far from the studio) just moments before the show would start. Letterman started banging on one of the candy machines, shaking it and nearly tipping it over. Many of us have done that at one time or another. The problem here was that David never deposited any money.

Usually he would look down at the floor or stare at an object. All this time, while pacing, he would never look at anyone. Bob Ostberg, our director, would follow him and, I guess, make sure that David didn't suddenly hop into his car and drive away. Somehow, I got the feeling that might have been on Letterman's mind at one time or another. When show time was within 60 seconds, Ostberg would say, "OK, David, let's go," and Letterman would bolt toward the studio and the show would begin. This went on night after night.

This particular night was no different than others. I went into the men's room just moments before the start of the show and found

David Letterman standing in full make-up with tissue papers still tucked around the inside of his collar so as to keep it clean from make-up before the show. He was trying to tuck his shirt in. Most men would take their jacket off and put it on a hook before attempting this. Letterman was trying to tuck his shirt into his pants without tucking his jacket in as well. All the time he was doing this, he had his eyes affixed to an imaginary dot on the wall. I tried not to look directly at him or say anything because I knew how intense he was before each show.

Not a word was spoken, and the only sounds from David were an occasional grunt of frustration and heavy breathing through his nostrils. Ostberg was standing in the doorway, and we all could hear *The Tonight Show* theme starting in the background. Bob told David, "30 seconds." Letterman bolted from the room—it was show time. I thought to myself, what would America think of David Letterman if they knew what strange rituals he went through night after night before entering through the curtain to entertain them? I sometimes wonder if he still does that kind of thing, now that he has his own program. He always has a look on his face when he first comes out to do his monologue as though he just started to feel sick, or that someone forced him to come out on stage. Maybe the real David Letterman would much rather get in his car and go home.

I never got to meet Clayton Moore. I did, however, come close to meeting him.

I was planning one of the Chamber of Commerce Fourth of July shows at Pierce College in Woodland Hills, California, and thought it would be great to have the Lone Ranger make a personal appearance. I obtained his phone number and address through Celebrity Service and gave him a call.

As the phone started to ring, I realized that in a matter of seconds I would be talking to the Lone Ranger. For a moment a cold sweat came over me, but it was replaced by a slight giggle when I realized that he might have an answering machine. The prospect of hearing that famous voice talking on an answering machine made me worry that I'd go into a fit of laughter. I didn't want come off sounding like a complete idiot. Then, suddenly, someone answered the phone.

It was his wife. She said she was his personal manager and that I could talk to her about booking him. When I told her who I was and why I called, she told me that Moore charged $5,000 for an appearance. I responded that we'd just want him to show up and sign a few autographs. She said it would still cost you $5,000. But it's for the community he lives in, I argued. Still $5,000 she said. She then told me that he puts on a whole show, horse included, and gives away silver bullets. (I guess the cost of silver had gone up quite a bit.) I told her I'd try to get the money and call her back. All I wanted to do was talk to him on the phone. I knew the Chamber didn't have any money to spend on a celebrity.

As time went by, I learned that Moore lived near one of my associates, Shelly Cohen. The semi-private community did not allow anyone to park campers or motor homes in front of their houses, but I'd heard that they gave a special dispensation to the Lone Ranger. He would travel from town to town making personal appearances in his first-class motor home. I actually had driven past his house whenever I went to Shelly's place. It was easy to find because of the motor home.

One day, at about 6:30 in the morning, I was delivering a music arrangement to Shelly's house and saw Clayton Moore walking his little dog, a Yorkshire terrier or miniature poodle. I wanted to stop my car, run over and introduce myself but came to my senses. I was looking rather scruffy that morning. I hadn't shaved in days and was wearing an old pair of sweats that had seen better times. I probably would have scared him and his little dog, too. I didn't want to risk the chance of being shot by one of his silver bullets. I didn't know if the Lone Ranger was packin' and I wasn't going to take the chance of finding out.

The Lone Ranger is one celebrity who eluded me. Hi yo, Silver, away!

Charles Nelson Reilly was one of the many guests that Johnny would have on the show just to talk. He had nothing to plug but was usually funny. There were some people who would say they couldn't stand Reilly. Every reason they didn't like him was one that made me appreciate him.

He would always be a nervous wreck when trying to tell a story. He'd constantly interrupt himself and go off on tangents but always try to finish the story he had started. When Johnny would interrupt him to tell him he had to break away for a commercial, Charles would act offended and start to stutter even more than usual to try to keep Johnny's attention away from the commercial lead-in. It was one of those routines that worked time and again, and people loved it.

Charles Nelson Reilly lived in Los Angeles and didn't work as much as some of the other guests, so he was almost always available to come over on a moment's notice to fill in for a star who at the last minute couldn't show for any number of reasons.

Charles and I would sometimes meet backstage at the bar that the prop man, Jack Grant, had hidden in a prop box backstage. Jack once told me that he had the bar built into the prop box so that he could easily close the doors on it whenever he needed to and roll it off. He had it made for the times that Johnny temporarily brought the show to Los Angeles from New York. When the show moved permanently, so did the bar.

Grant told me that on one occasion an NBC vice president called him after a show on which one of Johnny's guests was obviously drunk on camera. The executive asked if it was true that Jack had a bar backstage at *The Tonight Show.* Jack said to the executive: "Can you hold on a minute? I have to take care of something." He put the phone down, rolled the bar into the hallway outside of Studio 1 and came back to the phone. "I'm sorry, now what did you ask me?" he said to the caller. When the executive asked him the second time, Jack's reply was: "No, there is no bar backstage, sir." The bar remained a permanent fixture until Johnny's final show.

It was almost a ritualistic thing I did every night before the show. I'd get a few crackers and cheese from Jack Grant's snack platter backstage and grab a nice cold can of Budweiser to take to the greenroom while I watched the show. I would sometimes meet a nervous actress or a drunken actor in the process. Charles was not a drunken actor, but he did (as many did) enjoy a drink to loosen up before the show. Charles would always say hello and trade a joke or two with me at the bar.

Many years later (1996) I was appearing in Costa Mesa as part of the Earl Rose Trio, along with the Pacific Symphony Orchestra. Pianist Earl Rose, bass player Jeff d'Angelo (whose sister is actress

Beverly d'Angelo) and I went out for dinner before the concert. We walked across the street to a fine Italian restaurant but sat at the counter because we were in a hurry. The counter had a glass display with bread and pastries directly in front of us, and we couldn't figure out how anyone was going to take our order. It seemed that we would have to swivel around in our seats and order from a passing waiter. I looked at Earl and we both thought the same thing at the same time. So he turned to the man sitting next to him and asked, "How do we get a waitress to take our order . . .?" As the man turned towards us Earl recognized who he was and finished his question with, ". . . Charles Nelson Reilly."

Reilly was down in Costa Mesa rehearsing for an opera, of all things, and was having a quick dinner with his leading lady before rehearsal. We later found out it was a comedic opera. Charles was flattered that somebody recognized him, but he also recognized Rose. Earl had played piano for Charles many years ago, and Charles was actually a friend of the Rose family and had known Earl since he was a child. Charles gave Earl a big hello, and then he saw me. Charles said, "Hey, I know you, too." Earl said: "You ought to know him; he worked on the Carson show." Charles immediately made the connection and gave me a big hello as well.

I made it a point to tell Charles how good he'd been on a recent *The X-Files* episode. He really had been excellent. Before that, I'd only seen him in comedy shows and on *The Tonight Show*; yet he was always talking about directing plays at the Burt Reynolds Theater in Florida. It was good to see that he really could act in addition to telling funny stories on TV. Charles wished us well in our concert, and we wished him the best with his opera performance. As we were leaving, Charles said: "It's just like old times, only instead of standing at Jack Grant's bar backstage, here we are in a bar in Costa Mesa."

The young new hot property of NBC in 1977 was the Puerto Rican/Hungarian comic, Freddie Prinze. He was only 17 years old, had successfully performed as a stand-up comic on *The Tonight Show,* and became the star of his own hit comedy sit-com on NBC. I was trying to break into the business as a stand-up comic as well, and quite frankly, I was jealous of Freddie's instant success.

My friend Jerico and I were at the Comedy Store one night. At the time, Jerico was trying his hand at stand-up comedy. Jerico was writing a new comedy bit, and we went to check out the competition.

We sat through many stand-ups, some of whom were very well known. Comedian Gary Mule Deer was one of them. In between each comic, Gary would get up and assemble his props for when he would get up there later. Mule Deer built this elaborate set of pipes that looked like a set of monkey bars. On it he hung different colored buckets and was very intent as he meticulously set them in place. When it was his time to perform, he did the same routine I had heard him do before, except that whenever a joke didn't go over well, he would take out a golf ball and throw it into one the buckets. Whenever a joke received a large laugh or applause, he would throw a ball into a different bucket. It was insane, but entertainingly funny.

Jerico's routine was him pretending to be a blind comic. He was to come out wearing dark glasses and using a cane, as he would stumble his way on to the stage. He then would do a couple of blind jokes like, "I was driving down Sunset Boulevard the other day . . ." after a brief pause he would say, "Don't worry, I only drive at night." That's the direction this routine was going. After a few more jokes like that, he would then take off his dark sunglasses and say, "This doesn't seem to be working." He would remove his sunglasses to reveal two bulging eyes made from ping-pong balls cut in half with pupils painted on them. He would then tell the audience he was actually an extraterrestrial and do a few alien jokes. The experiment never happened, but compared to many of the other comics we all sat through that night, it would have been a highlight.

Normally, we would have left after seeing Gary Mule Deer's act. We were so curious as to why he was setting up all of those buckets. However, somebody announced that comedian Freddie Prinze was going to stop by. Out of curiosity, we stuck around. We wanted to see why everyone was calling him a genius.

We had to sit through several comics who were so bad, we felt we were being punished for something we did wrong in life. We stayed because we had great front row seats and were teased every few comics that Freddie was coming up shortly.

When Freddie Prinze finally took the stage, he began to just talk off the top of his head about a tour of the country he had just completed. He was traveling around the country visiting the NBC affiliate stations that carried his show, *Chico & the Man*. Freddie proceeded to tell us what it was like for a young Puerto Rican kid, who had never left New York City his whole life, to experience farmers and rural lifestyles.

When he spoke, it didn't sound like a well-honed stand-up act. He truly was just talking off of the top of his head about his experiences. Jerico and I sat there with our arms crossed and thinking to ourselves, "Come on kid, make us laugh." Pretty soon, our arms were unfolded and we were bellowing with laughter. Freddie was brilliant. He went on for about twenty minutes, sarcastically joking about tumbleweeds and tractors, pig slop and milking cows, all from a city slicker from Brooklyn.

As we left the Comedy Store that night, Jerico and I realized that the new kid on the block truly was a comic genius.

Chico & the Man taped directly across the hall from *The Tonight Show* in Studio 3. Most sit-coms would have a weekly routine of one or two days spent in one of the rehearsal halls at NBC before they took it inside the studio to block the show for the cameras. Because these shows were shot before a live studio audience, the cameramen needed to know where to be throughout the script to catch close-ups, and more importantly, not bump into one another or get into another camera's shot. The actors would rehearse camera blocking so that they knew where to stand for their close-ups and, more importantly, so that they didn't bump into each other or get run over by one of the cameras.

I was walking by the rehearsal hall where *Chico & the Man* was rehearsing and could see Freddie Prinze by himself, practicing karate moves with an imaginary opponent. He didn't see me coming toward him and suddenly did a karate kick into the wall in the hallway. He put a sizable hole in the wall with his foot. He came out of his karate-like trance and laughed at the hole he just made. He then saw me approaching and jokingly tried to stand in front of the hole to hide it from my view. Freddie went into a character of a small child and spoke in a whiny baby-like voice and said, "Please, mister, don't tell them what I did. I'm sorry. It won't happen again, I swear." I didn't know what to say. I just laughed and continued to walk on down the hall.

I had heard about Freddie's drug problems from news reports, newspapers and over-all buzz around the studio. Part of me wanted to turn back and talk to him. He was younger than me by almost seven years, but it was obvious to me that Freddie didn't have any friends his age. He was surrounded by agents, managers, producers, writers and other comics and actors who were all ten or fifteen years his senior. There were one or two cameramen or stage crew members who tried to look out for him, but he didn't have anyone to play with. Before I could get to know him, he was gone. Freddie killed himself. I don't know if he ended his life because he wanted attention or was just too drugged up to know why he put a gun to his head. We can only wonder where Freddie Prinze could have taken his career had he not taken his own life so early in his profession.

I had only been working at NBC for a year when music contractor Al Lapin hired me to play drums on *Chico & the Man*. Freddie Prinze's untimely death threw the show into a tailspin. In an effort to revive the show, a young boy, Gabriel Melgar, was brought in to play the part of Chico, and new characters played by Della Reese, Scatman Crothers and Charo were added.

In a nightclub scene, Chico's Aunt Charo was going to perform, along with Scatman Crothers and the show's star, Jack Albertson. Pat Morita was the club's emcee. I was hired to play drums in the little nightclub combo. We didn't have to back up Charo. She was scheduled to play guitar and sing a number all by herself. However, the producers discovered that Charo would be sitting in front of the band when Jack Albertson was performing a little soft-shoe dance to "Tea For Two." Pianist Gil Lieb was asked to show Charo the chord changes so that she could play along with us.

Gil, while playing the tune, was telling Charo the changes. He's saying, "Play C minor seven, then F seven, and C minor seven, back to F seven . . ." Charo stops him and says it is too difficult for her to understand his English. She asked us to wait until her guitar teacher arrived. So, we took a break. When the Spanish-speaking guitar teacher showed up, we played "Tea For Two" once again. As before, Gil relayed the chord changes to the teacher who relayed them to Charo in Spanish. Gil said, "Play C minor seven." The teacher says to Charo, "Ce menor siete." Gil said, "F seven," and the teacher said "Eff-ay siete." Charo was happy and Gil and I went away shaking our heads.

Charo is always Charo. She is genuine. What you see on the screen is what she really is like. Charo has a wonderful sense of humor and is an unbelievable performer. I had only seen her perform on *The Tonight Show, Bob Hope Specials,* or on *Love Boat.* Whenever she came on *The Tonight Show* and talked with Johnny, none of it was rehearsed. Her "coochee, coochee" trademark expression has always been part of her act. She may have had a pre-conceived idea of what she was going to talk about. Her comedic ability to twist the English language with her heavy Castilian Spanish accent was used to create many humorous misunderstandings.

I was somehow able to fully understand Charo when she spoke. Sometimes rehearsal would get a bit pressured, and Charo's accent got thicker and harder to decipher. She would say something to Doc about the way she wanted the music to sound behind her and Doc would have trouble understanding her. I would be the translator.

It wasn't until 2004 when I worked with Charo that I got to witness her Las Vegas nightclub act. Her act has received awards for the best family-oriented show in town. She is a fabulous classical guitarist. I knew she played guitar, and I knew she could sing. But she blew me away with how well she played guitar. She studied with Segovia! I wonder if Segovia knew how to play "Tea For Two"?

Every once in a while, the Tonight Show Band would be asked to play at a local function to accompany some major star at one of the high-profile hotels in the Beverly Hills area. The band was called to an event at the Century Plaza Hotel in Los Angeles honoring Bob Wright, president of NBC. As usual, I showed up early in the morning with the drums, amps, music stands and music for the band. The first person I met was a woman named Carol who was the NBC employee in charge of the event. She was a nervous wreck. This was supposed to be a simple local dinner with NBC entertainers such as Betty White and Rue McClanahan from *The Golden Girls,* who were going to sing as a trio along with Nell Carter of *Gimme A Break.* The entire cast of NBC's show *Fame* was also performing. Doc Severinsen and the Tonight Show Band would be featured along with several celebrities who would speak about Bob Wright from the podium. Several video clips were going to be shown on two large projection screens on either side of the stage. Carol told me the reason she was so uptight that morning was that the night before, at a production meeting for this event, they had a conference call with Bob Wright telling him how the event was all set to go. All was fine until Mr. Wright said, ". . . and we are videotaping this whole thing, right?" Although everyone at the meeting said they were all set to videotape, they scurried to make it happen overnight, hiring cameramen, having heavy recording equipment moved to the hotel, extra lighting, extra sound equipment and miles of cable. Just prior to me walking in, the fire marshal was completing his customary walk through to make sure all fire codes were met by this new addition to the event. He was an unusually unpleasant fire marshal who decided to push his weight around that day. There was one area where the video cable crossed in front of the stage, and he wanted it moved by the time he got back from having a cup of coffee. Carol's attitude was "just shoot me now and get it over with." She felt she had already lost her job.

Apparently the fire marshal just needed a little caffeine to listen to reason. When he saw that the crew was already rerouting the cable behind the stage, he signed off on the approval of the event. Carol felt a little better about being able to keep her job to make the monthly payments on her new car.

During the dress rehearsal I was summoned into a makeshift director's booth overlooking the ballroom. I was introduced to a director who worked for our local affiliate KNBC station, Jay Roper. Jay was a tall, friendly kind of guy with a very professional attitude about the whole adventure. He got a call late the night before to get over to the Century Plaza Hotel first thing in the morning to direct a live-to-tape program. He was just being given the particulars of the show. Jay was not used to cutting a live, musically based show. He told me about his lack of musical knowledge and said, "But you are going to get me through the musical segments of the show." Because I could read scores and music, he wanted me to read along with the musical portions and give him a "heads up" of what was going to happen next.

I have always thought that this was the way to cut musical numbers. I once peeked into the director's booth during a taping of a Bob

Hope special musical segment. There was someone sitting alongside of the director following the musical score letting the director know what was coming up next, and the whole booth was buzzing with enthusiasm and the excitement of the music. That's the way it should be done, I thought. And here I was getting the chance to do it.

We didn't have very much time during rehearsal to cut the musical numbers and we didn't have the privilege of production notes or even a production meeting. We were flying by the seats of our pants. Before we realized it, it was show time. The band started to play, singers were singing, dancers were dancing, and the band played on. Luckily for me, I was familiar with the pieces that Doc and the band played as features. Calling the camera shots for those numbers was a breeze. The other musical numbers were trickier, but we managed to get through them.

The program was as slick as any television special you would see on network TV. One of the segments I especially enjoyed was a pre-recorded piece done by the crew of NBC's *Unsolved Mysteries*. The show's host, Robert Stack, garbed in his trench coat and appearing out of a professionally lit, foggy alley scene, approached the camera and spoke with the straight-faced style Stack had perfected over the years. He proceeded to talk about the "unsolved mystery" of how Bob Wright managed to keep his job at General Electric. It was very funny and very well done.

When the show was over, Jay Roper shook my hand and congratulated me on a job well done. I was fascinated at the great work he had done. For a guy who was used to cutting the local news every day, I was impressed by how adept he was at cutting this live show. At the end of the shoot, he simply reached over into the tape machine and told a runner to get the tape to Bob Wright immediately. He didn't even run it back to see what it all looked like. Jay figured, we either did our jobs right or not. There wasn't anything we could do to fix it anyway.

This truly was a great learning experience for me and I made a great friend in Jay Roper. For years after that we would see each other in the halls of NBC and say hello and make idle conversation. When the news broke that Jay Leno was to become the new host of *The Tonight Show* upon Johnny's retirement, Jay expressed an interest in having a shot at being the show's director. Jay told me he would give his left testicle for that position. I told him I would put in a good word for him. When I talked with Jay Leno's manager, Helen Kushnick who was soon to be executive producer of Jay's show, about Roper for director, she informed me that Ellen Brown had already been signed for that job. When I broke the news to Roper I said, "I know you said you'd give your left testicle for that job. Well, the person who got the job doesn't have any testicles at all!" Ellen Brown has turned out to be a very good director for Jay Leno, but it would have been fun to see Jay Roper get a shot at it too without having to offer up any of his body parts.

4

Buddy Rich

Buddy Rich was appearing one time at a place on Long Island called The Riviera in Port Washington. My friend Joe Alquist and I took his mother with us. We were 16 or so, not old enough to get into this place alone because liquor was being served. Buddy and the band were late in starting. Buddy was there, the band was there and the drums were there, but one thing was missing—the music arrangements. Someone who had traveled separately from the band was supposed to bring the big band charts, but without them, it would be one big, unruly jam session. Apparently, the guy who was in charge of bringing the charts for the show had taken a wrong turn somewhere.

The Riviera was no cheap joint. For two guys who were part time ushers at the RKO Keith movie theater, making about $1.50 an hour, I think it cost us two weeks pay to go there that night. Joe and I treated his mother to dinner for escorting us. We figured it was the least we could do, but I think she too enjoyed the show.

I managed to speak to Buddy quite a bit that night while we waited for the charts to arrive, even asking him if he could give me drum lessons. Buddy said he didn't give drum lessons but knew someone who could. He pointed to a man seated across the room and said, "Talk to that guy over there, Ed Shaughnessy." Buddy then brought me over to Shaughnessy's table and introduced us. When the music finally arrived and the band began to play, I was still sitting at the table. Ed and I sat there and watched Buddy's every move. Ed told me to especially watch Buddy's right foot on the bass drum. He told me that was why he picked the table off to the side of the band. The two of us watched like little kids. Ed was as much in awe of Buddy as I was.

On one of the set breaks, I decided to leave Buddy alone since I'd been talking to him quite a bit that night. I decided to go to the bathroom. When I walked in, Buddy was there washing his hands and saw me coming in. He must have thought to himself that he couldn't even go to the bathroom to get away from this kid. He said to me, "Where am I?" I told him we were in Port Washington, Long Island. Buddy says, "I know that, but in relationship to Brooklyn, where is that?" I explained as best as a kid of 16 could. I realized that he was serious. It wasn't until I went on the road in 1990 for 30 one-nighters with pianist Earl Rose that I could fully understand that Buddy had no idea where he was that night.

When the performance was over, I realized that I'd forgotten to get Shaughnessy's phone number to set up my lessons. I ran out and found him at the hatcheck room putting his hat and coat on. Ed has always been noted for the bushy sideburns running clear down his cheeks, and this night he had the outfit to match. He was putting on a hound's-tooth overcoat with a cape attached to the shoulders as he offered me his phone number. Then he affixed a matching hounds-tooth hat similar to the one Sherlock Holmes would be expected to wear. To top off the outfit, Ed put a deep bowled-ladle-type tobacco pipe between his teeth and bid me good night. What a night!

A RARE VIDEO OF BUDDY RICH

On my way into work at NBC one day, I stopped at a video store on Ventura Boulevard in Studio City. There I found a video for sale that was said to contain rare out-takes of *The Tonight Show*. I bought the tape and viewed it when I got home. It had blurry kinescope versions of Johnny Carson and Ed McMahon doing impromptu commercials. In the earlier days of *The Tonight Show*, Ed McMahon would do live commercials. They were usually Budweiser beer or Alpo dog food ads. Johnny would do the lead-in to the commercial to give Ed the few seconds it took him to run to the commercial area backstage. Then Johnny would jokingly tease Ed by simply saying, "And now, here's Ed." Ed would dart around from the couch nearly breaking his neck to get backstage in time.

Sometimes, the dogs used for the Alpo commercials just weren't hungry, or they suddenly became camera shy and refused to eat the dog food. Much to everyone's surprise, Johnny came to Ed's rescue by pretending to be a dog and pretending to eat the dog food. These moments were recorded on this tape. I brought it to the attention of our associate producers, Peter Lassally and Jeff Sotzing. The tape also had Johnny singing a comedic duet, "Our Love Is Here To Stay," with Pearl Bailey. I played the tape in Fred de Cordova's office for Fred and the other two. When Lassally saw the tape, his reaction was complacent. He said, "We have all of this, and in color." "Then why don't we show it on the anniversary shows?" I suggested. Fred turned to Peter and Jeff and repeated my question to them. The clips magically appeared on the next anniversary show and the Pearl Bailey clip was included on a 15-minute tape of *The Tonight Show*'s memorable moments, which began to air every night before the show tapings, to the delight of the studio audiences.

After this meeting in Fred's office, Sotzing and I were talking about all the other memorable moments and that we should check to see if they still existed. I said to Jeff: "We should have the premier performance of Buddy Rich and his new big band on the show."

"Not Buddy's Band," Jeff said, "You mean with *The Tonight Show* guys."

"No," I said. "Buddy had his whole band on the show and they played the entire 15-minute version of the 'West Side Story' medley."

"Get out of here," Jeff said, "I'll have to look that up." I gave him the approximate dates that it would have been, and Jeff went off to search it out.

A few weeks later, Jeff came to my office all excited. He'd found the show with Buddy's big band on it. We both ran into his office to check it out. It was in black and white and looked like film, but it definitely existed.

Buddy and his entire 17-piece band had appeared on *The Tonight Show* in New York City on November 11, 1966 to debut his new big band. Historically and technically, Buddy actually had pre-taped the band on *The Mike Douglas Show* a few days prior to his *Tonight Show* appearance. But the Douglas show was a syndicated program and didn't air until a week after Rich had done Johnny's show, which in 1966 was a live show. Buddy came out and played a tune arranged by Louie Bellson titled "Apples." He then sat at the panel along with Soupy Sales and Joey Heatherton. After a brief commercial break, Buddy and the band played the "West Side Story Medley."

That night, Buddy, beyond a doubt, played one of the best drum solos I have ever heard him play. He was showing his new big band off to the American public that night and he knew he had to burn like he never burned before.

Jeff gave me a copy of the tape, which I still watch from time to time, to reminisce of the brilliance and genius of Buddy Rich.

GRAMPA BUDDY

Buddy's daughter Cathy had given birth to a baby boy and named him Nicky. He was Buddy's pride and joy. Buddy told me one time that he'd bought one of those small video cameras to take with him on his tours. He said he brought it along so that Cathy could send him videos of Nicky. Buddy could hook up the camera in any hotel room and see his grandson.

On one occasion, the proud grandfather had Cathy bring Nicky to a *Tonight Show* rehearsal. Buddy took Nicky, then about two years old, and stood him on his drum stool. Little Nicky, all of two feet tall, had a pair of sticks in his hands and leaned over to hit the snare drum. He managed to play what sounded like, "prrrr ump pum."

Much to the surprise of the entire band, when he did this little drum riff, it drew everyone's attention. The band members, who were talking and basically ignoring Buddy and his grandson, suddenly turned their heads in amazement. The proud grandfather smiled a wide grin and stated, "Of course he's got it. It's in his genes."

WE DON'T PLAY REQUESTS

When I was working at *The Tonight Show*, about 1983 or '84, I got a phone call from a man named Joseph Harvey. He was connected with someone named Doug Meriwether Jr., who was compiling a book on Buddy Rich. The first idea of the book was to create a discography on Buddy. But Harvey told me that because of all the stories and history of Buddy Rich, the book was turning out to be more of a biography. Harvey asked if I could help them do some research on the book. I was delighted to be included in any project that had anything to do with Buddy Rich.

Harvey and Meriwether would call me or correspond with me by mail, asking me to find out dates and songs from Buddy's numerous appearances on *The Tonight Show*. I actually enjoyed looking back and discovering what songs Buddy had played in shows gone by.

Many of *The Tonight Show* episodes were destroyed by NBC in the early 1970s in an effort to make room on their warehouse shelves. Not only did this make Johnny Carson furious and, later, bitter toward NBC, but resulted in so many classic performances and debut appearances being lost forever.

Even most of the paperwork was destroyed along the way. I called the head of NBC Music Rights in New York, trying to hunt down and confirm some of the dates I had. Many of the cue sheets were missing from the Los Angeles Music Rights office, but copies should have been on file in New York. Unfortunately, NBC Music Rights made some poor decisions, and most of the old records were tossed out to give them more shelf space.

Despite the missing files, I was able to furnish Meriwether and Harvey with quite a list of information for the book. When the book came out they titled it "We Don't Play Requests" after a quote that Buddy often used when joking around with the audiences at the end of his concerts. They sent me a complimentary copy along with a thank you letter for all my troubles. I was also mentioned in the book for my contributions. In the section where they displayed a separate listing of all of Buddy's *Tonight Show* appearances, they gave me special credit.

Upon Buddy's next appearance on the show, I took out my book and asked him to autograph it for me. When he saw me coming towards him with the book, he said, "Oh man, you don't really want my autograph, do you?" I said, "Yes. You bet your ass I do. Sign the book." He signed it for me.

I made sure that Johnny Carson received a complimentary copy, as well, from Meriwether and Harvey. They were glad to accommodate Johnny. Soon after I delivered the book to Johnny's office, he bumped into me in the hall just prior to taping one of the shows. Johnny commented on the unbelievable amount of recordings that Buddy had done during his career. It was then that Johnny said one of those phrases that only Johnny would say. He said to me, "What a property he was! What a property!"

NO MORE ENCORES

Buddy had a history of heart problems since the mid '60s. The first time I saw Buddy play was soon after one of his heart attacks. I thought I'd better go see this guy before he dies. Luckily, Buddy overcame several heart attacks and back pains over the next twenty-seven years, allowing me to enjoy his drumming and get to know him. That first encounter with Buddy was around 1968 at the Felt Forum in New York. Buddy's band opened for a group named Vanilla Fudge. I got to meet Buddy and shake his hand before the show. I'll never forget the shirt he wore. It was a turtleneck with a white-on-white paisley pattern, almost like an Irish linen tablecloth. He wore a navy blue double-breasted blazer that made him look like a million bucks. I have been searching for a shirt like the one he wore that night ever since and have never come close to finding one. I guess I am going to have to spend some bucks and have one hand-made for myself someday.

In early 1987, Buddy suffered a massive heart attack and stroke. He was hospitalized at the UCLA Medical Center in Westwood, and word had it that he had lost all feeling on his left side. I was told he was able to have visitors. I had to go and see him.

Following the taping of *The Tonight Show*, March 12, 1987 I went to the hospital. I wasn't used to the procedure of visiting people in the intensive care unit. I've always had to either sneak into a hospital or walk in along with other people.

I didn't want to come off as just another Buddy Rich fan trying to sneak in to see him. I was afraid I'd be turned away. Just then, Bob Dolce, the talent coordinator who booked Buddy on the show, walked into the hospital lobby. He was coming to visit Buddy also. Bob had been there several times before and knew exactly what to do. We went up together to see Buddy.

When we walked in his room, friends and family surrounded Buddy. Singer Jack Jones was there with a girl who looked to me like she was 12 years old. She was Jack's new wife, Kim. Buddy's wife Marie was there. This was the first time I met her. She was beautiful for a woman in her mid-sixties. You could tell that she must have been a model or actress when she first met Buddy.

Buddy was lying in bed and Bob went directly over to Buddy and hugged him hello. Bob then turned to me and said to Buddy, "Look, Don Sweeney came to see you." Buddy was not wearing his hair-piece. He had let his hair go snow white and it was nicely combed back. His new look reminded me of a young Toscanini (without the mustache). Buddy's speech was slurred and slow. He was heavily drugged from his cobalt treatments and the stroke had taken its toll. Buddy had a drumstick in his right hand and was constantly tapping it on the bed and anything he could reach from his bedside. His other hand, the left one, the hand that film cameras couldn't focus on without using high speed film, was motionless. He couldn't even lift it to scratch his leg.

Buddy managed to give me a smile and seemed happy to see me. I saw him tapping the drumstick, so in an effort to cheer him up I said, "I see you are practicing your Mommas."

It took a second for Buddy to get the joke. (When drummers are first learning how to hold the sticks and doing drum rudiments, one of the first things they learn how to play is a drum roll. When they play the roll slowly it is called the Momma-Daddy beat. The right hand taps two times and then the left taps two times. When you count it, you say Momma-Daddy-Momma-Daddy . . .) When Buddy got the joke, he turned to Jack Jones and said, "Hey Jack, did you hear that? I'm practicing my Mommas."

Buddy, with a lot of help from Jones, began to tell me of the concert they had both just finished taping before Buddy's attack. They recorded a television show for PBS, a tribute to Tommy Dorsey. Jones and Maureen Murphy sang with the band, along with a vocal group called The L.A. Voices, which managed to represent the Pied Pipers. Mel Torme hosted the event, and Buddy was billed as a special guest. It was taped at the Hollywood Palladium. Buddy said it was a lot of fun. He even stood in front of the band and sang a few songs. That was something he hadn't done in a long time. He also pointed out that it was at the Hollywood Palladium where he got his first gig with Tommy Dorsey's band. We all knew it was the scene for Buddy's last performance.

When the room got quiet, Buddy would start to ramble about starting up a singing career. Buddy said, "I'll do like I did when I broke my arm. I can sing as good as the next guy." He turned to Jack and said, "Even better than you. Sometimes." We laughed.

I asked Buddy when the last time was that he took a vacation. He thought for a moment and said, "Never." He had worked his entire life and never stopped to go anyplace for rest and relaxation—not even when he'd had a heart attack or a back operation. (He had a slipped disk and tremendous back pain for most of his life. He once told me that the only time his back didn't hurt was when he was playing the drums.)

I couldn't believe that he never took a vacation. I asked him out of all the places he had been in his life, what place did he enjoy the most. Buddy said, "Italy." He looked at his wife Marie and said, "Right?"

Marie was at the foot of his bed. She agreed they had enjoyed their stay in Italy.

So, I said, "Why don't you take a vacation? You deserve one. You've worked your whole life. It's time you got to enjoy life and take a rest."

"Italy, yeah," Buddy said. "I could go back there. Marie, do you want to go back to Italy?" Marie's answer was filled with tears. As she said yes, she excused herself from the room, and there was an uncomfortable silence.

Buddy said to me in a serious tone: "You see, my family is a little uptight right now. We just had a big talk with my doctor about this." He motioned with the drumstick like it was a magic wand. We all wished it could have been a magic wand that he could just wave over himself and walk out of the hospital. "The doctor said I have a tumor right here," Buddy said as he then took the drumstick and pointed it to the middle of his forehead. He continued: "The doctor says I'm not in any condition to undergo an operation. Yet, if I don't have it taken care of soon, it could be all over. The family thinks I should leave it alone. If I do that, I will be like this for the rest of my life. That's no way I want to live. I'm willing to take my chances with an operation."

The thoughts in my head were why is he telling me all of this? I think it was heavy on his mind and on the minds of everyone in the room.

I didn't know what to say. I changed the subject and started to talk about *The Tonight Show*. "Doc said to say hello," I said.

"That bum?" Buddy said. "He thinks he's a band leader. He's just a sideman who got lucky." I thought Buddy was being his usual insulting self until he said to me, "Where's my friend, Carson? I haven't gotten as much as a telephone call or a postcard from him since I'm in here." He had been in the hospital for over a week. I didn't have anything to make him feel better about that.

I felt I had stayed long enough. Buddy was due for more medication. He told me the cobalt treatments were the worst. He said, "They shoot it right at my face because of the tumor. It's supposed to help me, but it makes my face feel like it's on fire."

When I began to say good-bye, he asked me to come back and see him before the operation. I told him I'd be on the road but that I'd be back in 10 days and see him after the operation. I leaned over to hug him and he grabbed the back of my neck with his right hand. He hugged me and kissed me on the cheek and said, "Yeah, I'll see ya in 10 days." He smiled and gave me a wink, and I left the room.

As soon as I got back to NBC the next day, I went to Johnny's office and asked his assistant, Drue Ann Wilson, why Johnny hadn't called Buddy at the hospital. Drue said they had tried to call, but Buddy was always out of the room in therapy or asleep.

When I talked to Ed Shaughnessy and told him all that Buddy had said, Ed couldn't believe it. "He said all of that to you? Whenever I go to see him, he's so drugged up, he would go in and out of a sleeping state. Half the time I wondered if he even knew I was there." I explained to Ed that Buddy would undergo cobalt treatments in the mornings and he'd be on heavy medication to relieve his pain. By the time I got to see him at night, the drugs were beginning to wear off. Nighttime was the best time to go to see him. After talking with Ed, it all made sense as to why Johnny Carson had been unable to get through to him.

About a week later, I was in the middle of my West Coast tour with the Earl Rose Trio. We were driving from an engagement in Vernon, Canada, to the Seattle airport, where we had had to leave our band equipment and rental car. We couldn't bring any of that into Canada with us because of immigration laws and visa restrictions. We'd rented equipment in Canada. I was driving the car, and Earl and our bass player, Glen Richmond, were almost asleep when we approached the airport. Earl woke up and asked how I was doing. I was getting tired, but we were less than a mile from the airport, and I said, "I'm fine. Let's put on the radio and see what's been going on in the United States while we were gone."

I turned on the radio. It was like a scene from a bad television melodrama. In films, the actor always turns on the radio or television just as the announcer says whatever the screenplay wants you to hear. This was like one of those moments. I turned on the radio and the first thing I heard was the announcer saying, "Buddy Rich died today of a massive stroke." I nearly drove off of the road. I pulled off to the center divider and put my head down on the steering wheel. The three of us didn't say a word for about five minutes.

I was so depressed from losing my idol, my mentor, my friend, my buddy. I couldn't bring myself to listen to his music for about a year after his death. Then I came to my senses one day and thought, how stupid I was to deprive myself of the very thing I had enjoyed so much.

It was difficult at first to watch videotapes. Watching him play and joke with Johnny was tough. For a long time I had to imagine that Buddy would be back someday. I tried to think that he was just on a very long European tour somewhere.

Maybe Italy.

5

Jay Leno

Jay Leno wants to be, and quite possibly is, the nicest guy in show business. He goes way out of his way to prove to everybody that he has not let success go to his head.

One night, after a *Tonight Show* taping, as I was leaving the NBC Studio lot, an audience member was having car troubles near the front gate. Who had his head perched under their hood, getting his hands all greasy? Jay. As I passed by I rolled my window down and shouted to him, "You're not supposed to be doing that. You're a star!" He smirked, held back a smile and pooh-poohed my remarks. He then continued to help the helpless civilian. Jay loves to do things like that.

I was having a terrible experience with a van that I was leasing. I was getting a rubbing sound from the rear axle and brought it back to the dealer twelve times. I was about to get an attorney to enforce the "Lemon Law" when someone recommended I ask Jay if he had any suggestions. I approached him one day as he walked in from the parking lot. I briefly explained my car problem to him and he asked what the dealer was supposedly fixing when I brought it in. I told him that they kept trying to fix the rear bushings. Jay knew it wasn't the bushings and said it was probably my gear shift housing. He said he would have a look at it and asked if I could bring it over to his place on the weekend. Then, a moment later Jay asked if the van was still under warranty and I told him it was. He said I'd be better off having the dealer work on it but to have them check out the gearbox, not the bushings. Jay then said that if I still couldn't get anywhere with them that he would have a look at it.

As it turned out, I called my leasing agent and told him of my frustration with the van and with the service department. I told him I was going to enforce the Lemon Law. The agent asked me to bring it back to the dealer one more time. "Give them one more chance and if they can't fix it, then I'll help you put the paperwork through for the Lemon Law," he said. I took his advice and scheduled it for another visit. He must have called somebody high up in the auto business because they simply replaced the entire rear axle of the van at no charge and the problem went away. When I told Jay what had happened, he was glad I got rid of the noise but said to me, "It's too bad that they replaced everything for you," he said, "'Cause now we will never know what the problem was."

Jay was guest hosting for Johnny Carson on Monday nights for several weeks in a row. My friend Earl Rose called me and asked if I could let a friend of his in to watch the music rehearsal. He told me she was a female stand-up comic. I set it up for her to come and watch the rehearsal. This was nothing out of the ordinary. I was always accommodating people in this way. As long as the music artist of the day did not request a "closed door" rehearsal, there wouldn't be a problem. I usually had the time on my hands to give visitors, in cases like this, a personal guided tour of the studios.

Earl's friend was very excited and grateful to be there. She told me she knew Jay from meeting him a couple of times at the Comedy Store and wondered if she might be allowed to say hello to him. I told her I would check into that. I then went to Jay's dressing room and told him the comedienne's name and asked if it would be okay to bring her by to say hello to him. He said, "Oh sure. I know her. Sure, bring her by." A few minutes later I brought her to meet Jay. He gave her a warm welcome and asked her how her career was going. She told him she was performing at one of the comedy clubs on a regular basis. It was then that Jay asked her if she had a video reel of her act. When she told him she had one, Jay told her, "Get it to me and I'll see what I can do. I'll get it to de Cordova for you and maybe . . ." She was speechless. She asked Jay how to get it directly to him and he said, "Just give it to Don and he will get it to me." She thanked him profusely and said good-by to him. As I walked her out of the building she was still walking on air. She said she just wanted to say hello to him and he was so nice to pass her tape on to the producers. I told her to send me the video and I would get it to Jay when he returned the following Monday.

For a short time Jay must have considered becoming a staff writer and giving up stand-up. He may have also just needed the money. But in the mid-'70s there was a program on NBC called *Real People*. It starred John Barbour, Skip Stevenson and Sarah Purcell (she used to be one of many morning show hosts with Regis Philbin long before Kathie Lee or Kelly Ripa). Our *Tonight Show* production offices were in one of four one-story temporary buildings known as the bungalows area of NBC Studios. On one side of our bungalow was the guest relations bungalow, and on the other side of us were the NBC press bungalow and the *Real People* production offices.

One day, as I was walking toward our bungalow, I saw a young Jay Leno with pencil and legal pad in hand walking with John Barbour and a few other writers. (One of the other writers, Michael Mislove, was formerly one of the members of the Ace Trucking Company comedy team.)

Obviously, Jay did not stay with that show. Throughout my years at *The Tonight Show* I always speculated about who would ultimately replace Johnny Carson. When Joan Rivers became Johnny's permanent guest host in 1983, everyone assumed she would replace him when the time came. When Garry Shandling came along, he seemed to be the likely candidate. David Brenner came close to that seat, but I always thought that the replacement for Johnny Carson had not been discovered yet.

Although Jay's first appearance on *The Tonight Show*, March 12, 1977 was ten years before he got the chance to guest host, he had made a few appearances on the show. It didn't occur to anyone that he would even make a good guest host.

In 1987 Jay got his first chance at filling in for Johnny. He made a good impression with the NBC "brass," but he didn't "wow" us. I remember him as the comedian who did a funny impression of Scotty from Star Trek. Most of his observational humor struck a familiar chord with me because the things his mother would say sounded exactly like the things my mother would say to me. Jay and I both come from the East Coast, we are close in age (he is a year older than me), we both moved out to California around 1973 and we both got married in 1981. The difference between us is that he became a professional comedian and became the host of *The Tonight Show*, while I got all the good looks.

The first time I was introduced to Jay Leno was the day I met Branford Marsalis in Helen Kushnick's office in 1991. Helen was Jay Leno's manager who later would become infamous in the Late Night Wars when NBC had to make a choice between Leno and Letterman.

Helen had a temporary office in NBC's Catalina building which was a group of pre-fab temporary office buildings just east of NBC Studios. She thought that it would be a good thing for all of us to meet there. Jay sat in the corner on a sofa and shook my hand when Helen formally introduced us. Jay acted as if he had met me before. "Oh, yeah, yeah, we've met before. You had the office next to Jim McCauley's office back in the bungalows," he said as we shook hands.

Helen escorted me over to meet Branford. As we shook hands Branford said, "Do you know how to do Finale?" (a music writing program for the Macintosh computer). I told him I knew how to do it and he then said, "Good. 'Cause now you can teach it to me." I told him I had been using that program for almost a year but I hadn't mastered it yet. Branford reassured me that we would learn it together. I instantly felt that Branford and I were going to get along just fine and that we would soon become good friends. To this day, Branford and I still keep in touch.

Helen Kushnick led the discussion of how the show would run. The co-producer of the show, Bill Royce, was introduced to us all. He talked briefly with Branford about trying to get Jerry Garcia of the Grateful Dead as a guest. Bill asked Branford to use his "pull" to help get Garcia. Bill Royce was a segment producer for the *Arsenio Hall Show*, and Helen was able to entice him into doing Jay's show. Bill excused himself from the meeting to get back to work. Bill was lining up guests for Jay's opening week.

The meeting consisted of Helen, Branford, Jay and me. We looked at a mock-up of the set and some story boards of the opening sequence, and Branford played us a tape of the new *Tonight Show* theme. The theme was too long for the opening. I pointed out that the melody changed at midway just as the music changed, which would be the best point for Jay to make his entrance through the curtain. I demonstrated what I meant by reading the announce copy that Edd Hall (Jay's answer to Ed McMahon) would later read.

When I got to the part, ". . . and now, Jay Leno!" it timed out perfectly with the bridge of the theme song. Later, when we got into doing mock shows, I insisted on the song hitting as it did in Helen's office that day. Branford actually cut out measures to the piece and adjusted the tempo so that it worked every time. To this day, that is how the show still opens.

It was exhilarating for me to be a part of the early formation of the Jay Leno *Tonight Show*. As Jay sat there at the meeting, he explained how he didn't want a sidekick the way that Johnny had Ed and Doc to bounce things off. Jay explained that Edd Hall would not be seen on camera and that Jay would talk to Branford from time to time during the show, but not during the monologue. Jay said, "The monologue is my moment in the show."

He went on to explain how he did not know Branford very well and wanted to discover things about him "on the air." Jay said to Branford, "I'm not an actor. I can't read lines off of a piece of paper and make it sound like everyday talking. It will come off phony if I do that. I want to turn to you and say 'Branford, what did you do yesterday?' And then, however you react to that on the air will be real and much more entertaining." Well, that idea did not last very long.

After a week or two of taping the show, Helen Kushnick and the NBC executives wanted Jay to include Branford in his monologue. Soon almost every joke was bounced off Branford and the rest of the band to get their reactions. Before you knew it, Jay began doing exactly what Johnny Carson did in his monologues. Why? Because it worked.

Before NBC would approve my contract, Helen called me to tell me that I needed to have a face-to-face meeting with one of the NBC executives. It was just the usual protocol that I needed to follow. When I met with the NBC executive, he asked me how I saw my role in the new *Tonight Show* with Jay Leno. I told him that I saw myself as the music supervisor of the show overseeing any and all music elements of the program including music rights, hiring musicians, supervising all arranging and copying, and filing all union contracts and related paperwork. He said that was exactly what he had in mind for me. It was obvious to me that this vice president didn't have a clue what my job was and that was why he had me define it for him.

He then asked me if I knew of anyone who could lead the Tonight Show Band. When I looked puzzled at the question, he explained to me that Branford's contract negotiations were not going as smoothly as they would like and wanted to know if there was an alternative. I had been particularly impressed with record producer David Foster and suggested him for the job. David was well known within the musical community and highly regarded, but was not known to the general public yet. As I said Foster's name, the executive wrote his name down and said, "Yes, David Foster. We were considering him."

Immediately after my interview, Helen called me and asked how it went. I told her word for word what took place. I mentioned to her about the Branford contract negotiation. I told her I suggested David Foster. Helen gave me the same reaction as the NBC V.P. They were thinking about David Foster but quickly dismissed any problem with Branford's contract and assured me that Branford was going to be the new bandleader.

The next night, the Grammy Awards aired and David Foster won the award for Producer of the Year (1991). He produced the Best Song of the Year, Natalie Cole's "Unforgettable," and also produced the Best Album of the Year, "Unforgettable" again. I'm sure that Helen Kushnick and that NBC executive were home scratching their heads, wondering how I knew about David Foster before they did.

Jay's first show as new host of *The Tonight Show* aired three days after the nation bid a teary farewell to the much honored and beloved Johnny Carson. The entire staff squeezed into the greenroom to watch his first show. Jay was there with all of us prior to the broadcast and as he nervously exited the greenroom to start the show he said, "Let's hope I don't become an answer to a Trivial Pursuit question after this." He was reasonably nervous. Although he had guest hosted many *Tonight Show*s before this, he was about to either carry on the tradition as the new host of late night or become the person who ran the show into the ground after Johnny retired.

When the first show was over, I had arranged for my wife Cathy and her friend Linda to set up a few bottles of champagne and a platter of chocolate covered strawberries in an adjacent rehearsal hall for a small impromptu celebration. I only invited Jay, Branford, the members of the band, Helen and a few other key people on the production staff. Unbeknownst to me, Jay had a large number of friends and relatives in the audience that night whom he invited to this little bash. Suddenly this little private gathering became a huge corral of workers, relatives and NBC executives. We didn't have enough champagne or strawberries for everyone. We poured as many glassfuls of bubbly as we could until there was barely a drop left in the last bottle. I wanted to make sure there was something left for Branford who had not arrived yet. I covered the bottle with my hand and proceeded to tell those who wanted the last drop that I was saving it for Branford. One of our staff members came over to me and said that I just denied NBC president Warren Littlefield a glass of champagne. "Good," I said, hoping he would hear me, "Why didn't he arrange for NBC to spring for the after-party? Maybe there would have been enough champagne for everybody."

Helen Kushnick continued to rule *The Tonight Show* and Jay Leno with an iron fist. She once slapped Branford on his shoulder when he didn't see things her way. She would even put Jay down when he wasn't around. And when he was around, she talked to him as if he were a little child, in front of everybody. Jay took it too. She was like his mother and Jay listened to her and respected her as if she really was his mother.

Helen may have been on the road to "crazy" but she had some very good (and some very bad) innovations for the show. Some of her good ideas: She completely redesigned the greenroom in Studio 1. She had the room painted, re-carpeted and two large screen televisions were built into the wall high enough for everyone to have a good view from any seat in the room. She had a guy from the NBC commissary set up and serve hors d'oeuvres and soft drinks for all. (There no longer was any alcohol backstage as there was in the Carson days.)

The old pool room off of the greenroom, located directly under the studio audience bleachers, was a great hangout for crew members and band members. She had it converted into a sound-proof playroom for little children. (Sometimes guests and friends of the guests brought infants and toddlers to the taping and had to remain outside in the hallway or cooped up in the dressing room with them, until now.) The room was equipped with videogames and toddler toys and was painted to look like a nursery school room. Jay's monologues were longer than Johnny Carson's monologues and instead of throwing it to commercial when the monologue was completed, Jay acknowledged the band for a brief play-over and then did a comedy piece at the desk before the first commercial. *Tonight Show* guests would receive a basket of fruit and a terrycloth robe in their dressing rooms (because *The Arsenio Hall Show* gave out robes).

Some of the bad choices she made: The colors of the set and set furniture were hand-picked by Helen instead of leaving that up to the set designer. The ordeal of choosing the color combinations and the right plants to sit behind Jay went on for four months. Helen's way of dealing with anyone who dared get in her way was an "off with their head" approach. She would scream at people on the telephone and could be heard throughout *The Tonight Show* office halls. She thought that the sound problems we encountered in the first few weeks were sabotage attempts by the Arsenio Hall staff. Helen even sent a spy to Arsenio's offices to rummage through his files and report back to her in retaliation for the sound problems.

Helen would berate people in production meetings in front of the entire staff. She would announce to all what she said to Warren Littlefield, who was the NBC West Coast vice president; Bob Wright, who was the president of NBC; or any critic from the *New York Times* to *TV Guide*. If she told off some critic before a meeting, we all had to listen to her tell us how courageous she was in telling him or her to go to hell.

After Johnny retired, Ed McMahon continued to keep an office at NBC in one of the bungalows toward the back of the lot where the old *Tonight Show* offices used to be. He had this office until Kushnick found out about it. She called one of the NBC executives and ordered them to ask him to leave immediately. She didn't want anyone associated with Johnny Carson to have an office on NBC property. Even though Ed was renting the space on his own, Helen didn't care. She had him removed from the lot.

At one meeting Helen announced to the staff that we were going to get Jay an Emmy. "And here's how we're going to do it," she said as she unfurled her scheme. She asked how many of us were members of the Academy of Television Arts and Sciences. Several of us were already members, and when she saw a good show of hands she said that the rest of us would join and that the show would pay our membership dues. We would all nominate the show in our respective areas of the business, i.e., wardrobe would nominate for costume design, make-up for make-up, and so on. I nominated the show for best music performance, best music conductor and, because we were considered a new show, I nominated our new theme song. Helen then told us that after the show was nominated, we would call everyone we knew who was a voting member of the Academy. That was how we'd get an Emmy for Jay. Her plan seemed diabolical, but was basically the way most shows get nominated. The induction of several employees into the Academy at the expense of the show was out of the ordinary, and her self-assured attitude sounded as if it was a slam-dunk that we would get an Emmy. Her plan didn't work. We didn't win a single Emmy that year.

One of her biggest mistakes was how the band was paid. Back in her office in the Catalina Building, weeks before Jay took over from Johnny, Helen explained to me her innovative plan for screwing the American Federation of Musicians. When I began to talk about residuals and overtime, she interrupted me to tell me of her design. "We're not going to do things the old way. The new way of paying the musicians is this: We are going to pay our band a weekly salary that will be way over union scale. That way we don't have to worry about paying anybody overtime, or for sweetening, or doubles, and all that crap. These musicians are 'jazz' musicians. They love to play music all day long and all night long. They are used to that. We can have them play for hours and not have to worry about the costs getting astronomical." As she told me this I could feel my stomach churning in pain. If I agreed to this, it would mean I was selling out the AFM and all the musicians who come to visit the show. I knew that Helen was too proud of her idea to have me try to knock it down on the first day. I waited. And little by little I explained to her that not all of her illustrious plan was going to work. Each time I explained to her why we couldn't do things her way, I always put the blame on the videotape agreement that NBC had with the AFM. That way I could appear to be on her side, but point out that we had to comply with the agreement. The only aspect that remained was the way the house band was paid. They continued to get paid a weekly amount, and it was way over scale. This became a problem whenever we took the show out of town. The band had to put in many extra hours but received the same amount in their weekly paycheck. The only thing that went up on their weekly check was the 10 percent work dues they had to pay. I also tried to explain to them that when those shows were repeated, they would get more in their respective paychecks. Helen Kushnick created a monster. They should have been paid over scale, but that over scale figure should have been computed on an hourly basis. Pay them triple scale, or higher, but no matter how many hours they worked, they would all see an increase from the normal wage if they put in a longer-than-usual work day.

My office was situated about halfway between Jay's office and Helen's office. I would constantly see Helen walking to Jay's office or Jay walking to hers. One day, Jay came into my office and shut the door. He asked me, "What is Doc Severinsen's problem?" Doc had been saying a few negative things to the press about Jay's show, and in particular, the music. Doc was implying that he would never be asked to appear on Jay's show. In Doc's mind, he felt that Helen disliked him. Doc felt that Helen was the reason he wasn't asked to stay on with Jay. Whether that was the case or not, I felt that Doc had aggravated matters by saying things to the press and backstage that made him one of Helen's enemies (if he wasn't one before that).

I explained to Jay what had happened with Branford Marsalis and the Tonight Show Band prior to Jay taking over as host. Branford did not always think of the ramifications of things he would say off the cuff to the reporters who would approach him. Branford thought he was being honest, but sometimes honesty is not the best route of diplomacy. In an interview on the *Today Show* a few months before the change in command, Branford, in trying to talk up how good his band was going to sound, compared his band to Doc's band. He said something to the effect that his band was going to be hipper than Doc's band and would not be playing those "sorry old tunes" like the old band. I think you can imagine that this did not sit well with Doc and his band. When I explained this to Jay he said, "I can't have Doc on yet. It's too soon. If we were doing the show for a year or so I could have him and the guys on, but it's too soon." After he left my office, I got the feeling he thought I still talked to Doc every day and that Jay's sentiments would be conveyed directly to him from me.

One of Jay's earlier guests on his own *Tonight Show* was famous "Shock Jock" Howard Stern. Howard made a special trip to Los Angeles from New York just to appear on Jay's show. As part joke and part in honor, Helen Kushnick saw to it that a red carpet was actually laid out from the artists' entrance to Stern's dressing room to show our appreciation for his visit.

Howard is always controversial, if nothing else, and this time he was in rare form. Howard wasted no time in bad-mouthing Ed McMahon, Doc Severinsen and Johnny Carson. Howard was saying all the things Jay couldn't say. Whether or not Jay agreed with what Howard was saying didn't matter. The studio audience was howling at Howard's remarks.

The ratings for the Stern appearance went through the roof, but the critics had nothing good to say about the way Jay handled the situation. It made Jay look bad and that really cut Jay deeply. Remember, he wanted to be known as the "nicest guy in show business." I think Jay was disappointed in himself that he allowed Stern to take control of his show that way. Jay may have been told by Helen Kushnick to let Howard say all the bad things about the old show so that Jay didn't have to say them. I think Jay felt that he let Helen use him and his show to voice her animosities toward Johnny, Ed and Doc. That little trick would have its ramifications later when the Letterman/Leno wars began in December 1992.

Eventually, Helen Kushnick managed to get herself fired. She blamed part of her demise on the fact that she was a woman in a man's world. Male or female, you can't go around making public statements about the stupidity of your superiors and expect to keep your job. Helen made a call to the Howard Stern radio show and proceeded to tell Howard and all of his listeners what she thought of the top brass at NBC. She was a loose cannon that had to be harnessed. NBC had to fire her.

On the day that NBC terminated Helen, we proceeded with the show as usual. Word of her demise must have spread throughout NBC before she was fired. I got a call from the NBC Music Department that they just heard that Kushnick had been escorted off the lot. As those words were said, Helen and Jay walked by my office, and I could hear Helen telling Jay that NBC may try to pull her off the show during our taping. I told the music department that I thought they were premature with their gossip because she just walked past my office. Rumors of her saying, "What a world, what a world," as the NBC security walked her to her car were completely unfounded.

During the show taping, NBC security and a locksmith came up to our offices and changed the lock on Helen's door. When the show was over, she was escorted off the lot.

I had often seen news reports of CEOs of corporations arrested for embezzlement or fraud. Scenes of those executives being escorted out of their offices with handcuffs on and a coat draped over their head to hide from the cameras crossed my mind. I always wondered what it would be like to see your boss dragged through the media. An employee of such a company might wonder if they needed to go to work the next day or go straight to the unemployment line. We all wondered what was going to happen the next day and the days after that.

As music supervisor on the Jay Leno *Tonight Show*, it was my job to hire any outside musicians and backup singers whenever necessary. On this particular occasion, I was told to get a chorus for country singer Garth Brooks. He needed a 30-voice choir of young people with a good ethnic mix. The night that Helen Kushnick was fired, I had to forge ahead as if nothing had happened. As far as I knew, we still had a show to do the next day and Garth Brooks was going to be on it.

Where was I to find an ethnic mix? I needed to find a neighborhood where young people of all races would assemble. Then, it came to me—where I could find young people of all races in the form of a choral group? A college! I was about to pick up the telephone to call Cal State Northridge when my other line rang. It was the head of the Northridge music department, calling to ask for tickets to *The Tonight Show*. What a coincidence! When I told him what I needed, he said the university had just hired a choral director, Bill Lyons, who was forming a young-peoples' jazz choir. I called Bill, and he was delighted to help me out, as well as to be able to tell his new choir that they were to sing on *The Tonight Show* with Garth Brooks. I went to Northridge and checked out the choir in person. They were perfect. Lyons knew exactly what I needed when I said I needed an ethnic mix. The group looked the part and, thank goodness, they could sing, too.

It was arranged for Brooks to rehearse with the choir at the college the night before the taping of the show, and we all met at the campus.

Garth and his band arrived in a 12-passenger van along with all their equipment. He made it clear that he wanted to meet the choir before beginning the rehearsal. He walked in and shook hands with every choir member, putting everybody at ease from the very start.

Brooks was intense during the first few passes of the song, concerned with something his band was or wasn't doing that he couldn't quickly put his finger on. He apologized to the choir for making them sing the song so many times. The youngsters didn't care—they were still in awe of being in the same room with Garth Brooks.

When Garth felt comfortable with the song, it was time to pack it in for the night. Garth wanted to get back to the hotel to get some rest, since he and the band apparently had come straight to the college from the airport, and all were tired from the trip. Rather than making Garth wait around for his band to pack up the equipment, I offered to give him a ride back to the Sheraton Universal Hotel. I took Garth, his road manager and a woman publicist back to the hotel. Garth kept thanking me and kept asking if it was taking me out of my way. It was, but I wasn't going to tell him that. I felt as though I was getting a chance to chauffeur around the Elvis Presley of the '90s.

During the ride, a bit of *Tonight Show* politics surfaced. "Say, Don?" Garth said. "We heard something on the radio news tonight about NBC firing the executive producer of the show. Is that true?"

I was well aware of what had happened that night, but I wasn't about to go out of my way to tell Garth Brooks about it. But since he already knew most of it and was concerned whether the show was still going to go on as planned the next day, I had to tell him. Jay Leno's manager, Helen Kushnick, had indeed been fired from the show as he had heard.

It was one of the most extraordinary days I'd ever experienced during my then-17 years at the show. I assured Garth and his associates that *The Tonight Show* would survive and that tomorrow would be business as usual.

When the staff and crew came in the next day we found Jay heading the morning production meeting. He asked all of the workers in. He calmly assured us all that we all still had a job. He said we all still had a show to produce and that Helen Kushnick was a problem he had to deal with. He admitted that he had been in denial about a lot of the things she had done and he said he would try to fix anything she ruined and mend any fences she had destroyed.

There was a book called *The Late Shift* written about the fight for the late night throne that ended with the winner of late night TV undecided. It was up to the public to make the choice. The book was eventually made into an HBO movie under the same name. As we all know, Jay won Johnny Carson's show and time slot, but Johnny publicly favored David Letterman. A TV movie also tried to show the behind-the-scenes fight for Letterman and Leno in late night.

Helen definitely had a scary quality to her. She could be the nicest person one minute and a raving lunatic the next without warning. I think Kathy Bates did an eerie impression of her in the TV movie, except that the writer of the book and the producers of the TV epic portrayed Helen as a one-dimensional crazy woman. They left out the unpredictable change in character. They also forgot to mention that she died of cancer shortly before HBO released the movie.

She had a few tragedies in her personal life. Her three-year-old son was one of the first children to die of AIDS in 1983 due to a blood transfusion. Shortly after that, her husband, Jerold, died of a heart attack. Just before Jay inherited *The Tonight Show* throne, Helen got breast cancer (and beat it). Some of this might have explained a lot of her actions. But she riled too many men at the top, and they didn't want to give her an inch of sympathy.

It took a lot of mending, and some of those broken fences would never stand as they had before. Jay did a great job of gaining the trust of the staff and after Helen left, things calmed down considerably. The NBC executives had a little too much to say as far as production was concerned, but Jay coped with the Helen situation and eventually learned how to fend off the executive-producer-wanna-be's in his own way.

The first day after Kushnick's parting, Garth Brooks and his band showed up for rehearsal, as did the Northridge Jazz Choir, who sang their socks off. Garth and the new *Tonight Show* producers were quite pleased with the choir's performance. They did so well that the country star sent a crate of Garth Brooks T-shirts for the choir. Working with Garth Brooks was always a pleasure; he was a kind and courteous superstar. It was obvious to others that *The Tonight Show* would go on. There would be other hurdles to overcome, and the big one would soon be on the horizon: Who would eventually win the throne of *The Tonight Show*? In the coming weeks, Jay would joke that he already had the job, but NBC was deciding whether he could keep it.

One day, Jay's musical guest on the show was Robert Palmer. The writers thought it would be funny at the end of the opening monologue that Jay would announce his guests for the night with four models dancing behind him dressed in slinky black mini skirts. They were trying to do a satire on Robert Palmer's music video of the song "Simply Irresistible." At rehearsal, Jay was surrounded by the four leggy models who were hired to dance behind him. As they left the stage, Jay looked out to where his writers were sitting in the audience and said, "How much does one of those cost?" He took out his wallet and began to count off a stack of twenties. I was standing near where the writers were and walked over to Jay and said, "I'll tell you what one of those would cost you: your house, your car collection, all of your motorcycles . . ." Jay laughed and said, "You're right."

Jay once used one of my jokes in his monologue. His writers were much less uptight than Johnny's writers. Johnny's writing staff would resent anyone who approached them with a comedy idea or sketch as if we were going to take their jobs away. Jay's writers actually asked for ideas from the staff all the time.

Jay was doing jokes all week long about a man and a woman who each had a sex change operation. The man's parts were going to be put on the woman and the woman's parts were going to be put on the man. The scientists assured the couple that they would never know each other's identity. It's news stories like this one that comedians live for. The joke possibilities are endless. So, each night that week, Jay did a "sex change" joke. On Wednesday night, I was standing off stage watching Jay do his monologue. Joe Medeiros, one of Jay's head writers, was standing next to me. I said to Joe, "I'm surprised that Jay didn't do my joke, yet, it's so obvious." He asked me what my joke was and when I told it to him, he said, "That's a great joke. Have you told it to Jay?" Joe said Jay might use it in his monologue. I hadn't bothered to tell it to Jay, after the bad reaction I got from Johnny's writers years before. I didn't want to get the writers mad at me.

The next day Joe passed me in the hall and told me that he told Jay my joke and he liked it. He said Jay might use it in that night's monologue. I thought Joe was just pulling my leg. That night, Jay did not do my joke or any other sex change joke, so I thought that would be the end of them. But then, on Friday morning, Jay approached me on our way to the production meeting. He said, "Hey Don, I'm gonna use your joke in the monologue tonight." I was amazed. Not only did it confirm that Joe told Jay my joke, but he gave me credit for it. And, on top of that, Jay was going to tell my joke in the monologue.

That night, not only did Jay tell my joke and it received a big laugh, but it was his last joke in the monologue. Placing the joke at the end of his nightly routine meant that Jay felt confident enough that it would go over big enough for him to end on. This was the joke:

You know, that couple who had the sex change operation, his sex organs would be given to the woman and the woman's sex organs would be placed on the male. The doctors assured them that they would never know the identities of each other, and there was no chance that they would ever come in contact with one another. But, what if they were to meet somewhere and become intimate with one another. He might say to her, "Hey, I'll show you **yours,** *if you'll show me* **mine.** *"*

The joke got a very good laugh. I guess I could have tried to write more jokes for Jay, but I didn't want to wear out my welcome. There was no compensation for my efforts, but I wasn't looking for a buck. The problem was that the only people who knew I wrote that joke were a few of Jay's writers, me and Jay. I did, however, gain some headway with the writers on the show. They would listen to my occasional suggestions for bits and jokes from that time on.

I obviously had a few enemies at NBC (or I would still be working on Jay's show). About three or four months into the show I got word through my assistant, Steve Hull, that someone had accused me of stealing. Steve said he was questioned by the show's line producer about my practices of accounting. It seems the accounting department was questioning some of the ways in which things were billed to the show, and someone in the administration building thought I might be putting some of that money into my pocket. I was furious about the way this investigation was going on without my knowledge. If Steve hadn't brought it to my attention, who knows how far it would have gone? I decided to go directly to Jay. I couldn't trust anyone else. I told Jay what was happening. In another closed door meeting in my office, I explained to Jay that what they were accusing me of was virtually impossible. I said, "If anyone wants to look at my books, my filing cabinets are not locked. Check them out!"

Our billing system worked like a bank. If I made a mistake as small as a penny in any of my calculations, the accounting department would call me immediately on it. If the mistake would somehow get by the accounting department, our show accountant would question me on the mistake. And finally, if my mistake were to get by any of those accountants, the musicians union would catch it. It was a good system of checks and balances. I told Jay that because somebody in accounting didn't understand the AFM Videotape Agreement or someone in the administration office may have a personality conflict with me, they were trying to get me fired.

Jay said he would look into it. He could see I was reasonably upset and assured me that he would get to the bottom of it.

Jay certainly followed through. The next day he came into my office, closed the door and told me that everything was okay. He took care of it. Somebody made a mistake. He explained that whoever it was has been educated to the process and that they would leave me alone. I was very grateful that Jay went out of his way to save my job for me. He could easily have taken the easy way out and told me he didn't want to get involved. But, thankfully for me, he did get involved.

Months after Helen Kushnick was no longer with the show, Howard Stern was invited back as a guest. With Kushnick no longer calling the shots, Jay had to deal with Howard in his own way. Howard was touring the country and visiting all the talk shows that would have him. He was plugging his book *Private Parts*. His book was selling like none before, so he really didn't have to appear anywhere, but he was making headlines and was seen on the national news when near riots broke out among the 20,000 or more fans who showed up at the book signings. It was being equated to when "Beatlemania" happened in the '60s.

Why do the media always try to compare things to the success of the Beatles? Howard's book was a huge success, but it was nothing close to the phenomenon of the Beatles. Forty years later we are still talking about the Beatles. Ten years since Stern's book, people are saying, "What book?"

Jay knew he had to have Stern on or he would look like a wimp. Howard would soon be on his radio show badmouthing Jay. The "nicest guy in show business" could not have that happen. So Howard Stern returned to Jay's show. This time, Jay was more confident in his hosting chair. Jay's ratings had improved and he was occasionally beating out Letterman and Koppel. Jay decided not to let Howard get the upper hand.

Jay let Howard have his say, but would not let him get away with fabricating conversations. Howard loved to make things up that Jay supposedly said backstage that were completely untrue. I guess Howard simply fabricated stories to make the interview more edgy. Each time Howard tried this tactic, Jay stepped on his fingers. After a while, Jay was attacking Howard. Stern was caught completely off guard and even repeatedly asked what had gotten into Jay. He asked Jay why he was being so mean to him. Jay wasn't being mean. He was fighting back. And he was fighting back in the best way he knew how, through his comedy.

He outwitted Howard Stern that night. When the show was over, Howard didn't even stick around while the closing credits rolled. Howard made a "B" line for his limo and was out of there before the closing theme was over.

My office was just down the hall from Jay's dressing room and I heard some voices in the hall immediately after the show. I looked out to see who it was and saw Jay surrounded by several of his writers. Jay was telling them, "Did you see that. I beat him. Howard didn't know what hit him. He left without saying good-bye." One of the writers said, "Howard ran down the hallway and out of the building! You scared him off." Jay was almost giddy. He was acting like a little kid who finally slew the dragon that has been appearing in his nightmares. It was a fascinating sight for me to see.

Christmastime was approaching in the same vastness it always does year after year. Nonetheless, it seemed to creep up on us. My band was asked to play at the first Jay Leno Tonight Show Christmas Party, which was held in Studio 9 on the NBC lot. Previously, my band was asked to play many of Johnny Carson's anniversary parties, so I was thrilled that we were asked to continue a tradition with Jay.

The party was December 21, 1992, which was the day that NBC President Bob Wright was to meet in New York with David Letterman and decide who was going to be the host of *The Tonight Show*. Although Jay Leno was named Carson's successor and had already been hosting *The Tonight Show* since May 25th of that year, there still was a decision for Bob Wright to make. Somehow, although the results of Mr. Wright's meeting with Letterman would not be announced until Tuesday morning, Jay managed to get the results immediately following his show taping on Monday night, just prior to the office Christmas party.

As the office staff headed to Studio 9, Jay wound up having a shouting match with the West Coast NBC executives in front of most of the staff. The word got through to Jay that Bob Wright was going to announce NBC would go in favor of David Letterman over Jay. The men that Jay was shouting at had been on his side during this whole ordeal, but to Jay the bottom had fallen through. Jay felt betrayed and angry, and, unfortunately, the entire *Tonight Show* staff witnessed this ugly confrontation.

I was on the stage at Studio 9 playing with my band when all of this happened. I had no idea that any of this had taken place until the next day. I was puzzled why all of the people at the party seemed to be huddled at the opposite end of the room. And when we played our best dance music, no one seemed to want to dance. I dismissed it with the thought that staff members were being shy about dancing with other staff members. But then I realized that most of the staff had invited their spouses.

We tried everything to get them up dancing. It was the deadest party I had ever played. Unbeknownst to me, after hearing "the nicest guy in show business" screaming at his NBC adversaries, everyone thought that the show was over and they'd be out of work. Fred de Cordova told me that he was going to get up and say a few words. He tried to try to smooth things over with the staff. I was still puzzled and thought that Fred was kissing up to Jay in a way I had never seen him do before. His short speech sounded like a pep talk. It was something like, "I just want to tell you how proud Jay is of all of you and that this show, *The Tonight Show with Jay Leno*, will go on for many years to come . . ." My first thought was, "Oh man, Fred has become senile and totally forgot how to kiss up to his star. He's losing it!" After the party was over and I learned what had taken place, I could see why everyone was so numb and Fred said all those strange things.

During the following months, Jay had to fight the East Coast NBC executives to sway their opinion back to approving Jay for *The Tonight Show* host position. Johnny Carson's name came up quite often during those months and Letterman's camp let it go public that Carson was on Dave's side. It was later known that phone calls were made to Johnny Carson by Peter Lassally, David Letterman and Bob Wright. Even Jay made a call to Johnny to apologize for all the things that Helen Kushnick said in the past, and to reassure Johnny that it was not his doing. But Johnny was no dummy. He more or less told Jay that he had to take the responsibility for the actions of the people representing him. I'm sure that Johnny was thinking of the things Jay allowed Howard Stern to say on his show months before. Jay was going to have to sweat things out on his own. Johnny made it clear he didn't want to get involved. Funny though, every time I read that in print, there was usually another quote from Carson saying that he would not have let Letterman slip away to CBS.

6

Tonight Show Hits the Road

Ratings are the name of the television game. Sweeps weeks, the name given to the weeks when the ratings are measured, are seasonal. They come in February, May and November. The most important sweeps are in May. That's when the sponsors decide the value of a television show's commercial time. It is also the time when networks make decisions about their Fall line-ups. The Nielsen Media Research Company compiles the ratings in numerous ways using random surveys and families who are paid to log what they watch. Through phone calls and electronic boxes hooked up to home TVs, the Nielsen ratings are tallied and virtually rule what we see on television. If a show gets low ratings, sponsors start pulling out, the money to run the show goes away, and the network cancels the show. If the ratings are high, the cost of sponsorship goes up, and the network makes money, the show gets renewed.

When Johnny Carson hosted *The Tonight Show*, we rarely had to worry about ratings. Johnny's competition was knocked out one by one. Whenever someone was announced to be the "new competition for Johnny Carson," Johnny would sometimes have them on his show to wish them luck. He would also go on vacation the week that they debuted their shows. I think the strategy behind that was that any ratings they would accumulate would be reported as ratings against a "Best of Carson." Even with the boost of a week or two against a "Best of Carson" week or a week of guest hosts, Johnny's ratings would always spike when he returned and the competition would be crushed.

When Jay Leno took over *The Tonight Show*, ratings were an issue. He had competition. Arsenio Hall was well established but not much competition against Johnny. Arsenio was geared to a younger crowd. But when Jay came along, Arsenio and Jay were vying for the same younger audience. David Letterman may have lost the bid to succeed Johnny Carson on NBC, but CBS offered him a better deal to run against Jay. Eventually Arsenio bowed out of the late night race, but ratings numbers were now being taken every five minutes. This is one of the reasons why a late night guest rarely stays for more than two five-minute segments. Even if they are interesting and entertaining, they are moved out and the next guest, better or not, comes on. The remote control factor takes a role in the ratings ingredients. People click from show to show if a guest doesn't hold their interest. During the Carson years, remote controls were not a consideration. Most Carson viewers reveled in the fact that they liked to watch Johnny between their toes while they lay in bed. They weren't about to get up out of their comfortable place in bed to switch the channel.

When Jay took over *The Tonight Show* and was battling head-to-head with David Letterman, his producers watched Letterman to see what the competition was up to, which is the natural thing to do. But, instead of leading the race, we were mimicking the competition. David would do his monologue and comedy bits for the first half-hour of his show; Jay did the same. David was taking the camera out to the street to interview passers-by, a bit that Dave admittedly stole from the old *Steve Allen Show*. Jay developed "Jay Walking," where he would go out onto the streets of Los Angeles and talk to passers-by. It was even pointed out at a *Tonight Show* production meeting that Letterman had audience conductors—staff members waving the audience on during the opening applause when Dave came out. Jay's audience is told to stand up when Jay comes out, and a handful of hand-picked young people are asked to sit down front and come up to the edge of the stage to shake Jay's hand. Welcome to Hollywood.

One of the things that David Letterman did during sweeps weeks was take his show out to Los Angeles. Just as Carson did when his show was in New York, the jaunts to Los Angeles were a ratings booster. Naturally, NBC asked us to take the show out of town. Our first attempt was our trip to Boston.

We took the show to Boston for one broadcast when the NBC hit show *Cheers* went off the air. The show chartered a plane to Boston out of Burbank Airport. The entire plane was filled with the cast and crew of the show. As we taxied before take off, the flight crew gave the microphone to Jay and he comically did his own rendition of the safety procedures. We had to have a private jet so that we could fly into Boston, do the show, and fly back to Burbank in time to tape the show the next day.

We taped the show from inside the Bull & Finch, the actual bar that was used for the exterior shots on *Cheers*. It was undoubtedly the worst *Tonight Show* ever in the show's history. The *Cheers* cast was celebrating in the restaurant above the Bull & Finch in The Hampshire House, where they watched the last episode of their successful eleven-year run on NBC. There was much celebration going on all afternoon. We were going live to the East Coast and Central zone and on delay to the rest of the country. Our TV crew was crammed into this dinky little bar that resembled the décor of the bar set used on the TV series, but unlike the one on TV, this bar had a low ceiling and four walls much closer together than the set on *Cheers*.

Our guests were Ted Danson, George Wendt, Rhea Perlman, John Ratzenberger, Woody Harrelson and Kelsey Grammer. They all had had too much "cheer" during the afternoon and evening and were all giddy and childlike while Jay was trying to interview them. None of them could give him a straight answer. They also were shooting spitballs back and forth at each other, something they admitted doing to each other at rehearsals of *Cheers* from time to time. The show was an absolute disaster, which is a chance you take when it is done live.

The bar patrons that evening were the elite of Boston. A large contingent of Kennedys was there, and I was seated on a tabletop at one of the booths across from the bar. The young Senator from Massachusetts, John Kerry, was sharing a corner of that tabletop with me, and at one point he asked me, "Do you think this table is going to hold us?" I replied, "We're just going to have to hope so." During the show he continually asked me questions about the show, such as: what was I writing on my clipboard, what does that person do, etc. When the show ended, I had to scoot out the back door to get to a production meeting. As I got to the back door, there was a steep wooden ramp we all had to conquer in order to get down to the alleyway. I couldn't get past an elderly woman and her son, who was trying to get her down the ramp to her awaiting limousine. I offered to lend a hand on the woman's other side in an effort of chivalry—and so I could get by them quickly to get to my meeting. Halfway down the ramp I realized I was helping Joseph Kennedy and his mother, Ethel Kennedy, down to their car.

When Johnny Carson moved his show permanently from New York to beautiful downtown Burbank, the people of New York never forgave him. It was the same reaction they gave the Brooklyn Dodgers when they moved to Los Angeles. When it was announced that the new prince of late night was bringing the show back to New York (even though it was for just a visit), New York opened its arms to Jay. Of course, there was a lot of hype by the NBC press department and publicists. NBC paid for a giant billboard in the middle of Times Square announcing the return of *The Tonight Show* after a twenty-year exile. Jay was on every media outlet to talk about the return.

The media hype worked. The ratings soared. Being an ex-New Yorker, I was excited to see the show move to 30 Rockefeller Plaza for the week. I had always dreamed of having an office there someday, and for the week we were there, my dream came true.

One of the perks of doing the show from New York was that I was able to get a lot of my friends and family into the audience to see the show. My youngest sister Liz and her husband Tom Gardner were seen on camera to ask Iron Jay a question.

After our outing to Boston, the trip to New York was better planned. The publicity blitz worked to our advantage, and New York rolled out the red carpet for us. That week in New York was like the first week Jay took over Johnny's chair. It was terrific.

We used Studio 8H at NBC Studios in Rockefeller Plaza. I had been on the NBC tour so many times when I was a teenager, I knew my way around the hallways and back staircases. Unlike many years before, when I told an NBC page that my dad had an office upstairs and that he said it was okay for me to watch *The Tonight Show* rehearsal, now I was the one who had the office upstairs. It was my job to coordinate *The Tonight Show* rehearsals.

Studio 8H is where *Saturday Night Live* broadcasts its show and because it was the last week of May sweeps weeks, the *SNL* crew had wrapped up their season finale the Saturday before we arrived to do our week. Our set designer, Dennis Roof, designed a quick-changeover draped set that covered the SNL backdrops, so that the transition from Saturday night to Monday night could occur in a matter of hours.

Branford and the band had all day Sunday to get comfortable with the New York set. Branford also decided to enlarge the band for the week and doubled up the horn section with a couple of local

New York session players. Instead of the usual three horns (one trumpet, one trombone and Branford on saxes), we had two trumpets, two trombones and two saxes. The two trumpets were Sal Marquez and Chuck Findley, both from Los Angeles and both strong players. Branford was contemplating keeping both trumpeters and expanding the band. At rehearsal, the band was blaring through one of their charts and sounding good. I was standing out in front of the band near two NBC executives who had stopped in to check out the rehearsal. When the band finished a really kicking version of a Stevie Wonder tune, I heard one executive say to the other, "I like the look." That was the typical executive mentality toward music in television. They didn't hear the difference; they were only interested in two things: How does it look and how much is this going to cost?

These New York shows were loaded with top panelists and musical guests of the time. We had Madonna, James Taylor, Howard Stern, Spike Lee, Julio Iglesias, Mike Myers, Cindy Crawford, Farrah Fawcett and Kathy Lee Gifford and finished the week off with the Blue Man Group. It was a week of specials.

A sentimental favorite was a guest for veteran *Tonight Show* fans, the man who Johnny Carson replaced, Jack Paar. Paar was invited to be on the show because Johnny Carson had done a walk-on cameo appearance on Letterman's show when Letterman moved over to CBS.

Our announcer, Edd Hall, saw that I had a pocket camera with me and was clicking a few candid shots during rehearsal. Edd asked me to take a photo of him standing at the podium in the announcer booth. He said to me, "You'll get a kick out of this." The podium in the audio booth was a music stand not only used by *Saturday Night Live* announcer Don Pardo, but Arturo Toscanini also used it when he conducted the NBC Symphony in the 1940s. Those radio broadcasts were done from Studio 8H.

When we got back to Burbank after a successful week in New York, Jay told the NBC executives that he liked the way Studio 8H was laid out. He liked having the audience close to him and lit up so he could see them. At Studio 1 in Burbank where Johnny had performed the show since 1972 and Bob Hope had taped most of his NBC specials, the audience was in the dark behind the cameras. Jay taped his first two years in Studio 1 and moved across the hall to Studio 3 after NBC completely rebuilt the studio to Jay's liking, and that is where he continues to do the show today.

Letterman continued to take his show to Los Angeles and other cities, so we went to Las Vegas.

We broadcast the show for one week from the MGM Grand Hotel from a showroom called the Hollywood Theatre. It was a good size room, a little less than 750 seats. Studio 1 in Burbank holds about 500 people, but we would have no trouble filling the house in Las Vegas. The show was free.

My hotel room was near the showroom, but in order to get to the auditorium I needed to walk through the casino. If you've ever been to Vegas, you may have noticed how people walk through casinos. Or should I say, how they don't walk, they waddle. I call it the Vegas Waddle. They are not watching where they are going and they'll take one step to the left, then two steps to the right, and suddenly stop without warning. All the while they are carrying a cup full of coins looking for their lucky one-armed bandit. This Vegas Waddle was particularly frustrating to me because I was usually in a rush and needed to zip around the waddlers. To add to the madness, each time I traveled through the crowded casino, bells and sirens would be going off all around until I found refuge in my room or the showroom.

My wife, Cathy, did not come along with me on this trip, even though during the week in Vegas we would celebrate our thirteenth wedding anniversary. On the night of our anniversary I called her to wish her a happy anniversary. During our conversation she asked me if I was doing anything special to celebrate. I had turned in early that night, exhausted from working on the show all day, and was watching TV before getting some rest. She suggested I go out and gamble and pointed out it was our lucky thirteen. After our phone conversation, I got dressed and went out to the casino. I had heard from someone once, probably a casino owner, that the only way you win in Vegas is to bet big. So I got $500 in chips and went over to the roulette table. I'd never played roulette before in my life. I sat there and let one spin of the wheel go by without betting, and number 27 came up. I considered playing it safe with odd or even or black or red. But then, a little voice inside of me told me to put the chips on number 13. I placed a $100 chip dead center on 13. The casino man at the roulette table asked me if I wanted that to be straight up. I didn't know what that meant, but I coolly nodded yes. Most people put their chips on a line between two numbers or even on crossing lines so that they played four numbers with one chip.

From over my right shoulder I heard a sigh and turned to find an elderly couple standing there watching what I did. They smiled at me and nodded some encouragement as I told them it was my thirteenth wedding anniversary. I obviously was not paying attention to the wheel, because when I turned back to see how I did, the wheel had already been spun and the little white ball was sitting on number thirteen. The roulette man was pushing piles of chips in my direction. I asked him what happened and he told me I won. Playing the number straight up meant all $100 was on the number and that pays thirty-five to one.

I was shocked, embarrassed and elated all at the same time. I didn't know what to do. I had never won anything before, at least not this much. I felt guilty, so on the next spin I took another $100 chip and put it on four numbers and lost immediately. I quickly grabbed all of my chips and went over to the cashier's window and cashed in.

I had this euphoric feeling about me as I strolled through the casino. I only wish my wife could have been there with me to enjoy the excitement of it all. I thought how fun it was to win like that, but also thought, I won it so quickly I didn't get a chance to really gamble. I reached into my pocket and discovered four hundred dollars in chips there. They were the initial chips I bought prior to winning at roulette. I was going to go back and cash them in but thought I would experience some more gambling. So I sat down at a Black Jack table and started to play. After several hours of drinking, winning and losing, I eventually lost most of the four hundred, but I felt good about it. I turned in for the night with thirty-five hundred bucks in my pocket. I had found a way to celebrate my thirteenth wedding anniversary alone. For the rest of the week in Vegas I took that money and bought people drinks, paid for dinners and cab rides, and brought home an anniversary gift for my wife.

The rest of the week was filled with rehearsals and show preparation. The MGM Grand is so grand that it takes about twenty minutes to walk across the complex. Our production offices were at one end of the MGM and the showroom was at the other. I was one of a few people on the staff who had a cellular telephone. It sounds like this happened a million years ago, considering almost everyone has a cell phone today. Many of the segment producers asked to use my phone to call the other end of the complex. When we got back to Los Angeles, I submitted my phone bill to get reimbursed and NBC almost wasn't going to pay the bill. It was several hundred dollars due to roaming charges. NBC eventually paid, but only after I had several segment producers confirm that at times my phone was the only way to communicate with the rest of the staff.

We had a star-filled week of shows there. Some of our guests were Siegfried & Roy, Steve Lawrence and Edie Gorme, Phyllis Diller, Luther Vandross, Pattie LaBelle, Chaka Khan and Vince Gill. Each show was like a television special. The home viewers got to enjoy shows with out-of-the-ordinary *Tonight Show* guests in a way-out-of-the-ordinary setting, the glitz and glamour of Las Vegas.

Wayne Newton was scheduled to be one of the guests that week, and I had several telephone conversations with his music director, Greg Macaluso. Newton was appearing down the road at the Sands Hotel, and Greg invited me to come to his show. He added that if there was anyone I'd like to bring along, to do so. But most of the staffers at the Leno show were busy that evening.

I had always been curious to see Newton because of a story that Bill Cosby once told. Cosby said he was appearing in Vegas, and his nephew and a few of the young man's friends came to see the show. When they came backstage to thank him, Cosby asked them if they'd seen Wayne Newton's show yet. They looked at him, Cosby said, with sour looks on their faces and said, "Wayne Newton?" Cosby said, "Yeah, Wayne Newton! Tell you what! You guys go see Wayne Newton's show, and if you don't like it, I will pay the tab." The youngsters went off to Newton's show, and upon their return they all excitedly told Cosby: "Wayne Newton, yes!!!" So, I just had to see Wayne.

A few of my friends were in Vegas that week and also wanted to go, so Greg set up passes for all of us. The Sands Hotel was clearly one of the older casinos on the strip. Most all of the other hotels had rebuilt their lavish entrances. One had a fountain that erupted like a volcano every five minutes, complete with sound effects. Another had a pirate ship with live actors as pirates, shooting at one another until the ship exploded into two pieces and appeared to sink to the bottom of a man-made lake. The Sands had nothing like that. The showroom in which Newton was appearing looked more like a high school auditorium. There wasn't an actual stage; a stack of risers was assembled to simulate one. When we walked in the front door, the maitre d' escorted us all the way toward the front of the stage and sat us at Wayne Newton's table. He told us that Mrs. Newton would probably join us. We were quite impressed.

At that moment, silliness prevailed. As each woman in the vicinity was escorted to her respective table, we joked that she probably was Wayne's wife, no matter how old she was. The older they were, the funnier the game got. We had no idea what she looked like. I'm sure she was a model or actress type, but you never know.

Before we knew it, it was show time and, unfortunately, Mrs. Newton was a no-show. Suddenly the music rose to a fanfare and Wayne Newton burst upon the stage. He was huge. I mean he looked as if he was 6'5" or so (he's actually 6'2"). I couldn't help but notice his somewhat odd shape. His hips seemed to occur too high on his body, and his shoulders gave the impression of being as wide as the stage.

In his first number, he was smiling at all the old ladies (and indeed it was a room full of old ladies), and Wayne was kissing them, shaking their hands, kissing their hands, and winking at the ones he couldn't touch. He was working that room like a politician. Inside myself, I was laughing at him doing Elvis-like moves, throwing the microphone from hand to hand. Then I suddenly realized something. He wasn't imitating anyone else at all. Wayne was just being Wayne. It was that everyone else I've seen doing these kinds of things—they were doing Wayne Newton. Once I grasped that concept, I enjoyed the show much more.

Newton had a 15-piece band behind him, including a complete percussion section, horns, synthesizers and three back-up singers. It was quite impressive. The band played along with all of his gags and comedic pieces he did throughout the evening. Before the show was over, Wayne managed to play guitar, piano, trumpet, banjo, saxophone and every other instrument thrown his way. He left no stone unturned, pulling every entertainment schtick out of his collective bag of tricks. He had the audience in the palm of his hand from the moment he walked onto the stage. Wayne managed to make us laugh and cry several times during the show. Toward the end, when he introduced the band, he said that while almost all of the other shows in town have gone the route of prerecorded music, he insisted on having a live band.

Then he did the most unexpected thing. He began to introduce some prominent members of the audience to everyone and had them take a bow. One man was an author, another was an actor from an old TV show, and the third was, of all things, the music supervisor for the Jay Leno show. Yes, much to my amazement, he had me stand up and take a bow. I was near enough to the stage for Wayne to reach out and shake my hand. His grip was so strong that I thought he was going to pull me up onto the stage with him. I was honored and embarrassed and, of course, it impressed the hell out of my friends at the table.

We truly walked away from the Wayne Newton Show saying with excitement, "Wayne Newton, yes!!!"

The next night, Newton was a guest on the Leno show. I went over to Wayne at rehearsal and thanked him for the wonderful show the night before. Wayne said he hoped he didn't embarrass me by the introduction. I said, "Are you kidding? I'm a ham. You're lucky I didn't jump up on stage with you to finish out the closing song."

Surprisingly, toward the end of the week, our producers were scrounging around for a big finale. They didn't have one planned ahead of time. Our last minute production meetings were aimed at trying to come up with an ending. One or two NBC executives were running our production meetings. Bean counters and paper pushers were trying to be creative, and that could spell disaster.

We managed to create a parade of stars from the past week of guests along with a cavalcade of showgirls, circus performers and dancers on the Friday night finale of our week in Las Vegas.

Again, following David Letterman's lead, we planned another trip, supposedly to Chicago. Letterman had announced that he was going to try and take his show to each and every affiliate CBS station that carried his show. Eventually, he did us all one better. Instead of bringing the show to other cities, Letterman brought the townspeople to New York. It probably was cheaper to fly five hundred people to New York than to try to fly a camera crew and staff elsewhere in the country.

For one reason or another, the Chicago trip was not working out for us. The theater we wanted to use wasn't large enough or wasn't available when we needed it. Suddenly, it was announced that we were going back to New York during the November ratings sweeps. It was Thanksgiving week, which meant many of the staff and crew would be spending the holiday away from our families. I didn't mind because my parents and two sisters still lived in New York, and I could spend some of the time with them.

Our second trip to New York was a mistake. Unlike the first trip in May, we didn't have all the hype and excitement. Because the trip was hastily thrown together, it was not as well thought out as the prior trip. The New York media had just seen us in May, and here we were again five or six months later looking for attention. Instead we got a "Ho, hum" reaction, thus the ratings were "Ho, hum" as well. Even though we had a great lineup of guests including Barry Manilow, Celine Dion, Brooke Sheilds, Conan O'Brien and Bon Jovi, the ratings were not as impressive as when we visited the Big Apple in May.

We had the New York Jets and Giants football teams on, and I was in charge of teaching them how to sing Barry Manilow songs. Because Manilow was a guest on the show that night, the writers thought it would be funny to have the football team sing various Manilow hits going in and out of the commercials. We had a lot of laughs at rehearsal teaching these burly athletes to sing "Mandy" and "I Write the Songs."

One of the players on the Jets team was offensive lineman Jim Sweeney. I went over and introduced myself to him, and we compared family tree information to see if we were perhaps related to one another. He was a friendly guy with a good sense of humor, and if we would ever choose up sides, I would want him on my team. He must have been close to three hundred pounds, built like a bulldozer and had arms the size of my thighs.

At the end of that particular show, one of our stage managers, Roberta Savold, found me and said one of the football players was leaving and wanted to give me something. Jim Sweeney was out in the hallway near the elevators and was about to leave with the rest of the Jets. They had all changed into their street clothes, and Sweeney had his football jersey with him all rolled up in a ball. The team had worn their warm-up jerseys on the show. Each one was kelly green with white numbers and had the player's last name lettered across the back. It was soaking wet, for which he apologized as he handed it to me. "Here ya go," he said, "thought you might want this as a souvenir." It was so cool for him to do that for me. I still have that jersey and wear it once or twice a year for Super Bowl Sunday and St. Patrick's Day. It turned out that he didn't need it any longer anyway. Two or three days after Sweeney gave me the shirt, it was announced that he was leaving the Jets and being traded to the Pittsburgh Steelers.

Another one of the New York shows had a group of teenage hip-hoppers called the Knick City Dancers. They rehearsed the kids early in the morning and needed *Tonight Show* drummer Jeff "Tain" Watts to play a hip hop beat for them to dance to. Even though I told Tain about the early call the night before and left a morning wake-up call for him at the hotel, he was still a no-show at the early rehearsal. We called his hotel room several times with no answer. Our hotel was several blocks away from the NBC Studios, so we sent a runner to go bang on his hotel room door. I asked our director, Ellen Brown, if I could give it a try. I reminded Ellen that I was a drummer also, and she asked me to play for the young dancers.

I climbed up behind Tain's drums and asked the teenagers what tempo they needed. I could tell by the looks on their faces that they were thinking, "Who is this old guy and does he even know what hip hop is?" I proceeded to kick off a beat and soon the doubting teens were dancing their routine to the beat of this 41 year-old Irishman drummer. Eventually Jeff Watts made it over to rehearsal and took over where I left off. As I jumped down from the drums, the youngsters all thanked me for filling in. Somehow I felt like a dinosaur.

When we returned to Los Angeles, the producers decided we were not going to go back to New York anymore. They were blaming the poor ratings on New York rather than the fact that the NBC executives made a hasty decision. That put an end to *The Tonight Show* road trips for a while.

It was a sex scandal that turned the ratings race completely around between Jay and David in the summer of 1995 when Jay's guest was Hugh Grant. Grant was arrested for having sex in his car with a prostitute in Hollywood. The week that Hugh Grant's arrest became news all over the world, he was scheduled to appear on Jay's show. Despite his arrest, Hugh Grant kept his appointment to appear on Jay's show for a chance to apologize to his fans and his girl-friend, actress/model Elizabeth Hurley.

Hugh Grant saved his own career, and Jay's ratings went through the roof that night. He never had to look back on Letterman's ratings since that night, although after more than thirteen years, the ratings are closer, with Letterman sometimes ahead.

I had a three-year contract with NBC Productions that ran out shortly after Branford Marsalis made his exodus from the show. When it came time for contract renewal, my option was not renewed. It was no surprise to me when it happened. I was just saddened that my twenty-year career with *The Tonight Show* was suddenly over because of a change in command.

A few days after I left the show, I called Jay's assistant, Helga, to obtain a letter of recommendation from Jay. I already had letters from Supervising Producer Patti Grant, Line Producer Larry Goitia, West Coast Vice President Rick Ludwin and, best of all, a letter from Johnny Carson. All of these letters simply explained that I was an excellent employee and a hard worker. All I needed was a decent letter of the same sort from Jay Leno. Suddenly it was as if I was asking for a loan or a piece of scenery from the set. Helga told me that NBC would not let Jay sign anything without their approval. I explained it was simply a letter of recommendation, which should be common practice when an employee leaves a job. I wasn't asking for anything flowery or laudatory, just a simple: "He worked here, we liked him, we wish him luck." That's all. She said she would get back to me.

Two or three days later, I called Helga to see what was happening with the letter. She faxed me a copy of what NBC had approved Jay to sign and said that Jay was very sorry that they would not let him say anything more.

The letter read:

This is to confirm that Don Sweeney was employed as a music supervisor by our production of The Tonight Show for a period of over three years. During this time I have known him to be professional with pleasant manners and I wish him well in his future endeavors.

Sincerely, Jay Leno.

I told Helga that it was all I needed and it would be fine. She continued to try to explain how Jay wanted to do more, but couldn't. She said she would mail me a hard copy.

Later that day, I received a call from Jay Leno. He was very apologetic to me and expressed how he wanted the letter to say more to help me, but that NBC was his boss and he had to follow their orders. However, he said to me, "Tell you what I can do for you. If you are up for a job and the position is between you and someone else, if a call from me will cinch the job for you, I'll make the call." I was flattered that Jay would extend me such an offer. He certainly had bailed me out before and this was very nice of him.

I later hesitated to use Jay's offer for a few reasons. I wanted to ask for Jay's help only when the job was a position that I really had my heart set on getting. I hesitated calling Jay for fear that he might back down from the offer due to the long period of time that had passed since he made it.

When I tried to get the job of music supervisor for the *Howie Mandel Show*, it was the right time and job to ask Jay to make the call. I knew that Jay and Howie were friends from the '70s when they both were just starting out as stand-up comics. I had been told by the executive in charge of the *Howie Mandel Show*, Jeff Kopp, that Howie was "obsessed with this Johnny Carson thing." Howie was to tape his show from NBC Studios in Studio 1, which was the same studio that Johnny Carson had taped his show in for twenty years. If I got this job, I would be sitting in the same greenroom I sat in for sixteen and a half years when I worked for Johnny. Just the fact that I worked for Johnny Carson would be reason for Howie Mandel to want me to work for his show. A boost from a telephone call by Jay would put me into the job. After I exhausted all efforts to get the job on my own, I called Jay.

I called Jay early in the day and got his answering machine. Later that day, instead of getting a call from Jay, I got a call from Howie Mandel's bandleader, Steve (Goldy) Goldstein. Jeff Kopp had recommended me to him, and Goldy called me to set up a meeting. "Jeff says you are the man for the job," said Goldy, and I was hired a few days later.

The next day, after thinking that Jay had left me in the lurch, I got a call from him. He said he got my message and asked whom I wanted him to call. I told him what had happened and thanked him for getting back to me. I explained that I did not need him to make the call. I got the job on the *Howie Mandel Show* on my own. It was great that Jay took the time to call me back.

7

Branford Marsalis and the Tonight Show Band

As a drummer, I always aspired to play drums on *The Tonight Show*. Thoughts of tying Ed Shaughnessy up in a back room and pretending not to know where he was had crossed my mind from time to time.

When I first toured with Doc Severinsen's road show as a roadie, I got the chance to sit in. We were at Harrah's in Lake Tahoe and Shaughnessy was flying in separately from the rest of the group, and we heard that Ed had gotten snowed in somewhere in Colorado doing one of his drum clinics. We were told he was not going to make the gig. There wasn't enough time to fly someone in from Los Angeles, so Doc asked the band during soundcheck if anyone knew of any drummers in the Reno or Lake Tahoe area. None of them were coming up with anyone, so I stepped up to the plate. I asked Doc if I could have a shot at it. After all, I was a student of Ed Shaughnessy's and had heard the show often enough. Although I could sight read, I could play it without reading the parts. Doc gave me the chance, and I didn't have to tie anyone up in a back room to do it. I jumped into position behind Ed's drums. His set was monstrous with two bass drums, a row of tom toms and cymbals almost out of my reach. I made a few adjustments to the set moments before Doc kicked off the first tune.

The drum charts were no help to me. They had been scribbled on many times, were stained with everything from water to beer, and were dog-eared and torn. Some of the parts were missing pages, and I basically had to play by ear. Doc's bassist, John B. Williams, turned himself toward me and talked me through the tunes. I knew where to stop and where to change the feel, but it was helpful to have John leading me through the show. I guess I was doing okay, because Doc kept calling out other tunes until we pretty much ran through the whole show. At one point Doc said to me, "Well, Don, it looks like you're going to have to get us through the show tonight."

I certainly didn't want to take the gig away from Shaughnessy, but it would really look good on my resumé if I could play this show with Doc. Everyone in the band was supportive. One of the singers was even going to lend me one of his extra outfits to wear. The band and the singers all wore blue denim jeans with matching vests and white collared shirts. This was the mid-seventies; they could have been polyester suits. Doc wanted to go over one more song before we took a break before the show. As we started to play, I felt my heart melt and my dream fade away as I saw the door in the rear of the showroom open and Ed Shaughnessy walk in. Obviously he was able to get a flight out of Denver despite the snowstorm.

I stepped down from the drum set as Ed took the throne. I took a seat near the edge of the stage and sat there numb. When rehearsal was over, Doc came over to me and thanked me for filling in until Ed arrived. It was a thrill to play along with the big guys, even if it was only for rehearsal, and it meant a lot to me that Doc acknowledged my effort.

In contrast with that moment, the next time I sat in with the Tonight Show Band, it was a whole new cast of characters.

Branford and his Tonight Show Band differed a lot from Doc's band. Doc's band consisted of seasoned session players. They were "studio musicians," meaning that they were musical guns for hire. If you needed good sight-readers and great soloists, you'd hire a bunch of the best "studio musicians" that you could find to get the job done. Doc's band was a mix of studio players, hot soloists and tremendous sight-readers. These guys would read anything you threw in front of them. The expression, "they could read flies on fly paper," was true of them. I got the feeling that when I was talking to one of the members in Doc's band, they were picturing what we were saying in musical terms of notes and beats.

Branford's band lived, slept and ate music. They were jazz players, used to traveling around the world playing in small clubs and large clubs, even arenas, but playing the music they wanted to play, not music that someone else wanted them to play. Not all of them were sight-readers. They grew up playing in jam sessions and creating music in their heads. There is another expression: "I'm into jazz for the money." Playing in jazz clubs is a tough way to earn a living. So, when Branford asked them to come with him and play on television, it was the high salaries that lured them into it, not the music.

Branford eventually felt he was tricked into leading a band on television. He was told that he would be able to play whatever music he wanted as bandleader of *The Tonight Show*. "Even jazz?" Branford asked. "Whatever you want to do," was the response he got from the show's producers.

In the early days of Jay's *Tonight Show*, Branford played a little John Coltrane and a little Thelonius Monk and he would mix it up with "The Maple Leaf Rag" or an instrumental version of something he did with Sting. About a week into the new *Tonight Show*, I got a phone call from Henry Mancini, who asked me to pass the word on to Branford and the band about what a great job he felt they were doing. Mancini added that it was great for the younger people watching the show to be exposed to some of the jazz classics they were playing. Several other prominent people in the music world welcomed the new sound to *The Tonight Show*. Each time they complimented Branford's band, they would always add that there was certainly nothing wrong with Doc Severinsen's Tonight Show Band, but they were happy to see that music was still the dominant factor in *The Tonight Show* equation.

Unfortunately, when NBC fired executive producer Helen Kushnick from the show, the music changed as well. Branford was asked to play music that the average viewer could relate to. Branford translated that into having to play tunes by current artists and pop tunes from the '70s and '80s. He tried to have some fun with it by playing some of the tunes that he and the other band members grew up listening to, such as Jimi Hendrix, Led Zeppelin and James Brown. It didn't take long for Branford to grow tired of it.

Some of the other band members did not care to be playing television music either, but the money was so good, they put up with it.

Two of the band members, keyboardist Kenny Kirkland and drummer Jeff "Tain" Watts, were continually wandering off from rehearsal. Both of them smoked cigarettes and smoking inside of enclosed structures was no longer allowed, so they would step outside for a smoke. The problem was, they never just stepped outside. Sometimes they would hop in their cars and drive off the NBC lot.

Rehearsals for comedy skits usually involved the band for a music playon or playoff. The trouble was that Jay and his writers would spend quite a bit of time rewriting skits on stage. Some of the simplest of bits would take all afternoon. I would have the band ready to play on the bandstand, as requested by our director, Ellen Brown. The band would get bored waiting around and sitting there with their instruments in hand. The natural thing for them to do was eventually start jamming on a funky lick or familiar tune. I would soon get the signal from the director or writers to have the band stop. "We're trying to concentrate over here," they'd say. I didn't dare release the band for a break. On too many occasions I would have them take a ten, and as soon as they all were out of sight, the director would turn to me and say, "Now, where is the band? We're ready." I would have to run all over the NBC complex to round up the troops. Sometimes trying to keep up with them was like trying to balance marbles on a basketball.

At the production meeting before we were to embark on our mission to Vegas, the subject of the importance of catching an early Sunday morning flight out of Burbank Airport came up. Executive producer Debbie Vickers said, "How are we going to get the band members on a six a.m. plane? Kenny and Tain will never make it." Then she looked down the long table and pointed to me. "Don," she said, "You're the music supervisor. It's your responsibility to get them to the plane." As she said that, everyone protested that she not put that burden on me. They felt it was unfair. I came back with a simple plan. I said to Debbie, "Okay, I will get them on that flight, but I want a stretch limousine to pick me up at my house at four in the morning." I got my stretch limo. I should have put money on it; the odds were against me.

I went to Kenny and Tain and asked them not to go to sleep Saturday night. I had been out late with them before whenever they played in a jazz club in the L.A. area. They were true night owls. I said, "Stay out late and do whatever you want, but don't fall asleep. I will pick you both up at your house at five in the morning. When we get to Vegas, you'll have the whole day to sleep, because soundcheck isn't until seven that evening. You can block out the sunlight in your rooms when you get there."

Jeff and Kenny lived next door to one another in a duplex in the Fairfax District in Hollywood. It was only one stop to pick up both of them. Like clockwork, the driver picked me up in the dark of the morning hours at my house in the San Fernando Valley. I was in front of Jeff and Kenny's place just before five. All of us dozed on the way to the airport, but we made the flight.

When I attended the next production meeting in Las Vegas, Debbie Vickers congratulated me on getting them to the plane on time. "How did you do that?" she asked. "That's my secret," I said, and I never told her how I got it done.

Eventually, Kenny and Tain's tardiness would catch up with them.

In our first few weeks working together, Branford and the band were rehearsing with Angelique Kidjo. She was a well-known singer from Africa and a good friend of Branford's. That was one of the advantages of having Branford on the show. He had a lot of connections with performers who were not the usual talk show guests. He would invite them to either sit in with the band for the evening or have them come on as a featured guest. Angelique was one of those guests.

In the middle of rehearsal, Branford asked me to try and get a percussionist as soon as possible. I started calling every percussionist I knew, but at 3:00 in the afternoon, most musicians were not home, and all I got were answering machines. At one point I asked Branford, "What instrument do we need the percussionist to play?" Branford said he needed them to play a triangle. "Hello," I said, "I think I could handle that. I'm a drummer, remember?" Branford said, "You're right. I forgot." Moments later I was playing the triangle with the band.

I always get a laugh when I look back on that clip of me playing the triangle. The song Kidjo was performing, "Batonga," started out with a four bar intro of a triangle solo. The song was sung in the native tongue of Taal, which has many clicking and popping sounds in it, making it exotic to many of us. Director Ellen Brown started with a close-up of my hands and the triangle, and by the end of the four-bar solo, the camera shot widened out to show the entire band. There I was, this pink skinned white guy among a predominantly African American band. I am sure the viewers at home were wondering, "Who was that white guy?"

One day, I walked into Branford's dressing room to find him lying face down on the floor with the lights dimmed. At first I thought he was experiencing a migraine headache or something. As I stood there and asked if there was anything I could do for him, he said, "Shoot me." He moaned, "How did Doc Severinsen do this for thirty years?" I told him that he and Doc were coming from opposite ends of the rainbow. Doc, at one time, was one of the trumpet players in the brass section. I am sure he felt it was a step up to one day be the bandleader. Branford comes from a prominent family in jazz with his brother, Wynton, and his father, Ellis. All of Branford's siblings are enraptured with jazz. For Branford, he felt it was a step down to go from the jazz world into television. I am sure he was being pressured by his family to get out of television and get back to playing real music. He wanted out of his contract with NBC.

Branford managed to find a way to get out of the show and announced that he would be leaving in January 1995. It was also announced that Kevin Eubanks was going to succeed him. They could have switched out the entire band and replaced them with eager studio "session players" who would have been totally happy working for scale and playing anything that was thrown in front of them.

For the remaining weeks of Branford's contract, things went on as usual. This means that Kenny and Jeff were still wandering off whenever they felt like it, and some members continually complained about having to play hokey music for the comedy skits. They thought it was beneath them. Can you believe that some band members actually had the nerve to tell Jay that a skit or a joke wasn't funny? You can imagine how they would have reacted if Jay had told them how to play their instruments. Others in the band quietly did their jobs and were happy to be there.

One particular day, we needed to start exactly at 5:30 p.m., because we had a satellite feed and a lot of technical reasons for being punctual. It also was expensive if we were five or ten minutes off schedule. In the Johnny Carson days, we always started on time every single night unless there was a technical problem, which was extremely rare. Jay's show hardly ever started on time. They needed more time to work on the monologue or the audience load-in needed more time for security checks. We were always bumping the start time, but not this day.

At warm-up time, Kenny and Tain were nowhere to be found. I frantically looked in all the usual hiding places. Every two or three minutes I would report back to Branford, who was now on stage ready to play the warm-up number for the studio audience. Using sign language, I signaled from the sidelines that I couldn't find Kirkland or Watts. Each time, Branford would signal back for me to look in the rehearsal room, or the dressing room, or in make-up, or in the commissary, and each time I came back empty-handed.

I could hear our stage manager, Mike Schiff, telling Branford we had to start the show without them. From my point of view backstage, I could see Vicki Randle on her conga drums and hear Branford asking her to get on Tain's drums. Vicki looked over at me and motioned for me to jump up on the drums. "Fifteen seconds," the stage manager shouted. I jumped into position at the drums. I had never played on Tain's drums before. Playing on another drummer's drum kit is like bowling in high heels. I was trying to find a matching pair of drumsticks and heard Mike Schiff telling the production booth that we were ready to go, "Sweeney's on drums, so we're okay to go," he said. I'm glad Mike had more faith in me than I did. Trumpeter Chuck Findley and trombonist Matt Finders said to me that I was the one to count it off. Vicki on my other side tells me, "It's in four," just as I heard Mike Schiff say, "Here we go, in five, four . . ." This was much different than sitting in for Shaughnessy twenty years ago. In three seconds I was going out into millions of homes in America. While I am known to be the one who jumps into the pool before checking to see if it has any water in it, this was more like walking off the gang-plank blindfolded. I just counted ". . . three, four," and started mimicking what I had heard Tain play every night for the past three and a half years. With all the excitement, applause and bright lights, I don't know what I played, but it worked. It wasn't until the third or fourth joke into Jay's monologue that Branford looked up and saw me on the drums. He pointed and laughed quietly. I guess it was a good thing that he didn't notice it was me until after I played.

Somewhere within Jay's monologue, Kenny and Tain showed up and I slithered off to my office to watch the rest of the show. I continued to get high fives from staff and crew for the rest of the night, but the next day, Kenny and Tain's days were numbered. Because of this important, expensive satellite feed, there were a few executives in the director's booth that night, and they witnessed this whole fiasco.

They asked if this sort of thing went on regularly. The producers had taken all they could take with their tardiness and didn't try to make excuses for them. The executives gave the order to let them go.

Kenny and Tain explained to me after the show that they were down the road having some barbecue chicken and ribs. When they looked at their watches, they knew it was time to get back to the show, but they said, "You know how we never start on time . . ." They figured they had another ten or fifteen minutes before anyone would be looking for them. They just didn't know about the satellite feed.

Speaking of chicken, I was told to drop the ball on Kenny and Tain. I was the music supervisor for the show, but I didn't hire the Tonight Show Band. Why was I the one to go and give them the bad news? Because executives get paid big money to find ways to get other people to do their dirty work for them.

I walked into Kenny and Tain's dressing room. They could tell by the look on my face why I was there. Kenny said, "Aw, man, they sent you to give us the bad news?" Tain agreed, "That ain't right." I actually had developed a good relationship with the two of them over the years. Even with all the cat and mouse games that went on, I still enjoyed working with them. They knew they were getting the axe.

As we sat there talking about what had happened to make them late, we had a good laugh over how none of this would have happened if the service had been better at the rib joint. Kenny said, "It's just as well that we leave the show with Branford." They both explained how they joined the show to play with Branford because he said it would be fun, and it was. But they didn't want to stay if it meant that Branford was not going to be there. They took the bad news with a grain of salt, but they knew they would have left anyway when Branford announced he was departing.

A couple of weeks later we had a farewell party for Branford at B.B. King's Blues Club and Grill at Universal City Walk. We had a private terrace on the third level of the club above the stage. The entire staff was there for a wonderful send-off. I had edited a video for Branford as a farewell keepsake that we viewed toward the end of the party. It was a compilation of all the musical acts that Branford had reluctantly played over the years. I also popped in a few of the comedy sketches that included Branford and the band. We all had a big laugh over it and at the end of the clips, the video slide read "Branford, we're gonna miss you . . ." and the slide faded to another that read, ". . . don't leave us here!"

I had developed a good relationship with Branford in the short time we worked together. I never felt he was my boss; I felt like we were school buddies just doing the best we could to get the job done. We had a running gag going over the years when he would correct me about something like a song title or quote from someone. I'd say, "I hate it when you're right." And he always was right, not because he was my boss; he is just a very smart person. His genius extends far beyond his musical wisdom. We have remained good friends over the years since then, and even though we don't see each other as much, we call and write e-mails, and I go hear him play whenever he is in the Los Angeles area. But I truly miss working with him.

Shortly after Branford left the show, my contract was not renewed. During the Carson years I never had a contract. We never had to think about the thirteen-week cycle. Television shows are renewed in thirteen-week cycles. At the end of each cycle a show is told that the network is keeping you for another cycle, or, this is your last thirteen weeks. My contract was up and it was time to go. My blood pressure was taking a beating. I would get so upset that simple things took so much work to do. It took so much time and effort to accomplish the simplest of tasks, it would make my blood boil.

On my last day at *The Tonight Show*, Charo was a guest for a skit. I stopped by her dressing room to tell her it was my final day. When I knocked on her dressing room door, she said to come in. As I opened the door, Charo was sitting at the make-up table in her underwear. As soon as I saw this, I told her I could come back later. "Come in," she said, "It's nothing you haven't seen before." So, I came in and took a seat at the opposite end of the room. We joked about the old days with *Chico & the Man*. She told me how much she missed the Johnny Carson days with Doc and Ed. A few minutes into our conversation, the door opened and in stepped a tall handsome Scandinavian man. Charo introduced him to me. He was her husband, Kjel. As innocent as I knew I was, I still began to perspire. Her husband laughed at my uncomfortable nature and joked how Charo had no shame.

It was nice for me to spend part of my last day with someone as uplifting and light-hearted as Charo.

After nearly twenty years at NBC, I was dodging bullets for the last three years and was asked to leave because of a change in band-leaders. But, like Kenny and Tain, who came to work with Branford, I came to work at *The Tonight Show* because I wanted to work with Johnny Carson. I like Jay Leno, but he's no Johnny Carson. Johnny was a tough act to follow.

8

That's a Wrap!

In the early '70s I was invited to a party at the home of astronaut Buzz Aldrin. His son, Andrew, was a friend of a friend of mine, and he was having a jam session in the recreation room at his house while his parents were out for the evening.

At one point during the party, my friend Nancy and I sat in Buzz Aldrin's living room, leafing through a scrapbook filled with photos of Buzz and the other astronauts, Neil Armstrong and Michael Collins, from the Apollo 11 mission to the moon. They later embarked on a goodwill world tour, and this scrapbook was filled with photos from that journey. As we looked at a photo of natives standing by the side of a road in Kenya, Nancy pointed out to me how odd life is sometimes. They obviously waited for hours for the motorcade to pass them by, possibly not knowing who these men were, but knowing they were important. And then, here we were sitting in Buzz Aldrin's living room looking at his photo album like it was someone's vacation photos.

There have been many articles and books written about the difficulty Buzz had in living with the idea that he was one of the first human beings to walk on the moon. There was a blow-up poster on the wall in the recroom where the jam session was, that showed the front page of *The New York Daily News* with a photo of Buzz standing on the surface of the moon. The headline on the poster read "BIG DEAL!" Buzz had trained most of his adult life to become an astronaut, and the utmost for any astronaut of that time was to be one of the men chosen to go to the moon. At thirty-nine he had reached his life-long goal and felt he had no place to go.

Twenty years after seeing this poster, I could relate to Buzz's dilemma. I had spent a good deal of my adult life achieving my ultimate goal. When Johnny Carson retired, I didn't know where to go from there.

I had been to the moon and back and was left spinning in the parking lot of life, not knowing what to do. The headline on my *New York Daily News* would read, "WHAT NOW?"

Luckily I remained with the Jay Leno *Tonight Show* for a few years, which was not one of my goals, but managed to feed my appetite for working in television. I became a bit player in many of the Leno skits during the O. J. Simpson trial. I was one of the jurors. I wasn't about to tell the writers that there weren't any forty year old, red-headed Irishmen on the real Simpson jury. I was having too much fun.

During the week after Johnny's retirement, I was knee deep in helping to get the new *Tonight Show* off the ground. While running from a rehearsal hall to the studio I crossed paths with the former producer of *The Tonight Show*, Jeff Sotzing. Jeff stopped me and told me I might want to see what was happening in the midway.

The midway was the area between the studios and the executive offices of NBC, where the celebrities and V.I.P.s parked their cars. The parking spot closest to the studio used to have a sign on it that read "JOHNNY CARSON." Johnny had parked his car there every day since moving the show out from New York in 1972. The sign now read "JAY LENO." But that wasn't what Jeff wanted me to see. In the center lane of the midway, there was a large stake truck filled with scenery, which was not an unusual sight to see around Burbank and Hollywood. However, the scenery stacked into the back of this truck was that of Johnny Carson's show.

The teal blue dormer with Art Deco archways that framed the painted valley view for Johnny's familiar backdrop was folded to look like giant books tied together on the back of the truck. The rarely used gate from the midway that led directly out to Alameda Avenue was rolled back to make an easy getaway for this truckload of precious cargo.

I felt a chill of sadness come over me, as if I was witnessing a close friend get evicted from his home. Jeff and I stood there in silence as the truck revved its engine and slowly rumbled through the postern.

When it was completely out of sight and the sound of the truck engine had faded, I asked Jeff where they were taking it. He simply said it was going into storage at a warehouse but we all knew that the desk and the chair belonged in the Smithsonian in Washington, D.C. It would be in good company along with the *60 Minutes* stopwatch, the *Howdy Doody Show* puppet and Dorothy's ruby slippers.

After twenty years of working on *The Tonight Show*, I can now look back and see a lot of happy times and fond memories. There were a few bumps in the road, a few people to stay away from, but all in all, I was very lucky. I had so many people to look up to. How many people get to meet their idols? How many people get to work with their idols?

Four or five times a year the other idol of my life, Buddy Rich, would come by and entertain us with a raging drum solo. I was able to develop a relationship with him where I was no longer just another fan showing up at any Los Angeles area appearances he'd make. I was the kid from *The Tonight Show*. Buddy got to know my name, trade drum stories with me and invite me to some of his concerts when he was in town. What are the chances of me getting to know and work with two of my childhood idols?

I met quite an array of characters along the yellow brick road. We all know that the yellow brick road wasn't yellow and it wasn't even brick. This was Hollywood. It wasn't even really Hollywood; it was downtown Burbank. Everything in show business is held together with duct tape and glue. Everything is an illusion and make-believe. It's only natural that some of the people connected with the entertainment industry would be phony and plastic, but most of the people I remember were not that way.

I got to listen to the great Tonight Show Band every day. I was able to hire many of those same players to play in my own band and play some of the Tonight Show Band charts. I met Johnny Carson's son Cory and built a friendship with him that continues today.

I got to work with the greats of our business: Red Skelton, Tony Bennett, Bob Hope, Frank Sinatra, Sammy Davis, Jr., and Ray Charles. I met people such as Charlton Heston, Stevie Wonder, Charo, Jimmy Stewart, Dizzy Gillespie, Bob Newhart, Don Rickles, Bo Derek, Pete Fountain, Benny Goodman, Steve Allen, Rodney Dangerfield, Kenny Rogers, Raquel Welch, Olivia Newton-John, Steve Lawrence and Edie Gorme, Liberace, George Burns and . . . the list could go on for several pages.

Every day that I came in to work, there would be something to laugh about. Funny people, both on and off camera, surrounded me. Imagine a job where every day there is something to laugh at.

Nowadays I keep setting new goals for myself. Although these goals don't seem to measure up to working on *The Tonight Show*, they keep me going. I've learned to realize that the moon isn't as far away as I used to think. I just might have to go there someday to see if it compares.

Appendix

What the Al Pined

or

Oh C'mon, Did He Really Say That?!

The much loved and respected contractor Al Lapin was with NBC long before television. He was a drummer and a contractor in New York for many Broadway shows and lived to the ripe old age of 97. Al worked in radio, television, live theater, motion pictures and recordings.

Over his many years in show business, his mispronunciation of words may have been from his wearing of hearing aids. Comedian Norm Crosby used to ask me for the latest "Lapinisms," as we called them. I think Norm used some of Al's expressions in his act.

Musicians from all aspects of the industry compiled a list of Al's malaprops. This list has been photocopied and passed among session players for years. Much like lists compiled of expressions and mispronunciations performed by bandleader Lawrence Welk and conductor Eugene Ormandy, it is with respect and admiration for Al Lapin that this list was compiled. Although you might not know all of the people mentioned in the list, I hope you can still enjoy the humor.

1. "This situation is abdominal."
2. "The fire marshal might unconsciously come in."
3. "My bookkeeping problems are surmountable."
4. "I know a guy in Las Vegas who's a persecuting attorney."
5. "There goes another Masonic boom."
6. "That's water over the bridge."

7. Al was discussing Dean Martin's TV show cancellation and said, "Dean Martin suffered from over-expulsion."
8. "That's your provocative."
9. "You look extinguished."
10. "There's lots of stealage around here."
11. "In the finalysis . . ."
12. "He needs that like he needs a hole in his ass."
13. "The Union's doing an admiral job."
14. "This is a real dilemon."
15. "The three toughest parts of the restaurant business are spoilage, spillage and stealage."
16. "I need your W-4 number." (meaning your social security number)
17. "The leader from the Mac Davis Show is here today and I've told him about you guys, so tighten your shoes."
18. "I want you guys to move out of here smartly."(meaning fast)
19. "Are there anymore dubious checks?"
20. "That Mac—he's a real Bon Voyant."
21. "Put your nose to the grind wheel."
22. "Get that guy Lorenzo Alameda." (Lorenzo Lamas)
23. "The object of negotiation is to beat your component."
24. "If any of you guys don't like it here, I'd be glad to take your reservation."
25. "I flew back to New York on a TWA Consolation."
26. "Which one of you woodwind players left his contrary bass clarinet here?"
27. Violins were cut from 8 men to 4 on the Dean Martin Show. A violin player said, "Gee, Al, looks like we got a string quartet." Al answered, "Oh no, it's two violins and two violas."
28. "You really got us off the red carpet."
29. "That's not my bag of tea."
30. "I didn't want to give him apple-plexy."
31. "There's a brassiere in every back yard in Beverly Hills."
32. "Look for the trumpet part on 'Gentleman on My Mind.'"
33. "A bird in the hand is worth two around the corner."
34. "The stands and chairs and the ampleboxes are set up."
35. "The guy made a double out."

36. "This argument is open for debation."
37. "There is so much allergy in my pool."
38. "You'd better put a stoppage on that check."
39. "I got Bill Mays to come and play sympathizer."
40. "That remark is a double rotunda."
41. "We need a metrotone."
42. "My son is in St. Louis Obispo."(San Luis Obispo)
43. "That's the pimple on the watermelon."(frosting on the cake)
44. "That's Marcel Mazoo."(Marcel Marceau)
45. Referred to cartage as "drayage."
46. "His parents had a bad time. They shoved him around from pillar to post."
47. "I don't have any faith in that Transatlantic Medication." (Transcendental Meditation)
48. "You'd better look out. You're bruisin' a cruisin'." (cruisin' for a bruisin')
49. "You've got time for two margaritas."
50. "It's hard getting a bass player. It's busier than a hen's chicken."
51. "I knew Tommy Dorsey when he played trombone."
52. "Well, nobody's human."
53. Doc was co-hosting a telethon and Al told him, "You won't be able to play in the little group, you'll be MCA-ing." (emceeing)
54. "I take my car to the washmobile."
55. Al once told John Audino, "You ought to go eat at the Sally Rand Restaurant." (Tally Rand Restaurant)
56. "I have my pay stub from last year and it shows that I got double scale last Labor Day." Al thought for a moment and replied, "Don't tell 'em." "If they find out, they might make you give it back."
57. Al called *Tonight Show* director Bob Ostberg, "Bob Ostrich."
58. Al referred to Pete and Conte Candoli as "The Brothers Conti."
59. About Doc being angry. "Doc hit the Fan."
60. "Let's put the table right on the floor." (cards on the table)
62. "That 'Fingers' Carlisle can really play." ("Thumbs" Carlisle)
63. "Aaron Levine (New York contractor) sits in his two by nothing office."
64. "Watching the ocean is like mental telepathy." (therapy)

65. "Call that producer anytime. Call him until you're black in the face."
66. "Gil, I know you. You know that two and three make four."
67. He once went into the hospital for tests. He found out that his blood wasn't "coragullating."
68. The bass player didn't know whether to play acoustic or electric bass. Al told him to use his own "discrepancy."
69. "But before I leave we'll say hello."
70. The power went out in Al's house. He said, "I'll have to shop around for some frozen ice."
71. Al was talking to Nick Ceroli about Merv Griffin's financial status. "Merv doesn't have to take a back seat from Sinatra."
72. "The payroll department was so busy, I was hamstrung."
73. A leader asked Al to get trumpet player Al Vizzutti. Vizzuti's service told Al that Vizzutti was out with Chick Corea. When the leader asked why Vizzutti couldn't make the gig, Al said, "He's out with some chick in Korea."
74. Al to Don Ashworth, "You and Maurie Harris would give aspirin a headache."
75. "I don't mind my milk spoiling, but when my cream spoils . . ."
76. Referred to the Sisters Sledge as the "Sledge Sisters."
77. Referring to "top notch" players, he said, "When you can get those kind of players, you're really scraping the top of the barrel."
78. Don Sweeney told Al that they needed Bob Bain to accompany opera singer Beverly Sills center stage on *The Tonight Show*. Al said, "So, what you are telling me is, she and Bobby are going to do the song Acapulco."
79. "Les Brown is as fickle as a two dollar bill."
80. The solution to the gas shortage: "Keep your gas tank full."
81. "Wait! Let's not put the cart before the buggy."
82. "He was so tired he fell off his feet."
83. About smoking: "You are a chronicle smoker."
84. "A man of your statue."
85. "I'm getting a plate of soup."
86. "Stagnate the violins." (stagger)
87. "A great idea just went over my head."

88. "Norman's Clabertacle Choir." (Mormon Tabernacle Choir)
89. "Those insurance companies are an evil necessary."
90. "My wife has this crucifying pain."
91. Gil parked illegally. Al said, "He'll flip a cookie."
92. Al called Don Ashworth, "Don Ashford."
93. Al called Barry Manilow, "Barry Mamilow."
94. Al called Ross Tompkins, "Russ" and Russ Freedman, "Ross."
95. Ross "the Phantom" Tompkins was late for the gig. Al said, "He's the Phantom until you need him."
96. Dick Spencer and Bruce Paulson were both wearing navy blue velvet jackets. Al said, "You guys look like the Bobby twins."
97. When talking about someone's beach house, "He wouldn't sell that place for no tea in China."
98. Al referred to the piano player who would occasionally fill in for Ross Tompkins as "Beef." His name was Biff Hanna.
99. We were talking about how good Dionne Warwick's sound was the other day & Al said, "It sounded good because of the guy who played the Emmanuel Eater Two" (Emulator II).
100. Re: Union negotiations, "Let's not have a repercurrance."
101. After one of the guys in the band had surgery, "They had to go through his uterus." (urinary tract)
102. "Her father used to be an ex-cop."
103. "You're having mind-grain headaches."
104. ". . . for a fastitious (fastidious) man like you."
105. Referred to Carmelo's jazz club as Palmelo's.
106. ". . . anybody but his uncle could park there."
107. Referring to the Beverly Hilton Parking, ". . . you can park on the sun roof."
108. "Tea and Trumpets."
109. "My wife is an erotic fan of the Dodgers."
110. Al said to Dick Spencer, "Dick, were you on the show when Snooky (Smokey) Robinson was on?"
111. "Rick Honeycomb (Honeycutt) was pitching for the Dodgers."
112. When Marty Berman was ill, "his life was hanging on a nail."
113. "Yo, Zip!" (Yo, Cip!) Gene Cipriano.
114. "They took the big piano away and put a spinach (spinet) there."
115. "The Granny (Grammy) Awards."

116. "They're operating on a shoe lace budget." (shoestring)
117. "The world isn't crazy, it's the people who are crazy!"
118. Al to Don Sweeney when it was time to leave, "Let's go make a scene."
119. Al referred to Doc's short-lived band Xebron as "Exxon."
120. "Bob Hope is one of the richest comedians in captivity."
121. Ilene Shaughnessy wished Al a Merry Christmas and Al's reply was, "Yes, and the same for me from you."
122. "I'll give him the V.P.I. treatment."
123. "He's the greatest trumpet player on two feet."
124. "Each guy is responsible for his own expensability."
125. When talking about his son's poodles, "their feet don't touch the ground, that's how small they are."
126. "Vi is at Cedar Cyanide (Sinai) Hospital."
127. "Boy, Tom Rainier has lots of doubles today. He has one hand on this DC-10 (DX-7) and the other on that DC-10." (DX-7)
128. "A musician's life is a short one, but a long one."
129. "Wear your tux pants and your straight jacket."
130. Ed Shaughnessy called an 800 number. Al asked, "What part of the country is that?"
131. "That Steve Garvey is a first class baseman."
132. Watching a baseball game on TV, "They're hitting the ball, but they're catching it."
133. "When my car breaks down I call the AA."
134. "Treat everyone with respect and humidity."